Sentimentalism in Nineteenth-Century America

Sentimentalism in Nineteenth-Century America

Literary and Cultural Practices

Edited by Mary G. De Jong
with Paula Bernat Bennett

FAIRLEIGH DICKINSON UNIVERSITY PRESS
Madison • Teaneck

Published by Fairleigh Dickinson University Press
Co-published with The Rowman & Littlefield Publishing Group, Inc.
4501 Forbes Boulevard, Suite 200, Lanham, Maryland 20706
www.rowman.com

10 Thornbury Road, Plymouth PL6 7PP, United Kingdom

British Library Cataloguing in Publication Information Available

Library of Congress Cataloging-in-Publication Data

Sentimentalism in nineteenth-century America : literary and cultural practices / Mary De Jong.
p. cm.
Includes bibliographical references and index.
ISBN 978-1-61147-605-7 (cloth : alk. paper) — ISBN 978-1-61147-606-4 (electronic)
1. American literature—19th century—History and criticism. 2. Sentimentalism in literature. 3. Sentimentalism—United States—History—19th century. I. De Jong, Mary, editor of compilation.
PS217.S465S46 2013
810.9'11—dc23

ISBN 978-1-6114-7831-0 (pbk   )

2013004644

Printed in the United States of America

To Conor, Poppy, and Mackenzie

Contents

Acknowledgments

This volume owes much to the knowledge, exhortations, and generosity of Paula Bernat Bennett. One contributor expresses appreciation for her "inspiring tutelage in professional scholarship." My sentiments exactly. Other contributors likewise acknowledge her sound advice. Flaws that remain should be attributed to me.

A version of chapter 2 appeared in *Tulsa Studies in Women's Literature*, 25(1), Spring 2006; the author would like to thank the journal's editors, Holly Laird and Laura M. Stevens.

A slightly different version of chapter 3 was published in *ESQ: A Journal of the American Renaissance*, 58 (3), 2012. The author is grateful to the editors for allowing publication in this book.

The picture from *Godey's Lady's Book* in chapter 1 is from the author's personal collection.

The photograph of Lydia Sigourney with an unidentified young woman in chapter 4 is from Sigourney's *Letters to My Pupils*. The image was first accessed through Internet archive and, according to the Library of Congress website, it is now in the public domain.

Chapter 8 reproduces the cover of the 1855 edition of *Leaves of Grass* from Special Collections, University of Iowa Libraries; it is used by permission of the Walt Whitman Archive (www.whitmanarchive.org). The scan of the cover of *Album of Friendship* is used by permission of the University of Missouri-Kansas City Libraries, Dr. Kenneth J. LaBudde Department of Special Collections.

Chapter 9 reproduces two documents with permission: Figure 1: "Angel watching the Union and Confederate 'brothers' envelope." Envelope. Berlin & Jones. 1861–1865. The Library Company of Philadelphia, Civil War Envelope Collection. Figure 2: Sheet Music for "Glory! Glory! Hallelujah!"

Oliver Ditson & Co. 1861. Courtesy, The Lilly Library, Indiana University, Bloomington, Indiana, Sam DeVincent Collection.

Many thanks to Carole Bookhamer of Penn State Altoona for her support of busy teacher-scholars.

Mary G. De Jong
Altoona, PA

Introduction

Mary G. De Jong

Abolitionist Elizabeth Margaret Chandler urged readers in the antebellum northern U.S. to sympathize with the slave: if they would "imagine themselves for a few moments in his very circumstances, . . . enter into his feelings, comprehend all his wretchedness, [and] transform themselves mentally into his very self, they would not long withhold their compassion" (1836, 117). Chandler's appeal for sympathetic identification—entering into another's experience as if it were one's own—echoes a passage in the opening chapter of Adam Smith's *The Theory of Moral Sentiments* (1759, 9). Reprinted three times in northern American cities by 1822, Smith's influential treatise argues that individuals can form social and political communities because they are able, by an effort of the imagination and will, to understand one another's emotions (Clark 1995, 478–80). Other eighteenth- and early nineteenth-century moral philosophers as well as both evangelical and liberal religionists of the antebellum period agreed with Smith that persons who shared "sentiments"—meaning both feelings and opinions—could form "'families" linked by common sentiments, if not by blood (Clark 1995, 464–65, 471–73). Chandler, like many other early-nineteenth-century sentimental writers, especially reformers, used rhetorical strategies intended to cultivate fellow-feeling that, ideally, produced more than "streaming eyes" (a popular phrase of the time): they also sought to motivate the public to relieve oppression and pain. Such affective appeals were, and are, commonly called "sentimental."

If you ask literary scholars outside the nineteenth century how they recognize a sentimental text, it's a good bet most would say they know one when they read, see, or hear it. But nineteenth-century sentimentalism is not so easily pinned down. This introduction will briefly address the three components of any substantive discussion of nineteenth-century sentimentalism:

sentimentalism's origins in the eighteenth century, its protean nature in the nineteenth century, and the critical issues that have most engaged scholars of sentimentalism during the past thirty years, as they have sought to come to grips with sentimentality's many different aspects.

Literary sentimentalism originated in eighteenth-century Europe with the cult of "sensibility," as embodied in the "man of feeling," that sensitive, self-absorbed, emotionally expressive protagonist featured in works by Johan Wolfgang von Goethe, Jean-Jacques Rousseau, Samuel Richardson, and Laurence Sterne (Howard 1999, 69–72; Bernat Bennett 2003, 23–27). Like historian Elizabeth B. Clark (1995, 478), June Howard traces sensibility to Enlightenment moral theory, particularly that of the "Common Sense" philosophers, and the role of sensibility in the development of "modern subjectivities" (1999, 72). The value system and literary mode of sensibility debuted in late eighteenth-century America with the seduction novel (Barnes 1997, x–xi; Fisher 1985, 92–99). Acknowledging the eighteenth-century roots of sentimentality, Paula Bernat Bennett tracks its nineteenth-century history as "a bourgeois discourse of family, nation, and class" that at the same time was deeply wedded to domestic ideology—a position that would ultimately put it at odds with emerging "new women" (2003, 27). Although under heavy attack from a variety of quarters, not least from women themselves (Bernat Bennett, 2003, 56–61), sentimentalism outlasted the nineteenth century (Kete 2000, xiv–xix; Chapman and Hendler, 1999, 1–2). It persists today in efforts at persuasion dependent on empathy such as political speeches and calls for humanitarian aid for Third World children and the homeless in the United States. Manifestations of popular sentimentality—the nostalgia surrounding Stephen Foster's songs and the emotional appeal of stories about individuals who have overcome great hardships or of sad-eyed pets in need of "forever" homes—will be with us as long as there is an audience that vicariously participates in the suffering and joy of other beings, human and animal.

A nearly universal discourse in the nineteenth century, sentimentalism takes a multitude of forms, accommodating multiple internal contradictions and inconsistent manifestations that can reduce a scholar to tears. Walt Whitman's innovative "barbaric yawp" has been widely celebrated, but, as Adam Bradford demonstrates in chapter 8 of this volume, the poet's fondness for direct address–according to Mary Louise Kete, the signature rhetorical device of the sentimental text (2000, 39–47, 117)—can be traced directly to his early, and far from "barbaric," sentimental poems. Although sentimental authors favor certain tropes and themes (idealized intimate bonds, love won or lost, scenes of suffering and death) and share beliefs about human nature and morality, they take "a range of positions on social, religious, and political issues" (Baym 1998, 335), and these positions do not necessarily harmonize with each other. Views that may seem blatantly discordant can co-exist within a single sentimental work. Thus, for example, we find the assumption of Anglo-American superiority informing the characterization of African Americans in Harriet Beecher Stowe's *Uncle Tom's Cabin* (1852)—the most influential anti-slavery polemic published in the antebellum period.

Nor were all sentimental texts intended like Chandler's and Stowe's to serve social justice. Sentimental romances abounded, and, as Virginia Jackson argues, many sentimental poems by women (men also, we might add) turned inward instead, to explore what purported to be the authors' own subjectivity (2005, 210); such writers focused on their own psychic wounds, not those of others. Where sentimental texts did seek benevolent ends, moreover, their success was often mixed. Susan Toth Lord shows in chapter 5 of this collection how carefully Lydia Maria Child crafted *Letters from New-York* to generate sympathy for the city's outcasts. But other writers were less sensitive. The immigrant Hummel family in Louisa May Alcott's *Little Women* receives the March family's charity, but, as Kristen Proehl argues in chapter 6, the novel presents the Hummels themselves not just as hopelessly poor but also irredeemably foreign.

More ironically, sentimentality could also go bad when its universalization of human feelings blocked respectful recognition of the very real differences in experience between privileged observers and the objects of their gaze. By encouraging authors and readers to invest in the "fantasy of experiential equivalence" (Hendler 2001, 7), sentimentalism seemed to license privileged writers to appropriate others' voices and stories for their own ends, feeding racist and classist stereotypes in other, subtler ways. If Stowe's *Uncle Tom's Cabin* offers us the racist image of a "pickaninny" Topsy on the one hand, it gives us on the other the sublimely virtuous but not coincidentally totally passive Uncle Tom, a figure whose name has become a by-word for appeasement in the black community.

Nonetheless, for all its slipperiness as a discourse of compassion and reform, sentimentality did work effectively to bring about much progressive social change, especially for middle-class women. Drawing on sentimentality's alliance with domestic ideology—in particular, the latter's emphasis on women's virtue and their capacity to feel—female reformers like Child and Stowe claimed their right to help alleviate human suffering in society at large. For them and other reform-minded women, domesticity's privileging of women's putative natural morality and piety validated their participation, if only by writing, in the public sphere. Addressing this sphere, these women called for the rehabilitation of prostitutes, besieged Congress over Cherokee removal, and advocated for despised minorities. Well known for her work on behalf of Native Americans, Lydia Huntley Sigourney also championed the deaf, who, as Elizabeth Petrino observes in chapter 4, were likewise denied full humanity.

Despite and because of nineteenth-century women writers' now conspicuous assumption of race and class privilege, sentimentality contributed to the emergence of bourgeois subjectivity and helped authorize middle-class women's role as America's moral housekeepers and teachers. Unable to dictate public policy, women, through their gift for emotional suasion, influenced it, working at the local level for their own benevolent concerns but also, as Sarah Josepha Hale urged, to meet the nation's needs as well. As Kara Clevinger's study of *Godey's Lady's Book* in chapter 1 contends, Hale may have opposed women's suffrage, but she strenuously insisted that the welfare of both family and state rested on the foundation of well-educated mothers. Other child-rearing experts of both sexes agreed, as Ken Parille's study of antebellum maternal advice literature establishes in chapter 2. Contributors to the body of writings on female education such as Emma Willard and Mary Lyon deserve credit for the founding of intellectually challenging female seminaries that turned out aspiring teachers, writers, and reformers. Collectively, as writers and public speakers, women like Fidelia Fiske (missionary to Persia), Sarah Willis Parton ("Fanny Fern"), Helen Hunt Jackson, and Elizabeth Cady Stanton, all of whom attended female seminaries, used their education to help implement female sentimentality's reformist agenda.

In addition to enhancing middle-class women's social profile, raising expectations for female education, and contributing to the emergence of middle-class subjectivity, sentimentality increased women's potential for economic independence. It certainly made possible the career of Sigourney, one of the highest paid women writers of the century and America's first professional woman poet. At the same time, however, whether deployed by women or men, sentimental rhetoric, together with domestic ideology, reinforced the subordination of working-class women and minority populations, often making women, as Laura Wexler (1992), Amy Kaplan (1998), and Karen Sánchez-Eppler (2005, 186–220) have all argued, complicit in national aggression. In particular, the idealization of the middle-class Christian home that undergirded imperialistic tendencies supported the evangelical Protestant mission to resocialize others in order to save their souls, while extending the reach of American commerce. As a result, minority ethnic and racial populations in North America and abroad were educated, often by women, in ways destructive to their own cultures but productive of social subordinates and servants for white, bourgeois, North-American-born, Christian families (Wexler 1992, 17–19; Sánchez-Eppler 2005, 186–220). Such contradictions and complexities in sentimental values and practices speak directly to the inevitable ambiguities of a discourse that was at once a kind of rhetoric available to all comers and a sanctioned way to achieve progressive social reform.

Wexler critiques early domestically centered critical discussions of sentimentality such as those by Ann Douglas (1977) and Jane Tompkins (1985) for "ten[ding] to elide . . . the expansive, imperial project of sentimentalism" (1992, 15), an elision that later scholars have done much to redress. Often positioned as opposites, Douglas and Tompkins, who together created the foundation for modern sentimentalism studies, concur, as Wexler points out, that "sentimental fiction is a 'power' and a political 'force' too considerable to be neglected." Douglas and Tompkins also agree that "instruction of the literate middle class is the chief object as well as the chief subject of domestic narrative" (1992, 12, 13). Philip Fisher's *Hard Facts* likewise analyzes sentimental fiction as a valid and effective form of political rhetoric. "Radical" in extending sympathy to persons not usually respected as subjects, such fiction was viewed in some quarters as "dangerous" insofar as it took the promise of democracy seriously enough to urge that compassion be extended to all people (1985, 92, 98).

Needless to say, this bar was set too high for most writers and readers, so that in practice, eccentric or disabled individuals, racial and ethnic minorities, and working-class and enslaved people were often ignored despite authors' ardent affirmations of the essential sameness and rightful equality of all people before God. Ironically, such moments of aporia in the nation's (theoretically) liberal discourse became visible in part because Douglas, Tompkins, and Fisher raised awareness of the political uses to which sentimentality was put. Unsurprisingly, abolitionists were especially keen to hammer home the idea that the phrase "all men are created equal" was or should be a good deal more than mere words. Although coming from very different backgrounds, and writing in very different genres, authors such as poet Frances Ellen Watkins Harper, autobiographer Frederick Douglass, and essayist Lydia Maria Child all used sentimentality in equality's name.

The quarter century since the constellation of Tompkins and Fisher has witnessed a steady outpouring of scholarly work on late eighteenth- and nineteenth-century American sentimentalism in fiction and other literary and nonliterary cultural forms, such as photography and sculpture. What scholars have repeatedly discovered in working with sentimental texts is that sentimentalism is much more complex than we expected and more multifarious than we were taught. Certainly, we cannot dismiss it, as so many earlier generations of scholars did, as mere overwrought emotion and expression. What we do know is that sentimentality is not a genre, for it inhabits a multitude of forms; nor does it represent a particular political position, for as *Uncle Tom* illustrates, it can support liberatory or oppressive impulses and measures at once. One cannot even say that it is class- or race-biased since one finds sentimentalism used universally by oppressed groups as well as by persons of privilege.

In recognition of the language-based strategies literary sentimentalism deploys to achieve its goals, recent studies have called it a "rhetorical mode" (Harris 1990,112; Hendler 2001, 224 n 33; Bernat Bennett 2003, xxxvi;

Greyser 2007, 278). As such, it does have recognizable features—to name just a few, pictorial descriptiveness that makes the reader a spectator of others' affective experiences, clarity of style, authorial addresses to the audience—that reflect its purpose to move readers by changing their hearts and minds. Some sentimental texts are also "rhetorical" in that they overtly seek to persuade readers to identify with those in need of sympathy. For readers, sentimental elements can simplify, complicate, mar, or enrich a given work, depending on their own sentiments, personal and reading experiences, aesthetic values, and tolerance for being called upon to *feel*. Today's scholars recognize sentimentalism in a plenitude of texts, genres, and cultural practices and forms.

As a result, the terms "sentimental," "sentimentality," and "sentimentalism"—with no consistent distinction in usage between the latter two—have become ubiquitous in scholarly discourse on eighteenth- and nineteenth-century American literature, informing undergraduate and graduate courses, consistently earning space in national conferences of such professional organizations as the American Literature Association, C19, and the Society for the Study of American Women Writers and proliferating in dissertations, articles, and books. Sentimentalism is also examined by scholars of history, music, the visual arts, science and medicine, and the popular media, and it rewards interdisciplinary approaches. Robert Arbour's essay on Whitman's Civil War poetry, chapter 9, uncovers a trove of information on sentimental practices involving popular music, from parlor entertainment to singing beside army campfires.

Students of sentimentalism also find that it traverses boundaries devised by literary historians to demarcate periods and movements. From Emerson on the rhodora to Whitman on male bonding, sentimental elements figure in literary texts customarily classified as "romantic," "naturalistic," "realistic," or "(proto)modernist." According to Tara Penry, Melville's *Moby-Dick* opposes the "sentimental pairing" of Ishmael and Queequeg to Ahab's "Romantic self-absorption" (1999, 231, 233). As D. Zachary Finch demonstrates in chapter 3, Sarah Piatt's poems can sustain interpretations that would group her among romantics, realists, and sentimentalists. One could say the same of her near-contemporary Dickinson or of her Southern male counterpart, Mark Twain, a robust mixer of genres for whom sentimental culture had enormous if highly ambivalent appeal (Kete 2000, 146). Finding in naturalism "a dependence on the sentimentalism against which it defines itself," Francesca Sawaya supports her argument with Frank Norris's depiction of a "sentimental man/mother" in *The Octopus* (1999, 261, 266). In this volume, Bradford and Arbour trouble the placement of Whitman as a "modernist," while in chapter 10, George Gordon-Smith argues that ultimate "realist" Henry James engages "sentimental" issues in his fiction, albeit eschewing sentimental rhetoric in favor of his own intellectually analytical approach. These and other new interpretations, reclassifications, and aesthetic (re)assessments have multiplied in sentimentalism studies for at least three reasons: nineteenth-century writers' varied purposes and mixtures of modes and genres, feminists' interest in women's interactions with sentimentalism, and the ongoing challenge of defining sentimentalism itself.

Today's scholarship on sentimentalism is not confined to bourgeois experience and *belles lettres*. Influential studies such as those by Sánchez-Eppler (1992, 2005) and Bernat Bennett (2003) have inquired how sentimentality functions within a person who gives or receives sympathy, how it affects interpersonal relationships, and how sentimentality operates at various class levels within a social system. Sánchez-Eppler's "Bodily Bonds" asks us to view reading and sympathetic response to a suffering human being—or a literary representation of a person—as "bodily" acts (in Samuels 1992, 99–100). Attempting to bridge the bodily differences that mark sex, race, and class, sentimentalism has led to decidedly undemocratic consequences, subjecting the powerless to assimilation and exploitation. Naomi Greyser aptly remarks that although sentimentalism performed "ethical and social work," it also led to disillusionment and pain for individuals by valorizing what she calls "impossible intimacies," that is, personal relationships that could not overcome internalized social boundaries (2007, 278). Still, Frederick Douglass, Jarena Lee (Moody 2001), Zitkala-Sa (Carpenter 2008), and other writers of color co-opted Anglocentric sentimental literary conventions for their own purposes. This appropriation underscores sentimentalism's functioning as a rhetorical mode that can be adapted by writers at odds with each other on all other grounds. Grappling with the variability and seeming omnipresence of sentimentalism in nineteenth-century literature, scholars and teachers of sentimental texts and practices may well ask, "Was *everything* sentimental?"

With the multifarious potentials of sentimental literature established, we can now enquire what today's scholars mean by "sentimentalism." Since, as the foregoing pages indicate, they define it in numerous ways, it seems unlikely that that a single definition will satisfy them all. The very term "sentimentality," Howard remarks, is "so charged and pervasive, so plastic, precisely because our reactions to sentimentality are so deeply rooted in our ways of organizing the relation of self and world" (1999, 63). Defining sentimental affect in its interpersonal and social expressions therefore is no simple matter. Among the most often cited definitions is Joanne Dobson's theorization of sentimentality as affiliation based. Literary sentimentalism, she writes, "envisions the self-in-relation"; its "principal theme" is "the desire for bonding," for "affiliation on the plane of emotion, sympathy, nurturance, or similar moral or spiritual inclinations." Dobson identifies characteristic themes (prominent among them, the pain of loss) and formal features, noting that sentimental fiction and poems employ "conventional and familiar elements" in order to move "as wide an audience as possible" (1997, 267,

268). Having established what sentimentalism is, she then looks at how particular texts can be evaluated as art, a question whose many pitfalls—for example, who decides what is good or bad in art and on what basis—have led most scholars of sentimentalism to shun it (1997, 268–80).

Building on Dobson's foundation, Kete defines sentimental literature as "the written trace of a broad cultural discourse that [she calls] 'sentimental collaboration': the exchange of sympathy establishing the ground for participation in a common cultural or intellectual project" (2000, xiv). This shared practice enabled nineteenth-century individuals to "join together" in facing loss due to emigration, war, and death. Communal rituals helped them "[transform] their grief into restorative mourning" (2000, 7). Kete further argues that sentimentality functioned in the "construction of a personal identity that was not at odds with, but a necessary condition of, community" (2000, 7). Her emphases on collaboration and community, analysis of what sentimentalism "did for" readers and writers (2000, 4), and interest in the style, tropes, and techniques of poetry as well as prose have been widely influential, as the essays in this collection attest, especially those by Arbour, Bradford, Finch, and Petrino.

The meticulous definition of sentimentality and its various manifestations also entails disentangling it from other concepts, modes, and practices while retaining awareness of shared meanings and strategies. Exploring sentimentality's "limits," Maglina Lubovich's essay, chapter 7, designates "bachelor melancholia" as "a specific sub-set of sentimentalism" that needs to be read in light of its own separate history. Philipp Schweighauser acknowledges that "the twin topics of sentimentality and domesticity are deeply entwined in the scholarly literature as well as in nineteenth-century texts themselves," but he "separate[s] them": "Nineteenth-century domesticity . . . is best approached through historiographical research, as it has historical underpinnings that limit it to a particular time and place." Although nineteenth-century sentimentality too "has a history," sentimentality itself "is a question of aesthetics raised by a particular set of rhetorical conventions that writers can deploy at any time or place" (Bernat Bennett et al., 2007, 324–25). Elizabeth Dill, referring to "the false rift between the sensational and the sentimental [that] overlooks the dark side of sentimentality," challenges scholars to rethink their categories (2008, 707–8), a challenge germane to discussion of sentimentality in Edgar Allan Poe. Yet it is still too soon to redraw the lines in ink. As Penry observes, "domesticity and sensationalism may collaborate with sentimentalism" to advance the usual acknowledged sentimental ends of reform, "consolidation," and community building (2010, 235)—or to further different, even opposing, purposes, as we have seen. A particularly complex collaboration, the fusion of irony with sentimentality in Piatt and Dickinson, gives these two poets their own unique rhetorical brands and their force as cultural critics. The process of (re)definition continues as scholars offer fresh readings of canonized works and new studies of formerly neglected ones.

As noted above, the formal features and aesthetic quality of sentimental texts have not received the same kind of intense scrutiny as sentimentalism's ideological underpinnings enjoy. Critics are, however, beginning to examine sentimental writings as works of art. In a recent review of ten major critical books on sentimentalism published during the last quarter century, Hildegarde Hoeller argues that scholars now treat "the aesthetics of sentimental writing [as] inextricable from its ideological patterns or cultural work" (2006, 367). Penry's "Sentiment and Style" (2010) addresses without apparent effort many of the issues earlier scholars raised and evaded during the past three decades: rhetorical purposes, stylistic features (notably "transparency," "redundancy," and direct address), and aesthetic quality. In this book, the essays by Arbour, Bradford, Finch, and Gordon-Smith attend carefully to form—appropriately so, given their subjects: Whitman, Piatt, and James.

As mapped in this collection, sentimental discourse was ample enough to accommodate the questioning of its own ideologies. Evolving from moral philosophers' assertion that sympathy is the basis for community, and unstintingly protean in application, sentimentalism permeated nineteenth-century culture. Yet, as the essays collected here suggest, critique of sentimentality was never far behind. As the century wore on, exposing sentimentality's contradictions and failures to address common concerns, faith in its principles and claims crumbled.

The essays in Part 1, "Rethinking Sentimental Motherhood," interrogate the myth of the so-called empire of the mother, canvassing writings by a host of different authors who, far from celebrating what Ken Parille refers to as "the hallowed nature of the white mother-child relationship," called attention to maternal failures of knowledge and sympathy. Somewhat surprisingly, among these authors, Kara Clevinger argues, was Sarah Josepha Hale, literary editor of *Godey's Lady's Book*. Rather than portraying good mothering as an extension of women's natural inclination, Clevinger writes, "much of the content of *Godey's*, including essays on the theme of childrearing and Hale's own editorials, treat [it] as a professional activity that can be demystified, deconstructed, and taught to women." Insisting on the constructedness of mothering gave Hale the leverage to campaign for better education for women, whom she, like so many other authorities, saw as responsible for the nation's future leaders. Investigating complexities in "the category of 'the child,'" Ken Parille finds a debate among antebellum child-rearing experts over women's capacity to feel "affective sympathy" for their sons. Whereas sentimental authorities were uncritical of mother love, writers Parille calls "pragmatic" were profoundly concerned with the way in which gender difference unfitted mothers to discipline their sons, whose raucous "boy culture"

unnerved them. Some of these authorities urged mothers to be more sympathetic with their sons; others, skeptical of the efficacy of sympathy itself,
recommended stern discipline instead.

It was the mother's own ethical concerns that made mothering problematic for Sarah Piatt, a Kentucky-born poet who moved north at the outbreak of
the Civil War. Zachary Finch shows that Piatt's mother-speakers scruple to
pass on to their young the sentimental myths and ideologies of a culture that
depended on slavery and waged a bloody war to validate itself. Yet these
mothers' nostalgia for the Old South leaves them arrested in melancholy.
Finch applies Freud's 1917 distinction between mourning, which can be
completed, and melancholy, the result of unfinished grieving. "Reading Piatt
through the framework of melancholy," Finch explains, "allows us to observe that Piatt was not just exposing the limitations of antebellum sentimentality. . . . She was sincerely mourning the insolvency of sentimentality
itself."

Set in the antebellum period before sentimentality's insolvency was widely recognized, the three essays in Part 2, "Reform and Sympathetic Identification," all address sympathy as a political force. Sentimental authors generally agreed that the rhetor who cultivates in self and others a capacity for
sympathetic identification with unfortunate persons helps to raise the standard of public morality. Susan Toth Lord details the many ways in which
Child's *Letters from New-York* enacts for middle-class readers such moments
of compassion. In Lord's analysis, Child, "a cultural mediator," develops a
"collaborative relationship" with readers that encourages them to reproduce
her narrator's empathy with the downtrodden and to desire social justice as a
result. According to Elizabeth Petrino, popular author and revered pedagogue
Sigourney affirmed that the participation of deaf pupils in her classroom
provided hearing students with a model of sympathetic interaction and benevolent activity. She "celebrated" touch and the loving gaze as vehicles for
the "language of affections." But her observation of multiply disabled individuals, especially nonspeakers whose minds remained unfathomable, led
her to "interrogat[e] the limits of human understanding and the very definition of personhood" in ways she herself found profoundly disturbing. Forced
to scrutinize her own belief in the possibility of empathic communication,
Sigourney nonetheless maintained that education should be offered to persons who function, albeit differently, without verbal communication.

Kristen Proehl also raises questions regarding the power of sympathy to
bridge social difference in Alcott's *Little Women*, a book that, while intended
to teach young readers to care for persons not of their own race or class,
offers "contradictory messages about poverty" and social mobility. The novel's nonengagement with antislavery politics and Jo's condescension toward
her immigrant neighbors suggests that Alcott, in order to appeal to her white
bourgeois audience, ultimately "contain[ed] the political ramifications of

sympathy." As an adult philanthropic educator, Proehl writes, Jo "idealizes and infantilizes" her prospective impoverished students even while the novel purports to offer educational reform and racial integration as "viable ways to combat racial and class oppression."

Today we largely accept that sentimentality as a political discourse lost much of its valence after the Civil War. Did it also lose its viability as a preferred mode of feeling with respect to loss, grief, and death? The four essays clustered in Part 3, "Loss, Death, Mourning, and Grief," cut various ways.

A potent complex of sentimental principles, whose unifying effects led to shared views and feelings, was widely credited in the antebellum period with generating a national "family," which in turn conferred identity on individuals. So powerful was this basis for identity that, as Maglina Lubovich argues, it allowed even a melancholic isolato like Ik Marvel, the fictitious narrator of Donald Grant Mitchell's *Reveries of a Bachelor,* to participate in this family imaginatively through his fireside dreams of intimate love and loss. Lubovich coins the term "melancholic identification" for the psychological process by which Marvel's narrator seeks to legitimate his own citizenship as a single man within the polity. As "an unfinished language of *imagined* loss and grief," bachelor melancholia, Lubovich writes, "allowed Mitchell the opportunity to fold the self into community and into marriage, the markers of right citizenship in early America," thus claiming his manhood despite his unmarried status.

As Lubovich points out, death, especially the death of children, was a shaping phenomenon in nineteenth-century family life, and Americans relied on common memorial texts, customs, and objects such as locks of hair to acknowledge mortality, preserve memories of the dead, and affirm continuing communication with them. In his essay on Whitman's early poetry, Adam Bradford shows how Whitman drew on the antebellum "culture of mourning and memorializing," to which much of his early writing had been devoted, when composing the 1855 version of *Leaves of Grass.* Carrying forward the sentimental devices of apostrophe and direct address, Whitman learned how to create a sense of vital "presence" of and "perpetual" communion among the absent subject, the poetic speaker, and the reader holding the book. The volume's physical design linked it with "sentimental albums whose [cultural] work and look were in many ways similar to Whitman's own."

The cultural mechanisms for coping with loneliness, loss, and grief were strained to the breaking point as the Civil War claimed 620,000 casualties. Civilians and combatants alike found it difficult to credit the sentimental ideal of "national consensus." Although soldiers carried Bibles and hymnbooks, and revivals rippled though the northern and southern armies, American society was becoming secular. During the war and afterward, people became increasingly unable to believe in an affectively unified and divinely blessed Union or a heavenly reunion with loved ones, when faced with the terrors that sentimentality sought to dispel. Flaws and gaps in the sentimental picture of the world became evident and speakable.

Robert Arbour argues that an "ideological crisis" was already on its way to recognition as early as 1861. He examines thematic and figural connections between *Drum-Taps* and war-era popular music—the common property of Americans—that portrayed soldiers' experiences and idealized the bourgeois home and mother. Reading Whitman's 1865 collection "as a response to popular American concerns about the security of the nation and the legitimacy of sentimental consensus during the Civil War," Arbour concludes that "sentimentalism appeared to fail as a representational strategy for the Union, forcing poets and composers alike to search for different modes of representation." Whitman, borrowing from sentimentalism but revising it, offered "the poet" and his book as new means of gathering and reconnecting a ruptured nation.

Alone among the authors considered in this volume, Henry James eschewed overt displays of emotion, instead exploring consciousness and the capacity for nonverbal communication, especially through body language. George Gordon-Smith maintains that James the fiction writer, faulted in his day as coldly "scientific" and "unemotional," actually sympathized as deeply with his characters as did authors who portrayed the tragic seamstress and the blind boy. James dispensed with conventional overt signs of emotion and with explicit narratorial appeals such as Stowe had used with such conviction. Instead he worked out "a new ontology of sentiment" that recognizes "the role of the mind." For James sentiment was the product of mental processes—observation, imagination, and intellection—that were open to reason—much as Adam Smith had theorized more than two centuries earlier.

In revisiting nineteenth-century American sentimentalism, contributors to this collection assess authors' uncritical, revisionary, ironized, and anti-sentimental uses of sentimental themes and techniques. They confirm the rhetoric's pervasiveness. They ask us to see literary sentimentalism as a vital, energetic rhetorical mode that took a myriad of forms. Through discussions of writers like Whitman, Piatt , and James, they also suggest that both realism and modernism had deep roots in sentimental texts. Other scholars now have the opportunity to debate whether nineteenth-century literary sentimentalism died or whether it continued in other cultural forms. Above all, rethinking what we believe we know about it may help us better understand the modes and movements that coexisted with, borrowed from, and disowned it, down to our own day.

1

Rethinking Sentimental Motherhood

Chapter One

"These Human Flowers"

Sentimentalizing Children and Fashioning Maternal Authority in Godey's Lady's Book

Kara B. Clevinger

There is no subjection so complete as that which preserves the forms of freedom; it is thus that the ill itself is taken captive. Is not this poor child, without knowledge, strength, or wisdom, entirely at your mercy? Are you not master of his whole environment so far as it affects him? Cannot you make of him what you please? —Jean-Jacques Rousseau, *Emile*

In the July 1845 issue of *Godey's Lady's Book*, editor Sarah Josepha Hale included one of her own poems. The theme? "The Empire of Woman," which reiterated the nineteenth-century ideology of separate spheres in rhyming, sentimentalized terms. While the "outward World, for rugged Toil design'd" was "Man's dominion," women governed an empire "holier, more refin'd," and worked at "[l]ifting the earth-crushed heart to hope and heaven" (Hale 1845, 12). The four other sections of the poem are divided into a woman's ruling roles as daughter, sister, wife, and mother, all signified by their relational status. In the final section, "The Mother," Hale ends with an ode to maternal love: "Oh! wondrous power, how little understood,/ Entrusted to the Mother's mind alone,/ To fashion genius, form the soul for good,/ Inspire a West, or train a Washington!" (12). Although Hale characterizes mothering in this poem as a "wondrous power" that is "little understood," much of the content of *Godey's*, including essays on the theme of child rearing and Hale's own editorials, treats mothering as a professional activity that can be demystified, deconstructed, and taught to women. Not just imagining a power that was mysterious and divine—Hale's sentimental representation of motherhood[1]—Hale also presented a version of mothering that located a mother's success in proper education. Within this framework, a mother's power was not "wondrous"; it was acquired.

The model of mothering that Hale presented in *Godey's*[2] drew directly from and was in dialogue with the advice of contemporaneous child-rearing manuals, many of which also employed sentimental rhetoric to shape a vision of the home and the family that they ultimately unraveled. Taking the helpless child as the object of the sentimental gaze, domestic advice writers found language that emphasized the child's delicacy and innocence useful for insisting on the mother as best suited to protect children. Employing sentimental rhetoric, domestic advisors constructed the home, the family, and the child, in particular, as critically vulnerable sites in order to mobilize and legitimate the agency of the mother as protector. In the most popular women's magazine of the antebellum era, *Godey's Lady's Book*, sentimental pieces that involve children are a ubiquitous presence that range from the supportive to the frighteningly admonitory.

In the pages of *Godey's*, Hale's determination to make the rearing of children a primary vehicle for the expansion of women's public role as protector of the nation's children[3] played itself out in two versions of childhood that the magazine presented, those of the vulnerable and the free child. Sarah Hale recognized that these new meanings ascribed to childhood— symbol of both vulnerability and freedom—could be used to gain advantages for women. By drawing from the sentimental and didactic languages of domestic how-to guides, Hale helped to professionalize women's work in the home in ways that transformed the figure of the mother from passive and selfless to a firmly self-reliant nurturer of children.[4]

THE VULNERABLE CHILD

The success and popularity of the "empire of the mother" generated by *Godey's* and by domestic manuals like Lydia Maria Child's *The Mother's Book* (1831) and John S. C. Abbott's *The Mother at Home* (1833), along with the growing number of mothers' magazines in the 1830s and 1840s,[5] were contingent upon the vulnerability of the child. The overwhelming sentimentalization of the death of children—powerful iconography that drew attention to their innocence and vulnerability—spurred on not only a grotesque intoxication with the immense grief surrounding a child's death but also practical advice arguing that it was within the American mother's power to save her children, since death, while providential, was still preventable. This literature persuaded women that the health and well-being of their children was in their hands, but in empowering the mother, it also cast her as a potential threat to the child.

The figure of the dying or suffering child as a site of innocence and vulnerability was basic to antebellum sentimentalist projects, which often used elaborate death scenes to portray grief and inspire sympathy in readers. Demonstrably aware of these images, of their power to move readers, and of the anxieties about infant deaths they provoked, Hale employed sentimental images and rhetoric of helpless children in order to persuade readers that such deaths were evils that a qualified mother could eradicate. Numerous fiction pieces, poems, images, and statistics on the death of children in *Godey's* support Karen Sánchez-Eppler's observation that "Dying is what children do most and do best in the literary and cultural imagination of nineteenth-century America." Although childhood was typically conceived as a precious period in one's life, as a "distinct and special stage" (2005, 101, xiv) supposedly free from adult responsibility and hard labor, children were consistently imagined as dangerously close to disease and death at every hour. For example, a small item titled "The Little Hands" in the May 1861 issue of *Godey's* and characteristically syrupy in its tone encourages readers to "Cherish then the 'little hand' and guide and guard it while you may, for it belongs to an angel in your household, and you know not how soon their wings will unfold, and soar far away into the world of love and light, leaving you in your anguish to mourn and lament over their brief stay" (1861, 439).

For Americans who cared about childhood (and according to many women writers, mothers, clergymen, and education reformers, every American should), the delicate and ephemeral nature of the small, undeveloped child called for special attention and devotion toward the nation's young. The language of the child as an "angel in your household" whose "wings will unfold" is strikingly similar to reverential depictions of the domestic woman such as Coventry Patmore immortalized in "The Angel in the House," attaching the child as an object of sentimentalization to larger ideologies about the idealization of the home and those occupying it. While the home generally was (and often still is) considered a happy haven from the harsh, stressful realities of the rapidly expanding world of commerce and industry, its simultaneous construction in the nineteenth century as a site of vulnerability meant that the very forces it sought to repel constantly threatened to penetrate its welcoming doorway.

The vulnerability of the domestic sphere to outside forces from which it was said to be secluded was a fear circulating in a good deal of antebellum fiction and nonfiction, reflecting more general American anxieties about the stability of new American political and economic systems.[6] Lydia Maria Child, for example, dedicated her manual *The Frugal Housewife* to "those who are not ashamed of economy," framing the work around the possibility that men's fortunes might plummet and it would be up to thrifty wives to maintain solvency. Forty years later, Louisa May Alcott in *Little Women* invokes similar sentiments when she has Marmee caution her daughters to "stop complaining, to enjoy the blessings already possessed, and try to deserve them, lest they should be taken away entirely, instead of increased" ([1868–1869] 2004a, 43). Just as it was important to fortify the home's ideological armor against these cruel forces and to transform women into the custodians of household cheerfulness, new understandings of and values placed upon childhood, based on Lockean and Rousseauian principles of the importance of early childhood development, made it even more crucial to "purify the environments of the young" (Finkelstein 1985, 117).

Purifying and calming the home as the primary environment enfolding the child and making the mother the primary caregiver were therefore central to sentimentalist projects. The child, as a helpless being and a Lockean blank slate to be written on, needed to be sheltered in a warm, loving home in order to achieve not only a morally sound life but to sustain its life at all. Sentimental culture perpetuated this image as the goal and marker of middle-class whiteness.[7] In a *Godey's* editorial from July 1845, for instance, Sarah J. Hale quotes a young correspondent's piece called "Home" in order to express how impressive and enduring such a home is in the lives of her readers:

> How endeared to the heart of man is the soil where the footsteps of his childhood were first imprinted, when a father's smile and a mother's tenderness shed a halo around days of innocence and joy. . . . It is memory's cherished bower, and no distance can dim the brightness with which it blooms in the eye of the mind. . . . Home, when we leave it, becomes in after years the fairy-land of our imagination. (qtd. in Hale 1845, 46)

Home, as Americans understood and conceived it, was (or should be) the fairyland of the national imagination; it was an Elysian Fields that gained cultural capital by offsetting their fears of sweeping changes over which they had no control and the strokes of which pushed them toward an unforeseeable future. Child and others suggested that raising children in protective, isolated environments, far from producing weak and naïve adults, would actually provide children with the moral and spiritual strength needed to combat the corruption and depravity of the world they would encounter outside the haloed home. Of course, images of home as a heavenly haven and the larger world as a seedy sinkhole rested on a view of separate spheres that was more of an ideal than a reality. But this gendered binary was a powerful cultural force that influenced self-expression and meaning-making in American society. For the inhabitants of a "cherished bower" it meant being figuratively disconnected from and unaffected by the nation's economic, political, and historical processes.

In sentimental literature, the images of the home as a "fairy-land" and of children as delicate, angelic creatures raise their cultural value by their very transience: inevitably, children grow up and leave home. Neither the home nor the child is a stable, permanent thing. In part, because of this inevitable "death" of sorts, sentimentalists rarely treated actual death as an evil inflicted upon its victims. On the contrary, dying persons often exerted agency and purpose in their aspirations to depart from their corporeality, and suffering was generally depicted as meaningful and satisfying. The child in "The Little Hands" excerpt cited above, for example, is not struck down nor oppressed by illness, but unfolds its wings and soars away "into the world of love and light." From the sentimentalist's perspective, people are not torn from the world; they *want* to be taken from such an imperfect world. If sentimental literature urged readers to accept the death of a child as a blessing, a restoration of the child to its true home, this was hardly the end of the story for Hale. Even though Hale published and sometimes wrote these sentimentalized representations of a child's death, she ultimately insisted that such deaths were preventable by a well-educated mother; these images served her purpose of gender reform. For Hale and other domestic advice writers, children's deaths were warnings or instructive tools to the survivors. Jane Tompkins says of antebellum sentimental stories of deaths that they "enact a philosophy, as much political as religious, in which the pure and powerless die to save the powerful and corrupt" (1985, 127–28). Sánchez-Eppler argues that the death of children in particular "may be used to enforce a wide array of social issues, and any reader of nineteenth-century fiction can easily produce a list of the lessons—temperance, abolition, charity, chastity, and most of all piety" (2005, 101). The figurative death of children in *Godey's* sentimental pieces depicted children as vulnerable and thus valuable, stressing the real need to protect them.

In order for Hale and *Godey's* to construct women as guardians of the nation's children, however, they first had to cast women as threats to the child's safety and wellbeing. Thus Emma C. Embury, a popular periodical writer and one-time nominal editor of *Godey's*, declared, "Children may be beloved, and yet may suffer great injustice and cruel wrong at the hands of those whose privilege it is to protect them from harm" (1844, 80). And the magazine's "Health Department" column pressed home the same point when it questioned women's competence as caretakers of children's safe and healthy development.[8] Citing a quotation from *Hall's Journal of Health* that compared the death of children to that of flowers, which God "sometimes gather[ed] into heaven. . . lest some rude hand may despoil them of their beauty," the series's first medical expert, Jno. Stainback Wilson, rejects this sentimentalized version of children's deaths and writes:

> Some weak brother has been trying his hand to see what a beautifully sounding sentence he could make out of a whopper. The reason why children die is because they are not taken care of. . . . We don't think that the Almighty has any hand in it. And to draw comfort from the presumption that He has any

agency in the death of a child, in the manner of the quoted article above, is a presumption and profanation. (1862, 402)

As Wilson's response demonstrates, the fundamental point of exposing women's supposed inadequacies was to put within their grasp the tools needed to raise their children "properly." Wilson's notion of self-improvement relied on women's educability (a progressive move when considered in the context of a culture that was still debating the value of educating women). And to Hale's delight, no doubt, this encouragement of women's self-empowerment often could be used to advance women's status in American society. Indeed, the above excerpt appeared just below Wilson's comments in support of the medical training of women. If Wilson's condescending tone reflects the gendered limits of his liberalism, he nonetheless had "come to the conclusion that a woman doctor, educated after our fashion would be about as competent as most of our modern high-pressure MDs, and therefore as much entitled to the degree, though her practice might be confined to a particular class of disease" (1862, 402).

Domestic advisors were not alone in suggesting that the nation's children were at risk. The July 1858 issue of *Godey's* that contained the first installment of the "Health Department" also included a Hale editorial urgently titled, "OUR LITTLE CHILDREN, SHALL THEY LIVE?" Deploring the high rate of infant mortality, Hale argues that "infancy has not been cared for as it required"; there are numerous "little helpless invalids, whom their poor parents had not the means of making comfortable," and it is her readers who must "save little children from painful sufferings and a premature grave!" (Hale 1858, 81). Hale's "poor parents" evidently denotes impoverished parents who did not have the financial means to "care" for their infants and hence were unable to supply their basic needs. It then became the duty of upper- and middle-class parents to raise up impoverished children, who are designated as everyone's offspring: "our little children."

But contained within Hale's opening question is a broader uneasiness about the vulnerability of the nation's children. The various features of *Godey's*—editorials, essays, illustrations, fashion plates, the Health Department—all combined to augment this anxiety. The mother, whose primary responsibility was to purify the home and herself and make all things conjugal cozy and comfortable, was blamed if that environment was anything otherwise for her husband and children. While Hale's ideas about motherhood generally represented the normative ones for the rising middle class in the antebellum era, she also mobilized these ideas to advance her reform agenda, primarily her goal of improving women's access to education, including their access to such specialized knowledge as medical practices. Bringing about this improvement thus depended on depictions of incompetent mothers and on the vulnerability of children, which Hale used to underscore the high stakes, for the family, society, and nation, of reforming women's education, and to drive home this point, Hale also drew on the conventions of sentimentalized death.

THE FREE CHILD

Along with sorrowful images of vulnerable children close to disease and death at every hour—images that would seem to call for more vigilance and a tighter rein on children—were images of carefree children being indulged in full freedom of movement, images just as important for Hale's agenda.

All children "die" in the sense that they inevitably reach adulthood; childhood does not last and children cease to be children. The transitory nature of childhood made it a more valuable experience subject to nostalgic meditations; the growing tendency of families to have fewer children and the zoning-off of childhood as a special, carefree period of development meant that the individual child was a cherished object and particular interest was taken in creating peaceful, pleasant surroundings to preserve childhood purity. In *Centuries of Childhood: A Social History of Family Life*, Philippe Ariès is largely concerned with articulating a "silent history" by tracing the evolution of Western childhood as an idea from medieval to present times. One of the most significant arguments to come out of his landmark work was that childhood is not a fixed, stable concept; it was only "discovered" in a limited way beginning with fourteenth-century art.[9] Childhood was not just a dynamic stage in human life, but a shifting social force for Ariès. Attitudes toward children shaped, and were shaped by, changing historical circumstances. According to Ariès, preoccupation with childhood as a unique transitional stage in human development culminated in the nineteenth century's veneration of the child (1962, 11–12). While national awareness of children's issues meant that they enjoyed increased worth and benefits, Ariès criticized this more intense attention as restraining to a child's freedom. "Henceforth it was recognized that the child was not ready for life, and that he had to be subjected to a special treatment, a sort of quarantine, before he was allowed to join the adults" (412).

In the nineteenth century, child advocates did not see their advice as resulting in the confinement of children, but wished for and exalted their full freedom of movement. We are so familiar with the sentimentalization of children's vulnerability that it is easy to overlook that their lives, their carefree playfulness, are often represented just as wistfully. In a July 1842 "Editors' Table" essay, Sarah Hale constructed a fictional conversation between a schoolmaster, his pupil Ellen Marvin, and her mother, Mrs. Marvin, that in its four columns weaves in and out of seemingly disconnected thematic threads: it opens with the truth of poetry and its link to nature, shifts to the advantages of leaving the city for the country in the summer months, next deplores enclosing grass areas in Philadelphia that bar children from enjoying these natural spaces, then manages to squeeze in a soliloquy on women's education and their moral mission to use their superior goodness only in service to others, when finally the discussion makes its way back to what I think is ultimately its main point about facilitating children's outdoor play in the city. The zigzagging path over which this editorial traverses might seem random, meant simply to reflect the twists and turns of everyday conversation, but I hesitate to label as arbitrary anything from Hale's deliberate and meticulous mind. For, at the heart of this editorial, lying uncomfortably between the cry for children's physical liberty and the didactic reiteration of women's moral obligations, exists a tension in a mother's duty to allow children freedom while she must protect them. When does protection become confinement?

Under the guise of these three personae, Hale condemns policies that fenced off grassy areas in urban Philadelphia. As the male schoolmaster, she shaped her criticism with a metaphor that posited children as the more delicate wildlife in need of protection: "Those who framed these regulations doubtless thought they were acting wisely in thus guarding the beauty of these promenades. They did not take into account . . . the human flowers which might pine and droop on the hot gravel walks; and that these human flowers are much more precious than the grass" (Hale 1842, 58). If grass needed protection from children, children needed protection from overly zealous City custodians who sought to restrict their movement to "hot gravel walks" for the grass's sake—an argument that implicitly suggests that, intentionally or not, the current arrangement was inflicting direct harm on the children.

Hale's conversationalists blame male Philadelphia policy makers for enforcing measures deleterious to children's health, but speaking through the schoolmaster, she slyly swings the gender pendulum to point out how women also cruelly restrict children:

> But your sex are not always perfect in practice if they are infallible in judgment, otherwise we should not see such preposterous dresses inflicted on children. Look at little girls, especially, bedizened out in laces, flowers, feathers, and all extravagant finery of belles; and then their dresses often made so tight fitting as to preclude all benefit from the exercises or plays which are permitted them. (Hale 1842, 58)

It was not uncommon for Hale, in what was ostensibly a fashion magazine, to criticize the frivolity and fetters of the fashion and parlor cultures that *Godey's* promoted.

While offering affection and protection, disciplinary intimacy could stifle women and children. The genteel labor-free parlor assembled so beautifully in *Godey's* fashion plates often poised women at thresholds, their overlapping closeness and bulky dresses acting as a barricade between the parlor and the outdoors (see figure 1.1) effectively blocking the child (frequently included in these tableaux) like the fenced-off grass areas that draw the ire of Hale's "Editors' Table" group. In this discussion, the schoolmaster laments the lack of physical play and rural sports for children: "How I pity the poor little creatures who are confined in close dwellings during the pleasant weather. No matter if their parents are rich, I call such children poor; for they will never have the best feelings of the heart and mind cultivated and strengthened" (1842, 59). In general, concern in *Godey's* about the well-being of children centers on their mobility. Swaddling infants, keeping children indoors, and restricting their play were all seen as debilitating to their development, and Hale supported children's free movement. In an 1859 essay on "Precocious Children," for instance, the author urged mothers to circulate children under "God's free air, and in the open green fields": "Physicians tell us there are four hundred organs of motion in the human body; each of these requires, for its adequate development, free space and motion, and nature herself dictates it" (1859, 154). While much of the content of *Godey's* emphasized the vulnerability and mortality of children, the magazine's call for more freedom was meant to remedy their tender fragility. Mrs. Marvin in Hale's editorial asserts that she has "little doubt that . . . confinement is one cause of the great mortality among children born in cities," and the schoolmaster argues that "the health of the children of this city might be much benefited, even the preservation of many lives among them gained by allowing them the full freedom of the public squares" (Hale 1842, 59).

The physical mobility of children is one aspect of a larger theme of travel and progress that threads its way through the July 1842 issue of *Godey's* and many antebellum numbers of the magazine. In this number alone, one finds a sketch of life in Ireland, a story that recounts a day's journey in a train across Massachusetts, a list of literary notices that features books on Italy, on India and Afghanistan, a tour through Turkey, Greece, Egypt, and Arabia, and a history of the Lewis and Clark expedition. Just as development and progress improved the nation, so the health of the child was sustained by a program of unrestricted movement, vigorous activity, and physical growth. To borrow a phrase from Lora Romero, this "entanglement of child rearing and empire building" (1992, 117) meant that cultivating the child encouraged trespassing on the grass: breaking through enclosures and trampling over nature. Although Leslie Fiedler argues that nineteenth-century American literature was about fleeing feminine influence, escaping the "gentle tyranny of home and woman" (1966, 194), *Godey's* suggests that the child's freedom was actually the duty and goal of the mother's care.

One threat to mobility and progress was too much exertion concentrated in one area that weakened growth of the organization as a whole. "Precocity" was often characterized by antebellum commentators as an impediment to the proper development of the child. The *Godey's* essay "Precocious Children," for example, exploits the sentimental child-as-flower metaphor to make its point about the hazards of over-stimulating the child's mind:

> There are many small hillocks in churchyards, under which sleep many precocious children. The bud—as in a mild winter, the mistaken primrose—pushes out its colored point too prematurely, and the first frost kills it. Two results invariably occur from the too early development of the growing faculties. Either the child, which was the pride of our heart, and the light of our home, droops and withers from us when most interesting; or the overworked brain loses its power, and the 'portent' in infancy is the 'stupid' of maturity. (1859, 153)

Nineteenth-century attitudes toward precocity ranged from admiration for child prodigies to warnings like the one above prophesying that precocity would inevitably lead to either idiocy or an early grave.[10] In entertainment culture, "prodigy" referred to an adolescent "phenom" who exhibited immense talent in artistic or intellectual capacities. Medically, a precocious child lacked a proper balance between mental and physical activity; this fault was typically ascribed to parents who overworked the child's brain without allowing much invigorating exercise. A mother should not persist in showcasing her children such that "home, the child's home, which should breathe only of happiness, becomes an infant prison, and dyspepsia, deformed limbs, hysteria, and the thousand demons of disease, fatten upon young hearts, never to leave them" (1859, 153).[11]

This passage on precocity leads to a more sinister image of the home as a prison, an image that awakened the antebellum American imagination. The home as a potential prison centered dramatically in gothic fiction. (*Godey's* contributor Edgar Allan Poe's "The Fall of the House of Usher" is an example par excellence.) The *Godey's* passage quoted above evokes terrifying visions of demons, deformity, and children in possessed hysterics. Prevailing literary modes—the sentimental, the gothic—offered useful sets of conventions for *Godey's* nonfiction writers, including Hale, to engage readers and give them a clear picture of the consequences of bad parenting (here, the disastrous outcome of indulging precocity). By presenting the ominous, if fantastical, prospect of a home transformed into a gloomy prison, Hale and *Godey's* could then set about the work of raising the diligent, well-educated mother to the great role of liberator.

In order to free the home's captives, *Godey's* not only recommended circulating children in the open air; the magazine also endowed children with democratic rights that constituted them as "free" subjects of maternal governance. For example, "The Rights of Children," an essay by Emma C. Embury that Hale included in the February 1844 number, brings together discourses on motherhood and childhood with a political discourse on governing. The title alone evokes Enlightenment doctrines on the rights of man and classical treatises on the rights of citizens, philosophies that informed the principles and language in the political documents of the new American republic and with which *Godey's* readers would have been familiar. In its substitution of "children" for "man" the title also suggests a challenge to traditional Lockean beliefs of the emptiness of the child's mind. "The Rights of Children" would seem to indicate a declaration of children's independence and an assertion of their agency; it imagines them as entitled, not submissive, beings.

Like Jefferson's *Declaration of Independence*, Embury's article voices the grievances of a group whose power of speech has been discounted. She vilifies the parent who over-indulges, who ignores, who tyrannizes, who would "contaminate for ever the snowy purity of the infant mind." Indeed, she compares the physical abuse of children with the mistreatment of convicts in language that drifts very close to descriptions of American slavery: prisoners "dreaded the lash like base hounds; and amid the deep traces of sin and suffering written on their blasted brows, could be read the debasing influence of that system which sears the mind through the scars of the quivering body" (1844, 81). And similar to Jefferson's invalidation of the king's authority over the colonists, Embury's declaration, too, casts doubt on the prerogative of parents to assume absolute rule over their young charges. She points out that the

> guardians of infancy are usually selected with infinitely less care than we should bestow upon the qualifications of a cook, since a certain degree of skill is requisite to the proper pampering of our appetites, while any one is supposed to be capable of "tending baby." . . . And surely the child whose dawning intellect is clouded by the mists of ignorance and folly, through this gross neglect of a parent's highest privileges, has been despoiled of one of its most solemn rights." (80)

Embury (like her model, Jefferson) is not rallying for the complete freedom of her constituents but for the right of these dependent subjects to be governed fairly and knowledgeably. Ultimately her essay relies on sentimental rhetoric to describe the innocent infant citizen and rests on the assumption that political agency for the child can only be guaranteed by proper nurture, in this case affective mothering. Embury offers *Godey's* readers a maternal philosophy that values the child's obedience through "judicious" (not tyrannical) parenting. The mother exerts her authority through love, and loving authority is what makes the child want to obey. But affective parenting in Embury's paradigm does not merely promote strengthening emotional bonds between mother and child. It also involves cultivating the child's faculty of reason: "Children must be taught the principles of the laws by which they are directed, and they should be fully informed of the meaning of every variation from fixed rules" (1844, 81). If the parent instructs the child about his own governance and fuels his "expanding reason," the child "will not hesitate in his obedience" (81). Through informed consent, the child becomes an agent of his own submission.

Embury claims it as the child's right to be "governed by fixed rules of conduct" (1844, 80). It is thus through consistent affective mothering that the child becomes interpellated into the governing practices of American democracy. The figure of the child as an "emblem of freedom"[12] and a self-determined being commands the respect of the parent, who rules by a "code of laws" instead of despotic "whim" (81), therefore securing the happiness of a liberated childhood. The "happiest child is that one who has been fully disciplined in every duty," concludes Embury. "Obedience, deference, a subjection of the will to the gentle governance of affection, are all requisite to a sense of happiness in childhood" (83). The child seeking approval desires to say "Yes" to parental authority, and the parent in turn craves the child's consent. Similarly, the democratic state will provide a system of care that enfolds its citizens within its protective embrace in order to establish good public opinion. According to Gillian Brown, "the figure of the consenting child validates the consensual state of adults that itself emanates from childhood" (2001, 23). It is not surprising, then, that the model of affective parenting, reproduced and decreed by *Godey's*, placed considerable emphasis on the physical liberation of the child. A state of freedom for the child becomes associated with a maternal support structure that ensures a suitable, protected environment in which to enjoy that freedom.

Sarah J. Hale and *Godey's Lady's Book* use new perceptions of childhood to empower their women readers. Hale astutely recognized that moral authority in the nineteenth century—who could claim it and how to justify it—had shifted from the points of the king's crown to the warmth of the female heart. She helped to build the empire of the mother that was bolstered by an array of intersecting rhetorics: the domestic, sentimental, and political. For Hale, it meant melding multiple languages into a discourse on motherhood that relied on the vulnerability of children. If the sentimentalization of children's lives demonstrated how important early childhood development was in citizen formation and turned the figure of the child into a potent symbol of American freedom, then the sentimentalization of their deaths revealed how tenuous that freedom really was. Hale has been and continues to be useful to scholars as a conservative straw woman who designed and upheld a single, sentimental view of the mother in the influential pages of *Godey's*. But a closer analysis of Hale's writing and editorship reveals moments where she condemned the failure of sentimentalist literary techniques to represent women's work as mothers accurately and where she adeptly appropriated conventional depictions of mother and child in order to turn them on their head. By juxtaposing images of the dangers to children with images of benign freedom, Hale advanced a vision of women as protectors of children and as the arbiters of how the republic could best grow and thrive. If women were not trained and called upon to practice maternal benevolence, the very health and survival of the family and the nation were threatened.

NOTES

1. Mary McCartin Wearn warns scholars who read the sentimental representation of motherhood as "a coherent, monolithic, and essentially conservative cultural product" (2007, 11). In *Negotiating Motherhood*, Wearn analyzes how writers like Harriet Beecher Stowe and Harriet Jacobs complicated the maternal ideal, holding up their work against popular periodicals like *Godey's* that she deems prescriptive rather than progressive. The point that I want to make in this essay is that Hale and her magazine also offered a more complex picture of motherhood even as they propagated an image of divine maternity. Hale, the mother of five children, would have understood the difficulties of bearing the sole responsibility for a child's welfare as well as the pressure to conform to prevalent models of motherhood.

2. I do not wish to conflate the views of Hale and *Godey's*. Patricia Okker has observed that Louis Godey and Sarah Hale "had a clear sense of divided duties": Godey was the publisher and Hale the literary editor, and the "only feature that she evidently did not manage was fashion." While their "voices within the magazine did, at times, compete with one another, the magazine . . . did find a coherent identity, one that, significantly, celebrated Victorian ideologies of gender" (1995, 51). I examine various contributions to *Godey's*, Hale's and others', but my study of motherhood looks at how it is presented within the scope and mission of the magazine. For the most part they do complement each other and serve Hale's particular goal of advocating on behalf of women's issues.

3. This notion of motherhood was based on Benjamin Rush's idea of "Republican Motherhood," which reflected a post-Revolutionary desire to establish a political role for women. Linda Kerber reintroduced the term into scholarly discussions of womanhood in nineteenth-century America, explaining that Republican Motherhood "merged the domestic domain of the preindustrial woman with the new public ideology of individual responsibility and civic virtue" (1986, 269). I agree with Patricia Okker's claim in *Our Sister Editors* that "Hale would have likely found republican ideologies of gender limiting, for such rhetorics tended to define women primarily as wives and mothers and as occupying the domestic space" (1995, 50). However, I would add that perpetuating conventional models of motherhood established an ideal that, for Hale, would require reforms in women's lives and education if they were realistically expected to achieve it. Republican Motherhood thus became a platform upon which Hale argued for women's progress.

4. Conversations about Sarah Hale tend to revolve around the was-she-or-wasn't-she question of her politics: was she a radical in her efforts to expand women's education or was she a conservative in her unwillingness to press for women's right to vote? Hale's politics are not an easy either/or. *Godey's* presented women with the sentimentalized ideal of motherhood, the "perpetual Mother's Day" that Ann Douglas despised (1977a: 6), but Hale also used its pages to make the case that many women did not fit the bill. I show how Hale's demonstration of the unpreparedness of women to mother sufficiently became a powerful critique that used the child at risk to bring to light unfair gender practices and to show the vital importance of educating women.

5. 5 Mothering magazines began as organs for maternal associations. They were often religious in tone, publishing reports from meetings, missionary activity, parenting advice, and sentimental poetry. Popular examples include *The Mother's Magazine* (1833); *The Mother's Journal* (1836); *The Mother's Assistant and Young Lady's Friend* (1841); *Mrs. Whittelsey's Magazine for Mothers* (1850).

6. Amy Kaplan's landmark essay "Manifest Domesticity" (1998) points out the connection between the domestic as the space occupied by the family and the domestic as the entire nation in contradistinction to the foreign. Kaplan examines the "imperial scope" of Catharine

Beecher's *Treatise on Domestic Economy* and works by Sarah Hale, arguing that a reading of Hale "suggests that the concept of female influence so central to domestic discourse and at the heart of the sentimental ethos is underwritten by and abets the imperial expansion of the nation" (599).

7. The term "sentimental culture" is quoted from Karen Halttunen, who defines it as a "response to the poisonous hypocrisy being spread by the confidence man and the painted woman." As a result, "the conduct manuals concocted a sentimental antidote in the personal ideal of sincerity. More important, they insisted that the social forms and rituals adhered to in 'polite society,' where the proper people met face-to-face, ensure the sincerity of all participants" (1982, xvi). Halttunen is useful for recognizing that "sentimentalism" is not just a body of literature but a set of cultural assumptions (1982, 60).

8. The first installment of the "Health Department" in the July 1858 issue sought to "correct knowledge on the vitally important subjects of health and disease," directing its contents to the woman who was expected to assume "the duty of nursing the sick," but whose own "peculiar organization subjects her to diseases of the greatest gravity and complexity, diseases more often misunderstood and maltreated than any others" (Wilson 1858, 84). By 1860, Wilson's column shifted from concerns about women's health to the ways that women were inadvertently harming their children through uninformed medical practices and neglect of their maternal duties. "A mother who fails, without good cause, to discharge her maternal obligations," warns Wilson, "is guilty of criminal injustice to her offspring . . . which, in many cases, must result in the moral or physical destruction of her child, with a lifelong train of unavailing regrets over the sad consequences of her own folly and want of faithfulness" (1860, 80).

9. Ariès (1962) uses the "world of pictorial representation" as his entry into a discussion of the cultural significance of childhood. Thus it follows for Ariès that the lack of children as children in pre-medieval art means that "the men of the tenth and eleventh centuries did not dwell on the image of childhood, and that that image had neither interest nor even reality for them" (34). He proposes that a "completely new iconography" of childhood scenes appeared in the fourteenth century when "painters of religious childhood went beyond that of Jesus" (37, 36).

10. In an 1820 blurb about a "little living dictionary" for the *Euterpeiad, or Musical Intelligence,* the writer treats precocity as a trend, referring to a "rage for juvenile prodigies" ("Precocity" 1820, 119), while in the 1833 issue of *Mechanics' Magazine, and Journal of the Mechanics' Institute,* a writer alerts readers to the "danger of mental excitement": "On this point, the opinions of the most celebrated physicians seem to be unanimous. . . . 'Those highly gifted with precocious intellects possess miserable health and are generally short-lived; they are cut off by chronic inflammations, and disorganization of their viscera, or by acute inflammation of the brain'" ("Danger" 1833, 132).

11. According to Mary De Jong's *American National Biography* entry on the Davidson sisters, for instance, "Sarah J. Hale, an advocate of education for women, denied that rigorous schooling destroyed Lucretia, but she faulted Margaret's mother for allowing the child's 'imagination' to develop 'at the expense of her constitution when, by patient and prudent training, it might have been suppressed'" (2000).

12. This phrase is Brown's (2001). She argues, "Because the conception of the consensual child was a cornerstone in the founding of the United States, this figure attains a natural status, appearing as an emblem of freedom emanating from nature. Rather than standing as the conceptual figure that Locke imagines, the consensual child quickly becomes a literal entity, a being endowed with the full capacities and rights of self-determination" (23–24).

Chapter Two

"The Medicine of Sympathy"

Mothers, Sons, and Affective Pedagogy in Antebellum America

Ken Parille

Good mothers alone make *good men*. —E. N. Kirk, 1843

[We] base our plans for [a boy's] improvement upon the assumption of his total depravity. —"The Profession of Schoolmaster," 1858

A boy . . . does not readily find the medicine of sympathy.—Lydia Sigourney, 1853

As Joanne Dobson observes, "sentimentalism . . . takes as its highest values sympathy, affection, and relation" (1997, 283). Literary scholarship on sentimentality has been attuned to various relationships, such as those between mother and child, female friends, or whites and racial others, often focusing on the function of sympathy in writings about these bonds and on the performance of affect in social and political encounters. Scholars have looked less, however, at writings that undermine discourses of sympathy, especially those that interrogate popular beliefs about women and emotion.[1] Although antebellum culture celebrated the mother as a "fountain of sympathy," many maternal advice writers anxiously called this claim into question. They were eager to show that the "all-sympathizing" mother was a sentimental fiction, arguing that mothers frequently needed the most basic of instructions on how to generate sympathy in the management of children. As Michel Foucault notes, the celebration of sympathy has been central to a discipline based upon "the affective intensification of the family space" (1978, 109). It is easy to see, then, why domestic advice writers would be concerned, for they believed the mother-son relationship was the affective familial bond most crucial to domestic and national stability.

Critics often discuss the mother-child relationship without making the kinds of distinctions between male and female children made by many ante-bellum women writers. These authors saw gender as a problem that compli-cates the category of "the child," and they revised sentimental beliefs about the affective nature not only of mothers, but of children as well. In particular, they outlined crucial differences between the affective capacities of boys and of girls, noting that such distinctions undergirded mothers' approaches to discipline, even in ways that many mothers did not recognize. Among the numerous texts I explore, the writings of Harriet Beecher Stowe and Lydia Sigourney perhaps best represent this revision. Stowe's *Uncle Tom's Cabin*, which critics see as exemplifying antebellum sentimentalism in its celebra-tion of domestic affect and motherhood, narrates the complete failure of maternal sympathy as a tool for managing boys. Possibly the period's most dramatic commentary on the limits—and indeed the failure—of sympathy, the novel features two idealized mothers who raise the narrative's two most troubled sons. Like *Uncle Tom's Cabin*, Sigourney's *Letters to Mothers* praises "mother love" as a powerful and redemptive social force, yet she shows it to be an abstraction that bears little if any connection to the presence (or absence) of pedagogical sympathy within boyhood management. She believes that when a son was the disciplinary subject, most mothers simply did not act in accord with the convention of the "all-sympathizing" mother.

Arguments about maternal sympathy reveal that boyhood discipline was a profound source of concern for domestic theorists, and they speak to larger questions of sentimentality and affect, and to the tense yet intimate relation-ship between boyhood and domesticity--two cultural constructs that critical discourse, working within the logic of "separate spheres," often figures as opposites. Since the publication of Glenn Hendler and Mary Chapman's *Sentimental Men*, many scholars have noted that forms of masculinity are closely tied to questions of sentimentality, thus breaking down a traditional opposition between the two. Yet little work has studied boys as subjects constructed by domestic pedagogical discourses, ones that are decidedly dis-tinct from sentimental writings. It would be a mistake, therefore, to see recent studies of masculinity—which, as Judith Kegan Gardiner notes, have paid insufficient attention to "age categories"—as necessarily telling us about the content of boyhood masculinity (2002, 91).[2] Examining writing about moth-ers and sons exposes fears about the consequences of boys' nature. If boys were "mischievous," "troubled," and motivated only by self-gratification (as transcendentalist educator Bronson Alcott and many others said), then how could maternal sympathy—which relies on the moral nature of both the authority and her charge—be effective in managing them? Driving these anxieties were fears about the roles that boys would eventually inhabit, such as father, husband, merchant, or politician. If mothers failed to sympathize with boys, if they failed to act like the sentimental mother, it would mean disaster for the domestic and public spaces boys would populate as men.

Along with their interrogation of ideas about maternal sympathy and boys, Stowe, Sigourney, and the other writers I examine make varied and contradictory claims about the nature of sympathy itself. Some believed it flowed naturally from mothers to all children and was therefore the most accessible and potent form of discipline. Others agreed it was an involuntary response, but made an important qualification: it typically manifested itself only within the mother-daughter relationship. Mothers, they claimed, had an inherent tendency to disidentify with boys; because the nature of boys was so different from that of girls and women, mothers distanced themselves from sons. These writers believed that mothers could learn to generate sympathy and that it could be authentically performed if mothers recognized its disciplinary benefits. Although it might seem paradoxical given the many sentimental depictions of sympathy as natural and involuntary, these authors understood it as a learned, rational response to the problems of child management.

In the quotation I began with, Dobson makes a familiar association between sympathy and sentimentality, one that sees the former as intrinsically allied to the latter: discussions of sympathy are always about sentimentality because sympathy is the force that brings the world into accord with the objectives of sentimental ideology. Studies of nineteenth-century American culture almost always conceive of sympathy in this way, but I argue that many domestic theorists felt differently. They endorsed sympathy as a child management tool, while simultaneously revising or even completely dismissing sentimentalized beliefs about the nature of mothers and of sympathy. Critics have said that that culture fully embraced these beliefs (especially during the antebellum period), but the writings I look at undermine this critical position; they represent a widely disseminated approach that shares center stage with sentimental claims in debates about affect and child management. For many writers, sympathy had little or nothing to do with sentimentality.

In the eighteenth and early nineteenth centuries, American domestic theorists believed—as John Locke and others had argued—that the father was responsible for his children's moral education. But in the decades before 1850, "the custody of children was transferred . . . officially from male to female," and the theoretical and practical implications of this transfer were developed in maternal advice literature, a body of writing instrumental in shaping women's beliefs about motherhood (Ryan 1982, 56). Given domestic ideology's tendency to figure the mother as the locus of familial sentiment, it is not surprising that maternal affective pedagogy—the management of children by appeals to their moral and emotional bonds with the mother—occupies center stage in advice literature's theorizing of affective discipline. Beliefs about mothers' sympathy are expressed within this literature in discourses that I will call "pragmatic" and "sentimental." Pragmatic discourses typically appear in educational journals and advice writing, and they examine the relationship between white mothers and their children by focusing at length on particular disciplinary approaches. Articles such as "Mothers, Do You Sympathize with Your Children?" (1856), "The Comforts of Playing 'Hookie'" (1856), and "What is to be done with Charley?" (1860), which were staples in books and magazines directed at mothers,[3] outline the skills a mother needs to teach her child and suggest numerous forms of motivation and discipline. The five-part epistolary series, "Training of Boys," published in 1845 in *The Mother's Journal and Family Visitant*, for example, details the "moral and physical training" of sons, discussing "boy-nature," how to create a domestic environment that adapts to this nature, and how to use an affect-based discipline (1845a, 117).

Perhaps the most popular way of talking about maternal sympathy embodies a mode of thinking about culture that in nineteenth-century studies has been called "sentimental." This ideology is visible in the popular encomiums to "eternal mother love" and the "hallowed" nature of the white mother-child relationship, such as often appear in novels, poetry, sketches, and women's magazines. Sentimental discourses tend to be less explicitly instructional than pragmatic ones. They celebrate the mother's capacity to generate sympathy and govern children with it: "What a fountain of love is a mother's heart," an anonymous author in *The Mother's Magazine* writes in language typical of sentimental discourse, "and how it pours out its streams upon her offspring . . . how tender her sympathy in his misfortune" ("A Mother's Love" 1845, 115).[4] Like mother love itself, the ability to sympathize is seen as "unquenchable" and innate to women. In a similarly titled essay in *Godey's Lady's Book*, published in 1852, Mrs. Ellis refers to this love as an "instinct . . . that we have no power to control or subdue," which "imbibes the mind with equal tenderness for her infirm child . . . as for him who gives early promise of personal as well as mental beauty" (1852, 163). As these writers understood it, mothers were equally likely to sympathize with healthy or sick children and with sons as well as daughters.

Although sentimental and pragmatic discourses typically agree about mothers' inherent ability to sympathize with daughters, in theories of boyhood management, these two discourses are often completely at odds.[5] Mary Ryan suggests that "the sexes intersected in such a way as to create, at the level of ideology at least, a tight knot between mother and son," but pragmatic ideology insisted the opposite was true (1982, 58–9). The mother-son bond is almost always figured as the most unstable family structure. Pragmatic writers offer two distinct objections to sentimental discourse. Some claim that mothers are inherently unsympathetic toward boys yet can learn to use sympathy when disciplining them. Others argue that the very use of sympathy with boys is at best ineffective—a boy's nature is such that he can't respond to it—and at worst dangerous—boys will manipulate it to avoid punishment.[6] While pragmatic discourses occasionally portray a mother as unsympathetic toward her daughter, they almost never suggest that mothers possess a natural tendency to be so. Paula Bennett has said that the second half of the century witnessed "profound changes [in] women's self-construction" that revised the "sentimental discourse" of writers including Sigourney (1995, 592).[7] As I show, however, Sigourney and many other pragmatic antebellum authors constantly critique and reimagine popular definitions of women and sentiment, especially those about mothers and sympathy.

Animating writings about sympathy and maternal nature are theories of what was often called "boy-nature," which was seen as a particular disciplinary challenge to mothers. While literary critics often characterize "the boy" as a figure admired by nineteenth-century culture, boys were understood in complicated and contradictory ways, not only within discussions of the mother-son bond, but throughout antebellum culture itself. Though "the boy" was celebrated in sentimental sketches and poems (as "the child" and "the girl" were), in educational discourses boys were repeatedly characterized as "mischievous," "troubled," and "depraved." Sympathy, as David Marshall notes, depends on one's "capacity to feel the sentiments of someone else," thus making the "depraved" and self-directed boy inherently a troubled category. Boys were seen as far less able (or completely unable) to respond to affect than girls because they lacked girls' sympathetic and moral nature (1988, 3). The anecdotes of misbehaving boys that appear in advice literature rarely depict male children producing contrition or tears, sentimental emotional responses that figure a child as capable of acknowledging a breach of familial bonds and her own moral negligence. In "Mothers, do you sympathize with your children?," a piece in a popular 1856 collection *The Mother's Rule*, a boy misbehaves in ways typically associated with the limited emotional range of boys. He "has an irritable temper. A trifle would make him angry, and then would come an outburst of passion" (1856, 127). Like an animal, the boy is easily triggered; he has difficulty recognizing that his own desires should be subordinated to the desires of others and to the needs of family order. In "The Bright Side," also from *The Mother's Rule*, the author contrasts the mothers of the two discourses—the sentimental and the pragmatic—connecting their ability to sympathize to their notions of boy-nature. The author sets the mother "whose heart is ever ready with . . . abundant sympathy" against the hostile mother often found in pragmatic discourses who refuses to identify with boys (1856, 196). Echoing the understanding of gender difference endorsed by the woman who believed men and boys would be "savage creature[s] . . . without the meliorating offices of the gentle sex," this mother exclaims, "*All* boys [are] noisy savages," and "are, as a matter of course, to be snubbed, and stinted, and *put down!*" (196). It is important to note that she generalizes only about boys: although some girls are "frivolous," "*All* boys [are] noisy savages." She simplifies boys' emotions in order to justify her harsh disciplinary "course." Her ideas about girl-nature do not lead to a discussion of any discipline that might result from these traits, whereas her beliefs about boys are connected to an endorsement of repression: since boys can't respond to maternal sympathy, they need to be "snubbed . . . and *put down!*"

Although the harshness of this mother places her on the extreme end of bad mothering as seen in pragmatic discourses, she nevertheless represents one of this discourse's central tenets: the belief, echoed throughout antebellum culture, that mothers often failed to sympathize with boys because they believed boys, like savages, were either devoid of morality or had less developed sympathetic natures than girls. Horace Mann, perhaps the most influential American educator in the nineteenth century, proposes that "the differences of organization and temperament which individualize the sexes" meant that girls "need kindness and not force. . . . They can feel a thing to be right or wrong . . . and hence, appeals should be addressed to their sentiments" (1843, 28), and the popular fictional and pedagogical writings of Jacob Abbott repeatedly define girls as both more "reasonable" and "affectionate" than their male counterparts. (Abbott 1841a, 66, 70, 97; and Abbott 1841b, 75–76.) Prominent Cambridge, Massachusetts, doctor Morill Wyman and many others argue for banning the corporal punishment of girls because of their ability to respond to reason: "certainly . . . whips . . . can be dispensed with in the case of a reasoning girl" but not, he insists, in the case of boys (1867, 6). Corporal discipline theorist Lyman Cobb similarly claims that girls "certainly *can* be *persuaded* to do what is right," while boys often cannot. Cobb believes that very young boys are essentially good, but often in "*boyhood*," he says, "they become BAD" (1847, 205): "many boys are rather *unfeeling*," and "are not, at that time, suitable company for men, women, or children" (1847, 210–11). Cobb's ideas about boys' development accord with standard nineteenth-century child-rearing philosophies, which held that boys and girls as infants and young children possessed similar natures and therefore should be disciplined in similar ways. Though nineteenth-century adult males are often characterized by their capacity for reason, this was decidedly not the case for boys, for boyhood was a distinct stage. The boy was not yet a man, but he was also no longer the generic sentimental "child"; he had entered boyhood, becoming "unfeeling" and unreachable through affective bonds, and therefore a chronic problem for maternal affective pedagogy. For some of these writers, boyhood was the antithesis of sentimentality. Laura Wexler has argued that any "enlargement by sentimentality of the percentage of the population who can come 'inside' the magic circle of domesticity still leaves behind the vast numbers who cannot qualify for entry under moral standards" (1992, 17). It was precisely on the grounds of these standards that some writers argued boys could not always participate in a domesticity created by sentiment—boys had a limited capacity to reproduce in themselves the emotions of others. Wexler sees forms of sentiment as allied with the project to acculturate "savages," yet does not note that ante-bellum boys were often described as "savage" in pedagogical theory, a popular trope that had implications for boys' discipline and acculturation. Although the treatment of white boys was far removed from that of marginalized nonwhite groups, the metaphor suggests a kind of cultural stigma attached to boys that was similar to one often attached to Native Americans. Scholars who discuss this metaphor cite its use by post-Civil War male authors as a way to celebrate the boy, yet such examples do not represent antebellum uses. Kenneth Kidd claims that "savagery was often a less pejorative concept than we might assume, associated with self-reliance and entrepreneurial spirit" (2004, 63). Similarly, Gillian Brown says that "nineteenth-century Americans often characterized the sphere of boyhood . . . as a state of savagery," and she cites Mark Twain's friend Charles Dudley Warner as representative of those who, like many late-century male writers, saw the metaphor as ennobling: "every boy who is good for anything is a natural savage" (2003, 26).

Brown and Kidd may be correct about the late century, but they do not note that antebellum educators and mother's advice writers repeatedly invoke the metaphor to explain why boys could require corporal punishment and be immune to affective appeals. In a series titled the "Training of Boys," the author worries that readers might find the very discussion of sympathy "incongruous with my general subject" of managing male children, an understandable concern given that boys' discipline was often identified, not with "moral suasion," but with corporal punishment (1845c, 164); as one educational writer observes, "Ask what is meant by a good disciplinarian . . . and the general reply will be, 'the teacher who knows how to . . . make boys learn . . . by a liberal use of the rod'" (Richards 1855, 108). In "The Profession of Schoolmaster," the author makes it clear that ideas about the "savagery" of boys were closely connected to their pedagogy: we "put him into that class . . . *fera naturae* . . . and base our plans for his improvement upon the assumption of his total depravity" (1858, 41). Theories of boy-nature, then, determine the practices of boyhood discipline.

While I am not equating the social status of white boys and Native Americans, I am suggesting that the parallel between them is meaningful to women's advice authors. For many, this nature means that boys' participation in sentimental "family circles" is a vexed question in a way that girls' involvement is not. Advisors want to see that mothers, to adapt Stowe's famous words, "felt right" about boys in the ways that Stowe and others want them to feel right about slaves or other marginalized figures such as Native Americans, asylum patients, or prisoners, all of whom are not part of the world of white middle-class authors. When the figure is a boy, who as a future man appears to be the least marginalized figure in antebellum culture, the parameters that often define domesticity and what it excludes—such as race or class—disappear. The ostensible goal of affect-producing narratives such as *Uncle Tom's Cabin* and Sedgwick's *Hope Leslie* was to humanize nonwhite others and present them as subjects worthy of white sympathy and a place in American public life. Similarly, boys were often characterized by pragmatic writers as liminal figures, unfairly cut off from mothers' sympathy and exiled from home, a separation that only sympathy could repair. [8]

Most advice writers understood the exile of boys as a problem, and that belief about the relationship between boyhood and domesticity challenges the current critical view represented by historian E. Anthony Rotundo, who makes an often repeated "separate spheres" argument. The physical and ideological exile of boys from women's spaces and women's sympathy, he says, was solely intended for boys' and society's benefit. They were left alone to explore "boy culture," a carefully constructed masculine world outside of and antithetical to the domestic and sentimental "circle" and a world whose rules prepared boys for a place in public life and for the competition of the market (Rotundo, 63, 80).[9] Rotundo and many scholars cite the relationship between boys and maternal authorities visible in Huck Finn's and Tom Sawyer's desire to escape the civilizing influence of women as representative of the relationship between boyhood and the domestic endorsed by authors and educators throughout the century. Yet writers in *Mother's Journal* often criticize genteel culture for banishing boys to "the streets, that mamma and sisters might play on the piano and write letters in peace" ("What is to be done with Charley?," 1860, 15). In "Look at the Results" the author argues that not only do many mothers and sisters attempt to exclude boys from domestic life, but every family member will display "a want of *consideration*" when dealing with boys (1843, 56). She tells an anecdote about the mistreatment that boys often suffer: immediately upon entering his family's house, a dirty and disheveled boy is chastised by the servant and his sister, threatened with a whipping by his mother, and scolded by his father. The author, who claims to have observed this scene, lectures mothers on how to be affectionate to neglected boys and "win [their] kind feelings" (58). The debate about discipline represented by the conflict between the views of the author and the family she discusses reveals that antebellum theories of boyhood masculinity are a contested site within, not outside of, domestic spaces and theory, and that such patriarchal structures, rather than always celebrating boys, express contradictory and often condemnatory ideas about them.

Poet, advice author, and essayist Lydia Sigourney was deeply interested in boys and showed far more concern for them than did many educators and authors; her *Letters to Mothers* was one of the most popular of the numerous antebellum maternal advice books to counsel its readers about boyhood management and sympathy. In the opening of Letter XI, "Idiom of Character," it appears as if Sigourney is going to construct an individualized, gender-neutral disciplinary theory, one aware of the "different dispositions of each subject" (1838, 118). It soon becomes clear, however, that her theory is based on "the barrier which an Unerring Hand erected between" the natures of boys and girls and on a key belief about maternal nature: mothers have difficulty providing "affectionate mother[ing]" to boys (1838b, 121). Sigourney cites a poem that offers a typical characterization of boy-nature and its uneasy relationship to maternal discipline:

> boys are driven
> To wild pursuits, by mighty impulses.
> Out of a mother's anxious hands they tear
> The leading-strings.
> (1838, 122)

Although the word "savage" is not used, the poem's language invokes the content of the trope. Like the savage, the "wild" boy is not controlled by reason; instead he is "driven . . . by mighty impulses," and his actions tend toward expressions of violence, as he "tear[s] / The leading-strings." Because of this aggressive and physical nature, "in the discipline of sons," she warns, "mothers need a double portion of the wisdom that is from above" (1838, 121). This assertion stands in stark contrast to Sigourney's sentimental figuring of mothers and daughters, repeatedly saying that their sympathetic relationship flows from female nature itself and is reinforced by participation in activities that take sympathy as their primary subject: together they "visit the aged, go on errands of mercy . . . [and] sit by the side of the sufferer" (120). With girls, sympathy comes naturally, but with boys, it must be calculated. The mother needs to train herself how to "keep hold on his affections" by demonstrating affection toward him herself (123).

In pragmatic writing on boys like Sigourney's, then, sympathy becomes denaturalized; it does not arise spontaneously from the mother as sentimental discourse claimed, but rather it must be learned or unlearned and employed or rejected. The series "Training of Boys" reveals a deep anxiety about sympathy that is not immediately apparent in the writings of Sigourney and others, an anxiety that reflects sympathy's valorization throughout antebellum culture. Something that can be so transformative, so powerful a means of control, could, if misapplied, be destructive; although sympathy could have a "salutary influence . . . on boys" (1845c, 164), "even this best principle," the author warns, can "degenerate into a morbid tenderness, subversive of the best interests" of boyhood discipline (1845b, 148). Calculating the proper amount of sympathy to use on a boy was the mother's difficult task, one that

presented numerous problems as she struggled to find the precise mean between a "morbid tenderness" and a "cold and distant manner" (1845b, 148).
When a sentimentalized sympathy produces too great an identification with
the disciplinary subject, it fails to fulfill its promise to curb the excesses
associated with the savagery of boyhood masculinity, becoming the "false
tenderness" that "is the fruitful source of very much of the misrule . . .[and]
unsubdued passions . . . which stalk abroad unabashed at the present day"
(1845b, 149).

Like the pragmatic writers discussed earlier, authors skeptical of using
sympathy with boys also criticize sentimental beliefs about the natures of
mothers and children. They do not argue, however, that mothers lack sympathy, but rather that the sympathy, which comes naturally to them, represents a
threat to proper management; the sympathizing mother would likely be lax in
her application of discipline. For these writers, sympathy is an unreliable
emotion that can negate discipline. An essay that dramatizes this concern is
"The Comforts of Playing 'Hookie,'" which appeared in *The Mother's Magazine for Daughters and Mothers*. To provoke an emotional response in
readers accustomed to the sentimental staple of bodies in pain, it begins with
a picture of a "poor" suffering boy followed by a series of questions interrogating the reader's reaction to the image. The first question asks, "Have you
any sympathy with this poor boy?" and, worried that readers might answer
yes, the author quickly undermines this identification by showing it to be
dangerous (1856, 91). The boy has skipped school and, though he shivers in
the cold, he does not deserve any mother's sympathy. The author talks to the
boy, modeling the way that mothers should manage misbehaving sons and
warning them that boys can manipulate maternal affect. Questioning the
authenticity of the boy's "sorry looks," she views them as a performance for
readers/mothers; his appearance of suffering and remorse seems to be an
index of genuine contrition but is marked as false, just as to respond to it
would be "false tenderness." For her, the sole sign of repentance should be
for the boy to "run home [and] take a whipping" and not to hope that his
performance will moderate or eliminate the stern discipline he deserves
(1856, 92). Whereas the author of "Training of Boys" sees only excessive
sympathy as a "morbid tenderness"(1845b, 148) that could work against
discipline, this author views even the slightest amount of sympathy with the
disciplinary subject as harmful, thus rejecting any affect-based discipline for
boys.

Not only is corporal punishment and physical suffering endorsed in "The
Comforts of Playing 'Hookie,'" but more importantly, it is coupled with the
denial of sympathy, a disciplinary tactic the mother in "The Bright Side"
implies is foremost in her arsenal when she recommends "snubbing" boys
(1856, 196). Whereas affective pedagogy was supposed to situate the disciplinary subject within familial bonds as a way to control him, here the denial

of sympathy becomes a form of discipline. Tellingly, this piece appears in a section of the journal called "The Family Circle," a recurring feature that often dramatized principles of familial discipline by offering anecdotes of domestic life. For this author and many others we have explored, the boy's participation in the family circle is not a given, and the withholding of sympathy essentially bans him from affective domesticity. The author believes that the boy's "sorry looks" expose a weakness in the claims of those who endorse affective discipline; if mothers cannot distinguish between a boy's real and performed suffering—and boys were often described as "deceitful"—then affective discipline cannot succeed. Boy-nature was more powerful in its ability to deceive than maternal nature was in its capacity to govern with sympathy.

As a writer acutely aware of the connection between sentiment and suffering bodies like the one in "The Comforts of Playing 'Hookie,'" domestic novelist Catharine Sedgwick understood the effect that such an image could have on readers. Elizabeth Barnes has noted that nineteenth-century readers were trained "to put themselves in the character's position in order to experience the full effects of the punishment meted out" (1996, 608), and Sedgwick worries that the opening scene of punishment in her novel *Home* could trigger exactly this kind of identification between maternal reader and disciplined boy character. Unlike the author of "The Comforts of Playing 'Hookie,'" however, Sedgwick is not concerned that boys will manipulate sympathy, but rather that maternal sentiment will compromise punishment. She fears, as does the author of "The Comforts of Playing 'Hookie,'" that her readers might empathize with Wallace Barclay (who has thrown his sister's cat into a tub of hot water) because of the stern discipline—indefinite isolation from the family—that his father orders. So she quickly counsels them to think of him not as a child, but as a body infected with "moral consumption" (1835, 17). This rhetorical move depersonalizes Wallace, reducing him, as other writers reduced boys, to a complex of urges and desires unmediated by a moral sense ("driven by mighty impulses," as Sigourney's poem described them); thus Sedgwick attempts to diminish, if not completely erase, the possibility of identification with him.

Sedgwick wants readers to agree that stern punishment is inarguably the correct treatment for this body's disease and therefore should be administered quickly and without reservation—and repeated by readers when dealing with their sons. Her scene shows that some authors believed strategies of sentimental control that would work for girls were not applicable to boys. During his two weeks of disciplinary isolation, Wallace is not allowed to talk to any family member, a punishment difficult to imagine Sedgwick advocating for girls, whom she often describes in generically sentimental terms as "gentle" and "compassionate." Such traits make the management of girls by means of sympathy a strategy consistent with their nature. Sedgwick's endorsement of isolation recalls Lyman Cobb's belief in boyhood as a kind of contagion for which he also recommends separation: in childhood, "many boys . . . are not, at that time, suitable company for men, women, or children" (1847, 210–11). The harshness of Sedgwick's treatment of Wallace suggests the value she places in swift punishment, and it displays opposition to the sympathetic disciplining of boys, an opposition rooted in a specific belief about boy-nature: that the boy is morally insensitive and emotionally coarse. Indeed, Sedgwick calls the only kind boy in the novel "unboyish," fully severing any connection between boys and sympathy (1835, 16). When Sigourney laments that "a boy . . . does not readily find the medicine of sympathy," perhaps she is thinking of the stern pedagogy of advice writers like Sedgwick.

No matter what approach sentimental or pragmatic writers take toward questions of maternal sympathy and boyhood discipline, they justify their position by discussing what they believe to be domestic and national benefits. Boys are the focus of these debates because they are the future patriarchs, and affective discipline could generate in them the moral sentiment they lacked and would need as men. But if maternal sympathy can produce such powerful, lasting results, its absence can be equally profound. "The mother," domestic theorist Catharine Beecher warns, "forms the character of the future man . . . for good or evil" (1842, 67) and Sigourney likewise proposes that bad mothers are responsible for bad men, such as Benedict Arnold, and good mothers for good men, such as George Washington. Nonetheless, the most popular novel of the period makes a case that complicates both sentimental and pragmatic claims about the effectiveness of maternal sympathy itself. Stowe's *Uncle Tom's Cabin* argues that even a pious mother who embodies sentiment offers no guarantee of producing a morally upright son. It is the son of such a mother who is the novel's, and perhaps the period's, greatest villain. Stowe recognizes that white male power, ambition, cruelty, and callousness bring into being the kind of material and moral conditions necessary for slavery, and *Uncle Tom's Cabin* everywhere critiques these forces and depicts their damaging effects. Nevertheless, she makes mothers and their pedagogy crucial to sons' proper upbringing: if they "had all felt as they should . . . [their] sons . . . would not have been the [slave] holders" (1981, 624). It is not only that mothers need to feel right, but as domestic theorists often said, that the affective bond they create with their sons model the way sons should feel toward others. Yet the boyhood narratives of *Uncle Tom's Cabin*'s two most prominent slave owners—Augustine St. Clare and Simon Legree—show that even perfect mothers, those capable of immense sympathy with slaves and sons, can fail. Part of the power and horror of Stowe's examination of motherhood is that the text's most intelligent and demonic slave owners have its most idealized mothers.

Stowe's characterization of St. Clare's mother evinces what Eva Cherni-avsky has called "essential motherhood," the ideology of sentimental writings about the mother (1995, ix-xi). "*She* was *divine!*," St. Clare exclaims, and "as far as I could ever observe there was not a trace of any human weakness or error about her . . . [and everybody] say[s] the same" (1995, 333). St. Clare's mother was an "angel," "a direct embodiment and personification of the New Testament—a living fact . . . to be accounted for in no other way than by its truth" (1995, 333). Stowe wants readers to understand a crucial point: this sentimental mother is not the cultural fiction of maternal encomiums, but a "living fact," a literal realization of the loving, sympathizing mother. St. Clare's relationship with his mother replays the close affective tie that many advice writers believed could be so effective in managing boys, and the bond between them is reproduced in their bond with their slaves. They "formed a committee for a redress of grievances" through which they tried to ease the abuse of slaves by St. Clare's father's cruel overseer (1995, 336). While they were occasionally successful, his father, an aristocrat with "no human sympathies beyond a certain line in society," eventually asserts his patriarchal right to determine how the slaves will be treated (1995, 335). In spite of his flawless mother, St. Clare—perhaps Stowe's most eloquent critic of slavery—becomes complicit in its operation. Though his mother has the primary responsibility for his moral development until well into his late boyhood, she ultimately is unable to see that he truly "feels right" about slavery. Here the ideal mother leaves unfulfilled the promise offered by the sentimental discourses that created and celebrated her: the promise that she would raise a moral son.

Stowe's most compelling portrait of a mother and son and her strongest revision of sentimental claims are visible in the relationship between Legree and his "gentle" mother. Stowe describes Legree's boyhood mothering as similar to St. Clare's: he was raised "with prayers and pious hymns. . . . Far in New England that woman had trained her only son, with long, unwearied love" (1981, 528). Yet Legree, like St. Clare, follows the trajectory of his cold, unfeeling father, upon whom his mother "had wasted a world of unvalued love" (1981, 528). Despite his mother's training, the "magic of the real presence of distress" that transforms Stowe's Senator Bird as he witnesses the suffering of the fugitive slave, Eliza, is lost on Legree (1981, 156). He eventually rejects his mother and is never reconciled with her. Although she is dead, her powerful presence is still with him, but instead of providing the lifelong moral guidance that advice authors claimed she would, the "angel" of sentimental discourse becomes a ghost. As an echo of unrealized maternal power, she haunts Legree as well as the sentimental discourse she represents, "turn[ing] things sweetest and holiest to phantoms of horror and affright." Legree is tormented by his rejection of his mother, imagining a "pale mother rising by his bedside" in retribution (1981, 529).[10]

Stowe provides these two male characters with a history almost solely about their boyhood bonds with their mothers, and she is a sentimentalist insofar as she celebrates "essential motherhood" and argues for the social benefits that follow from proper maternal bonding with sons. Critics have rightly noted that Stowe's text valorizes mothers and their power to effect change, and the novel has many examples of strong motherhood; Mrs. Shelby, Rachel Halliday, Aunt Chloe, Mrs. Bird, and others influence husbands and sons, "rul[ing] more . . . by persuasion than command" (1981, 143). Mrs. Shelby, who is never described in the sentimentalized language used for Legree's and St. Clare's mothers, is able to raise a model son, George, whose final act in the novel is to free his slaves. Yet when presented with antebellum culture's ultimate challenge—raising abolitionist sons—Stowe's ideal mothers (Legree's and St. Clare's) are surprisingly ineffective. While readers—and mothers in particular—would have likely been appalled by St. Clare's cynicism and horrified by Legree's cruelty, not only to his slaves but perhaps even more so to his perfect white mother, they might have been terrified by Stowe's two portraits of ideal, yet ineffectual, motherhood. Stowe's dramatization of the powerlessness of maternal sentiment reminds us that, as Glenn Hendler has argued, questions of sympathetic identification were complicated by authors throughout the century (Hendler, 1991). In *Uncle Tom's Cabin*, the power of maternal affective pedagogy was compromised by the corrupting influence of the "peculiar institution." Although Stowe believes that these mothers are, as St. Clare notes, without "a trace of any human weakness," it's possible that she did not fully consider the ways in which her descriptions of these mothers and sons conflicted with the claims of sentimental ideology about sympathy and the mother-son relationship. Typically, pragmatic discourses revise sentimental writings by arguing that mothers are not icons of "affection" and tend to be unsympathetic toward boys. But by putting two sentimental mothers in a narrative that celebrates their seemingly inexhaustible sympathy with their sons *and* representing their impotence, Stowe offers perhaps the most devastating critique of sentimental discourse found in antebellum writing.

The author of "Training of Boys" warned that excessive sympathy could create "a morbid tenderness, subversive of the best interests" of both the mother and her disciplinary charge (1845b, 148). Perhaps unintentionally, Stowe seems to suggest that the excessive sentiment St. Clare's mother directed toward her son may in some way be responsible for his failure to adopt an abolitionist position. St. Clare himself says of his boyhood, "there was morbid sensitiveness and acuteness of feeling in me" (1981, 334), the kind of perversion of sentiment that some pragmatic writers saw as the outcome of an improperly performed sympathy; such "an acuteness of feeling" tended to manifest itself as a narcissism that precluded identification with others. Though it might seem incongruous with Stowe's praise of St. Clare's mother and maternal sentiment, her narrative nevertheless rejects the belief that if a mother learns to calculate and employ sympathetic management, she can be certain of an ethical son. In a description of the "unusually gentle and sympathetic" Mrs. Bird, who is "the most indulgent and easy to be entreated of all mothers," Stowe says that maternal sympathy possesses a kind of instability that can allow it to devolve into its opposite, in the same way that the ideal mother could generate the cruelest overseer. Bird's extreme tenderness can quickly become an "inexplicable" kind of rage: "anything in the shape of cruelty would throw her into a passion, which was the more alarming and inexplicable in proportion to the general softness of her nature" (1981, 143).

It is unlikely that Stowe intends for us to believe that St. Clare's and Legree's mothers should be held accountable for the actions of their sons. Yet the novel dramatizes a fear that forces beyond a mother's control—from male cruelty and paternal influence to social institutions—can negate the effects of even the most perfect mother's sympathy, a fear that undermines Stowe's belief in the spiritual redemption promised by the sentimental power of maternal love. In her pioneering work on Stowe's novel, Jane Tompkins claims that *Uncle Tom's Cabin* is "the *summa theologica* of nineteenth-century America's religion of domesticity . . . [and] the story of salvation through motherly love." Tompkins centers on mothers like the Quaker Rachel Halliday, whom she calls Stowe's "God in human form" (1985, 142). It is true that the novel exalts Halliday as a mother whose household and domestic ideology represent a kind of a matriarchal utopia, yet Tompkins overlooks the mothers I discuss, two figures who complicate her argument. Indeed, Stowe specifically calls St. Clare's mother—not Halliday—"God in human form": she was "a direct embodiment and personification of the New Testament." Yet she failed to deliver on the promise of salvation. Tompkins and many later critics have seen the novel's endorsement of maternal sentimentality as representing a way for Stowe and women readers to access a form of power tied to beliefs about sentimentality. Hendler has called *Uncle Tom's Cabin* an "apotheosis" for "the culture of sentiment" in nineteenth-century America, yet I would argue that Stowe's celebration of sentiment is destabilized by narratives of idealized mothering that suggest the best of mothers can raise the worst of sons (2001, 3).

Boys were guaranteed a central role in antebellum domestic and public life, but perhaps—if many writers' concerns reflect actual conditions—only when they were no longer boys. The boyhoods of male characters like those in Stowe's novel and the boys in pragmatic discourses show that this stage was considered a crucial time for the affective molding of a male's domestic, social, and political character. But writers did not agree about the disciplinary value of many forms of management, especially sympathy: some praised it as the most successful (though underutilized) kind of discipline.

Others rejected it as ineffective and endorsed corporal punishment because it spoke directly to boys' physical nature and desires. Yet others warned that all maternal sympathy was dangerous—either boys would cleverly manipulate it to avoid punishment or the sympathizing mother would withhold the stern discipline a boy deserved. This complex field of reactions reveals the widespread anxiety about the relationship between boys and their mothers and just how troublesome interactions between maternal emotion and boy-nature could be. Debates about boys and discipline demonstrate that boyhood should not be seen as either a stable component of domesticity or a male-only counterpart to it. Maternal advice writing suggests that boys' connections to social structures such as sentimentality were always far more tangled than that. The strong conflicts between sentimental and pragmatic discourses reveal that mothers' advice writing figured both the mother-son bond and sympathy as cultural sites subject to constant investigation. The integration of boys into the "domestic circle" and the moral reformation some writers believed was necessary to accomplish it show that the relationship between ideas about mothers, boys, emotion, and tropes of sentimentality were always under negotiation. Not surprisingly, all of these arguments circulated around one of antebellum culture's most cherished sentimental conventions: the all-sympathizing mother.

NOTES

1. Recent scholarship on sentiment has continued to complicate our picture of the ways in which nineteenth-century culture theorized sympathy. The following essays look at authors who dramatize sympathy's inability to bring about desirable results; they do not, however, explore texts that fully reject popular notions of sympathy: Roberts (2004), Parris (2003), and Steele (2001).

2. Shamir and Travis (2002), an important collection on masculinity and emotion that builds upon Hendler and Chapman (1999) is, like its predecessor (and despite its title), not interested in boys. Both these collections explore masculinity and emotion without acknowledging that their claims may not be true for forms of boyhood masculinity. Similarly, Crain (2001), a study of literary representations of male friendship in the eighteenth and nineteenth centuries, looks only at adults. In an essay on Melville, masculinity, and domesticity, Sarah Wilson says that "[b]y masculinity, I mean the white, middle-class gender identity that is the focus of recent masculinity studies" (2004, 81). But the gender identity she equates with masculinity is not sufficiently aware of age categories, a problem that persists throughout work on masculinity in the nineteenth century. See also Adams and Savran's adult-focused *The Masculinity Studies Reader* (2002).

3. See for example *The Mother's Rule* and *The Mother's Magazine*.

4. For an overview of sentimental discourses about mothers, see Lewis (1997), Grant (1998), and Hays (1995).

5. And it is important to note that I am not setting up pragmatic and sentimental discourse as opposites; rather, I am saying that they discuss the mother-child relationship at different levels of specificity and are typically in conflict in ways that are revealing. Writers of both discourses often (but not always) wanted the same outcome: for mothers to sympathize with sons.

6. Even though pragmatic discourses describe a more nuanced understanding of sympathy and the mother-son relationship, like sentimental discourses they typically do not record details

of actual relationships, such as would be the case in letters, diaries, and memoirs. Both discourses are, therefore, largely prescriptions about child raising. My primary interest in this chapter is to explore writers' beliefs about maternal sympathy and boyhood pedagogy, not to discuss actual conditions. It is true, however, that authors of pragmatic discourses believe they are writing about the actual treatment of boys, and they often use real and fictional anecdotes as case studies of typical problems in mother-son interactions.

7. Parris has said that "postbellum realities" led to a revision of antebellum beliefs about the effectiveness of sympathy, though I argue that this revision had been underway for decades (2003, 25).

8. For white boys as Indians and "savages," see "Boyhood and Barbarism" (1851) and "The Bright Side" (1856). For white boys as slaves, see Cobb (1847). For a description of boy behavior that invokes both of these comparisons, see Sedgwick (1835, 17).

9. In an essay on children and play in the nineteenth century, Dawson echoes Rotundo by repeatedly describing boys as "unfettered" and "carefree" (2003, 64), ignoring that they were the subjects of numerous disciplinary theories and pedagogical practices.

10. Cherniavsky (1995) claims that because Stowe's Cassy, an African American, successfully performs white motherhood when she imitates Legree's mother, Cassy undercuts the discourse of "essential motherhood" because that discourse is figured as exclusively white. But I would argue that Cassy is only able to imitate white motherhood in the eyes of the paranoid, guilt-ridden, and drunken Legree, and thus her impersonation represents no threat to Stowe's beliefs about white mothers. What is a threat, I argue, is the failure of Legree's and St. Clare's ideal mothers to bring about spiritual and political change through the affective mothering of sons.

Chapter Three

The Ethics of Postbellum Melancholy in the Poetry of Sarah Piatt

D. Zachary Finch

Sarah Piatt composed a body of postbellum poetry profoundly volatized by the fault lines of American history. Born into a family of slaveholders in Lexington, Kentucky, in 1836, Piatt moved north of the Mason-Dixon Line just months after the Civil War began, and never again returned to the South, memories of which defined her poetry in complex ways.[1] Her starkly psychological work, the result of a melancholic relationship with losses that were both historical and personal, patently refused to offer formulaic moral conclusions to readers during the Reconstruction era. Eschewing the pedagogical function common to late nineteenth-century American poetry, Piatt instead exposed her readers to a precarious ethical space, in which idealism and irony, nostalgia and skepticism continually coexist in unsettling and unpredictable ways. Such unwillingness to seek rhetorical resolutions to the facts of death and loss defied the ideological stances and sympathetic identifications normally found in sentimental poetics, a tendency in Piatt that struck many contemporary readers by its radical ambivalence. "Wayward, abrupt, enigmatic, and prolific in hints and innuendoes," as one reviewer phrased it, Piatt's poetry is riddled with "questions it neglects to answer" (*Scribner's* 1880, 635).

For most of the twentieth century, when she had largely disappeared from the chronicles of literary history, it was the questions Piatt had asked but refused to answer that became entirely neglected.[2] Only in the decade since her work was returned to print in Paula Bernat Bennett's edition of *Palace-Burner: The Selected Poetry of Sarah Piatt*, published in 2001, have literary critics begun to reconsider how deeply Piatt's questions reflect the changing status of sentimentality in the years following the war. More dramatically than any other poet of the Reconstruction era, Piatt provides us with a divided picture of sentimentality, on the one hand rejecting its utopian promises as misleading and even morally insupportable, while on the other hand remaining nostalgically attached to its antebellum ideals. In a period marked by trends toward prose realism that repudiated sentimentality altogether, Piatt continued to write in the sentimental idiom even as she documented how the fundamental values of its ideology were eroding. It is above all the unrepressed melancholy of Piatt's work within this setting that reflects the growing divisions of the postbellum decades, when a rising tide of skepticism concerning sentimentality was accompanied by waves of nostalgia for an antebellum past underwritten by sentimental ideals.

While melancholy has been recognized as an important factor in Piatt's poetry, recent critics have emphasized her work as that of a cultural critic deliberately subverting sentimental ideology. Paula Bernat Bennett has called attention to the acute self-consciousness and "searing self-knowledge" with which Piatt deployed irony as a tool to complicate the naïveté of sympathy politics (2003, 140). Mary McCartin Wearn, building upon and refocusing Bennett's scholarship, has written more specifically of motherhood as the "fulcrum of [Piatt's] cultural critique" (2006, 164). Phrases such as Bennett's "deconstructing the Angel" and Wearn's "dismantling the maternal icon" ask that we recognize the critical agency of a poet who was for too long mistaken as just another writer of generic late nineteenth-century poems (Bennett 2003, 139; Wearn 2006, 165). However, rather than continue to insist upon Piatt as a defiant countercultural figure, it is crucial that we remember the acutely melancholic aspects of her poetry, those that flow from the Latin *passio*, to suffer. For Piatt's historical value as a poet springs from her openness to portraying, in highly crafted public performances, effects of mourning and melancholy that are highly representative of the increasingly ambivalent attitudes toward sentimentality that defined postbellum America. Reading Piatt through the framework of melancholy allows us to observe that Piatt was not just exposing the limitations of antebellum sentimentality from the vantage of a postbellum ironist. She was sincerely mourning the insolvency of sentimentality itself.

LOSS BEYOND REPAIR: PIATT'S "BROKEN TALK"

The idea that sentimentality was being mourned during the postwar years has been advanced by Mary Louise Kete in her important study *Sentimental Collaborations: Mourning and Middle-Class Identity in Nineteenth-Century America* (2000). Kete defines sentimentality as a mode that "empowered the creation of a certain sense of self (a collaborative self) which was oriented toward community and toward cohesiveness and at odds with the definition of self as essentially isolated and alienated from others" (149). During Reconstruction, however, certain strains in American literature and in political rhetoric reveal a gradual sea change, an increasing skepticism as to "what might be called the ideological . . . functions of sentimentality" (148). Owing to the ways in which cultural changes placed "[s]tresses on the culture of sentimentality" in the years after the war, it is possible, Kete writes, to see a turning away from collaborative acts of mourning (151). "Reconstruction as formulated after Lincoln's death," she insists, "betrayed the sentimental promise of mourning; the rituals of mourning failed to effect a utopian reunification of the national family" (157). Although Kete doesn't include poetry in the postbellum section of her book, Piatt would have been the best possible example of the ways in which Reconstruction-era culture was indeed "Mourning Sentimentality," to quote from the title of her book's final section (145). This is because the prospect of successfully mourning the loss of sentimentality's own mourning tactics poses a peculiar problem for Piatt. For as Kete points out, sentimentality's strength had always been its wide array of practices, whether literary or customary, designed "to rebind the mourner to the community" in the aftermath of private loss (55). To mourn the passing of this collaborative practice effectively would require a replacement for sentimental discourse, one that Piatt has not yet fashioned—a predicament that leads to the paradoxes and isolations that darken her work.

This impasse is no more plainly pronounced than in Piatt's poem "Army of Occupation," one of her most direct representations of the war's immediate aftermath and a key point of departure for understanding how mourning and melancholy dovetail in her *oeuvre*. First published in *Harper's Weekly* in August 1866, this poem features a group of women explicitly unable to complete the work of mourning. This difficulty may be partly because of the enormity of what they are confronting, for they are standing over a mass grave in Arlington National Cemetery that contains the remains of over two thousand unknown soldiers. Even as the speaker characterizes the nameless dead with profound empathy, her thoughts are less concerned with the burial of the past than with the possibility of its recurrence. Thinking of these unnamed soldiers, she says,

> They had been sick, and worn, and weary, when
> They stopp'd on this calm hill beneath the trees:
> Yet if, in some red-clouded dawn, again
> The country should be calling to her men,
> Shall the r[e]veil[e] not remember these?
>
> Around them underneath the mid-day skies
> The dreadful phantoms of the living walk,
> And by low moons and darkness with their cries—
> The mothers, sisters, wives with faded eyes,
> Who call still names amid their broken talk.

> And there is one who comes alone and stands
> At this dim fireless hearth—chill'd and oppress'd
> By Something he has summon'd to his lands,
> While the weird pallor of its many hands
> Points to his rusted sword in his own breast!
> (2001, 5–7)

As this scene with its inarticulate mourners and ghostly presences suggests, the prospect of sealing the grave and moving on into a future that is different from the past does not seem at all likely. Even the poem's title implies that the "occupation" of this army of women and children may be a permanent deployment. The gathering does not resemble a ceremony, because no one steps forward to deliver a eulogy, or any other conventional performative that might provide the words necessary for some degree of closure. The final stanza's spectral figure is the apotheosis of the muteness of real grief, for he cannot even name the "Something" at whose hands they have all been "oppress'd." Here Piatt was probably imagining General Robert E. Lee, whose former estate had been recently converted into the grounds of the Arlington National Cemetery. In stark contrast to Lincoln, the typical choice for a Civil War elegy, Lee represents the burdens and the schisms of the past that he had helped to "summon." Lee was a border figure not unlike Piatt herself, with the major difference that he decided to side with the South, taking command of the Army of Northern Virginia after turning down command of the Army of the Potomac.

To register the difference between Piatt's open-ended melancholy and a more sentimental, indeed successful, expression of mourning at the war's end, we may pause to compare "Army of Occupation" with one of the most popular sentimental elegies of the era, Francis Miles Finch's "The Blue and the Gray." Finch's poem was based upon a report originally written in the *New York Tribune* about a group of women in Columbus, Mississippi, who had performed a successful act of mourning. "Animated by nobler sentiments than are many of their sisters," these women "strewed flowers alike on the graves of the Confederate and of the National soldiers" (1867, 369). In a reiteration of this cathartic gesture, Finch pronounces the national conflict ended once and for all. Because of the women's ceremonial gesture, he writes,

> No more shall the war-cry sever,
> Or the winding rivers be red;
> They banish our anger forever
> When they laurel the graves of our dead!
> Under the sod and the dew,
> Waiting the judgment day;—
> Love and tears for the Blue,
> Tears and love for the Gray.

(370)

The difference between Finch's and Piatt's poems indicates the sharp difference between the perpetuity of Piattian melancholy and the more definitive closures attempted by normative sentimental mourning techniques. If "The Blue and the Gray" depicts a conventional action that fulfills a moral imperative, then "Army of Occupation" depicts a condition that precedes and imperils the ability to perform such acts. The apparent spectrality of the mourners in the Piatt poem is reflected by their inability to act and to pronounce on the world. This deprivation is a form of unalleviated privacy: the "one who comes alone" is the plenipotentiary of the female specters, partly because his isolation is so complete. Someone with "his rusted sword in his own breast" suggests that suicide, as the ultimate confirmation of individual isolation, may be the most decisive action available in a world that denies the closures of successful mourning acts.

The cultural capital of Finch's elegy differs dramatically from that of Piatt's poem. "The Blue and the Gray" would become one of the most popular poems of its time, recited over and over again in the years following the war. It possessed a meaningful currency not only because it consecrated the end of national division, but because it helped invent a new kind of solidarity, in the form of a new national holiday. The flower strewing of the women in Columbus came to be understood as one of the origins of Decoration Day in large part because Finch's poem elevated this particular action into a universal that could live on in public consciousness, through endless reiterations and recitals. In contrast, we cannot imagine "Army of Occupation" ever functioning in such a practical way. Owing to the abjection experienced by its speaker, it displays a profound and irremediable skepticism with regard to public rhetoric.

PIATT AND THE ETHICS OF MATERNAL MELANCHOLY

In referring to the ethics of melancholy in this chapter's title, I mean to emphasize Piatt's willingness to inhabit a realm characterized by ambivalence, vulnerability, impasse, and irresolution. When R. Clifton Spargo writes in *The Ethics of Mourning: Grief and Responsibility in Elegiac Literature* of the "threshold of an incapability or impossibility from which ethics arise," he defines the location of many of Piatt's poems, in which we find the experience of loss to be more crucial than its transcendence (2007, 7). Spargo's description of "literature's capacity for irresolutions that challenge the normative, often reductive, capacities of the social rules presiding over representation" applies to Piatt's own relationship with the conventions presiding over sentimentalism's representations of loss and grief—experiences that can no longer be healed through collaborative tactics (10). To point out the ethical orientation of Piatt's work is to place her at the cusp of a modern relationship with loss, in which melancholy is equated with an ongoing process, without a foreseeable terminus. In recent years, David Eng and David Kazanjian, editors of *Loss: The Politics of Mourning*, have defined melancholy as just such a "continuous engagement with loss and its remains" (2003, 4). Similarly, Anne Anlin Cheng has argued of American racial politics that "the desired goal may not be to 'work through' or 'get over' something but rather to negotiate between mourning and melancholia in a more complicated, even continuous way" (2001, 94). Piatt's poetry exposes us to this same ordeal, not bent upon overcoming loss so much as it is compelled to inhabit the contradictions incurred by it.

The difficulty of this awareness is related to the fact that Piatt's speakers are usually mothers. Raising children obviously entails the transmission of values, one of the celebrated duties of nineteenth-century middle-class women. As Wearn's article "Subjection and Subversion in Sarah Piatt's Maternal Poetics" shows, maternal grief and bereavement play a decisive role throughout Piatt's *oeuvre*. Piatt dramatizes the visceral ongoingness of mourning by refusing to offer the programmatic deathbed scenes that provide transcendent consolations to mothers facing the deaths of young children. Piatt's child elegies reject closure, Wearn argues, and as a result they seem "at times, narcissistic, heretical and even nihilistic in their grief"—effectively "powerless to offer moral instruction" to either the mother or to readers (2006, 170; 169). Piatt presents motherhood as a raw, troubling, realistic, empirical experience. Her representation of motherhood follows an emotional economy that defies ideological attempts to regulate it or make it socially profitable. If such an economy is defined by loss more than by redemption— motherhood as a site of continual dispossession rather than eventual enfranchisement—this is mainly the case because of the ruling cultural paradigms that have constructed an idealized version of maternal nature in the first place.

Sarah Robbins reminds us in *Managing Literacy, Mothering America: Women's Narratives on Reading and Writing in the Nineteenth Century* (2004) of how consistently the domestic education subgenre of sentimental literature promoted the idea that women's most important work was the cultivation of the character of the nation's children. For Piatt, however, this obligation involves a recurring ethical problem since the transmission of positive moral values is what her melancholic mothers find so difficult to perform. Most importantly, since Piatt always associates children with both her own antebellum childhood and with sentimentality in a general sense, their ubiquitous presence in her poems triggers a variety of conflicting responses. Often, her mother-child dialogues voice a deep distrust of, even hostility toward, what she came to view as cultural myths and fantasies, including romantic love, religious faith, and childhood innocence—the myths and fantasies to which Piatt's young are immediately drawn. Piatt's melancholic refusal to perpetuate such ideals therefore places her in an impractical position with respect to child rearing. At the same time, however, Piatt's child interlocutors sometimes catalyze in the poems' maternal speakers an uncensored longing to restore the vanished antebellum past. That is, Piatt's speakers occasionally *wish to return* to a world defined by the slave economy that supported her planter-class family and helped to provide the economic and social security she experienced as a child. The apparent irresponsibility and inconsistency of these poems may come as a surprise when compared with the more politically acceptable aspects of Piatt's poetry. At times, it may even appear that Piatt wrote two absolutely different kinds of poems—those that are fiercely inhospitable toward antebellum sentimental ideals and those that long to defect back to an imaginary homeland. In view of this difference, I suggest that what Bennett has called the "split consciousness" of Piatt's speakers must be extended to account for a split between the two types of poems which seem, at first glance, nearly irreconcilable (2003, 138).

Piatt's expression of this contradiction predates Sigmund Freud's analysis of melancholy by several decades. Nevertheless, her tendencies correspond with uncanny accuracy to the division in the psyche that Freud first observed in "Mourning and Melancholy." Therefore, before turning to a detailed analysis of both types of Piatt's poems, it is well worth recalling the split that Freud thought characterized melancholic individuals as well as those attempting to negotiate the work of mourning. Published first in 1917, toward the end of World War I, Freud's paper argued that in both mourning and melancholy, the ego suffers a significant bifurcation. Unrealistically attached to an object that has been lost, the subject's libido withdraws into itself, where it sets up an introjected version of the lost object and there "establish[es] an identification of the ego with the abandoned object" ([1917] 1948, 159). What results from this identification is a regression from the state of the healthy libido, turned outward toward existing objects, to a kind of infantile narcissism. "In this way," Freud concludes, "The loss of the object becomes transformed into a loss in the ego, and the conflict . . . transformed into a cleavage between the criticizing faculty of the ego and the ego as altered by the identification" (159).

Across Piatt's work we see different halves of this divided ego take over at different times. Often, the critical faculty is in the ascendant, in poems that would disabuse children of their sentimental beliefs. In the poem "My Dead Fairies," for instance, a mother responds to her child's question "Do the Fairies ever die?" with the chilly response, "Why, yes, they are always dying. / There, in the freezing dark close by, / A thousand, dead, are lying" (2001, 19). Likewise, in the poem "Answering a Child," Piatt checks a child's belief in God's inherent goodness by completing the poem, "But He cannot undo / The terrible darkened gate / Which the fire of His will went through, /

Leading the Dead away; For the Past it is vain to pray" (60). Still again, when a young daughter unleashes a litany of twenty-four consecutive questions concerning angels, rainbows, and fairy godmothers in the poem "Questions of the Hour," the mother's total silence, followed by her curt demand that the child go to bed, prompts one final, frustrated question from the child—
"Mamma, are you—my stepmother?" Acknowledging the underlying truth of an "unnatural" relationship with her child, the speaker ends by confessing how this "innocent reproof crept to my heart" (10–11).

The ethical impasses in Piatt's mother-child poems take on added importance if viewed in the context of Theodor Adorno's essays on the ethics of education in the years that followed World War II. Adorno's essentially Freudian orientation was based on a belief that parents and educators should reflect upon their own internal conflicts in order to avoid a repetition of the past, since "what is conscious could never prove so fateful as what remains unconscious" (1998, 100). This notion of self-reflection, inspired by Freud's *Group Psychology and the Analysis of Ego* and *Civilization and Its Discontents,* linked the formation of the ego-ideal in early childhood with the influence of the super-ego. For adult arbiters of the super-ego, "The only education that has any sense at all," as Adorno wrote in "Education After Auschwitz," "is an education toward critical self-reflection" that might lay bare those psychic mechanisms that permit ordinary people to allow injustice to occur (193). For teachers and parents, this kind of reckoning may be painful and protracted when compared with the desire to just get on with things. However, educators "should not repress their emotions only then to vent them in rationalized guise," Adorno insisted in "Taboos on the Teaching Profession" (187). "Instead," he suggests, "they must acknowledge the emotions to themselves and others and thereby disarm their pupils" (187).

THE CRITICAL SIDE OF PIATT'S MELANCHOLY

A revealing example of how Piatt's melancholic candor invokes a disarming kind of cultural critique is "Love-Stories." This dialogic poem opens with a child asking her mother a familiar question: Can you tell me a love-story? The poem's first lines establish the mother's total refusal to do so. "Can I tell any? No: / I have forgotten all I ever knew" (2001, 35). In the stanzas that follow, the stakes of this refusal become increasingly clear. We come to see that the romance of "love-stories" is just one of a series of illusions which this melancholic mother does not wish to perpetuate.

> "Rose's grandmother knows
> Love stories?" *She* could tell you one or two?
> "*She* is not young?" You wish that you were Rose?
> "*She* hears love-stories? Are they ever true?"

Some time I may ask you.

I was not living when
Columbus came here, nor before that? So,
You wonder when I saw the fairies, then?
The Indians would have killed them all, you know?
"How *long* is long ago?"
And if I am too old
To know love-stories, why am I not good?
Why do n't I read the Bible, and not scold?
Why do n't I pray, as all old ladies should?
(I only wish I could.)

Why do n't I buy gray hair?
And why——
Oh! child, the Sphinx herself might spring
Out of her sands to answer, should you dare
Her patience with your endless questioning.
(35–6)

Here the poem voices a series of reproaches that American culture might make of any mother unwilling to engage in customary, sentimental, or religious practices. Indeed, her injunction against love-stories is tantamount to her refusing to collaborate with the culture in the raising of her child. We hear in the speaker's tone of voice a real bitterness with respect to Rose's grandmother, who is not just telling love-stories to Rose and her friends, but filling them with reprehensible myths about American history. To say that Indians committed a genocide of all the fairies is quite obviously to eclipse the fact that Native Americans were the object of ongoing cultural genocide (a truth which had a particular claim on Piatt, the great-grandniece of the "Indian-killer" Daniel Boone). Rather than speak against such myths through an alternative act of storytelling, Piatt's melancholic mother remains silent, while her child, who holds forth throughout the first half of the poem, admonishes her for not praying, for not reading the Bible, and in general for not playing a motherly role in the little girl's life.

Only in the last three stanzas of the poem does the mother finally imagine her response to these accusations. If the Sphinx could talk, "if her lips were not all stone," she says, "there is one [love-story] she must remember well,

One whose long music aches—
How sharp the sword, how sweet the snake, O Queen!—
Into the last unquiet heart that breaks.
But the Nile-lily rises faint betwe[e]n—
You wonder what I mean?

I mean there is but one
Love-story in this withered world, forsooth;

> And it is brief, and ends, where it begun,
> (What if I tell, in play, the dreary truth?)
> With something we call Youth.
> (36)

Because of the ambiguous use of quotation marks throughout the poem, it may be unclear whether or not she has spoken these lines aloud, or whether the whole conversation is now being imagined as an interiorized "play." Nevertheless, the poem contains what William Dean Howells, in a review of Piatt for *The Atlantic Monthly*, called an "allegory for older hearts" (1874, 104). First, the allusion to *Antony and Cleopatra* reveals the speaker's belief that all *true* love-stories are tragedies. She then implies that all tragedies are but variations on a single theme, the death of Youth. Her reluctance to tell her child this particularly tragic story speaks to her desire to protect and to preserve what remains of the youth of her daughter—to shelter her from tragedy. What we encounter in this poem, then, is the tale of a double bind. The mother does not want to end her child's childhood too quickly by informing her of "the dreary truth." And yet, this attachment to the ideal of youth requires that she remain cut off from her child, as well as from the sentimental culture that the child represents.

This difficulty, however pervasive, did not deter Piatt from inhabiting the problem deeply, or from composing a more extensive range of poems about (not simply for) children than any other American poet.[3] Indeed, several of her collections were organized exclusively around the sentimental topic of child rearing. In 1877 she published *Poems: In Company with Children*, reprinted without changes five years later as *A Book about Baby and Other Poems in Company with Children*. One wonders, however, whether the ironies of this book's poems were fully registered by all of her readers. One reviewer from the *N.Y. Evening Post* offered a whitewashed sense of *Poems: In Company with Children*, reporting that "all of her Songs to or concerning little ones are full of the heaven which lies about us in our infancy" (Piatt 1882; see "Extracts From Reviews, Etc." in the back matter of *Book About Baby*). Piatt herself probably would have heard a double entendre in the phrase "the heaven which lies about us." The first stanza from the opening poem, "A Book About the Baby," begins,

> If I could write such a book for you,
> What a pretty book it would be!—
> And the prettiest things they would all be true.
> ——But *can* I? Ah, you shall see.
> (11)

In the volume that ensues, Piatt does appeal to a stereotypical sense of adoration associated with babies. But a powerful undertow of skepticism disturbs the apparently sentimental veneer of the book. Instead of reworking fairy tales for her children, for instance, she writes a poem called "At Hans Andersen's Funeral." Likewise, in a poem that converses with children about the precious smallness of an infant's hand, the final stanzas compare the newborn with the Greek titan Atlas, who holds up the world in all its gravity.

> How is it the Baby's hand can hold
> The world?——Yes, surely I ought to know;
> For oh, were the Baby's hand withdrawn,
> Down in the dust the world were gone,
> Folded therein as you might fold
> The sad white bud of a rose—just so—
> For the Baby's hand to hold.
> (40)

Despite the book's sentimental trappings, the shadows cast throughout *A Book about Baby* darken its otherwise pure intentions. The book's final poem "A Walk to My Own Grave [with Three Children]" reveals that Piatt's ultimate aim is not to represent death as a means to spiritual enlightenment or a collaborative sense of community. Rather, with the book's lesson is death itself—"Every step that we go / Is one step nearer, you know" (1882, 160–2).

Such unredeemed melancholy opposes the celebration of childhood innocence and national unity that Angela Sorby has discussed in *Schoolroom Poets: Childhood, Performance, and the Place of American Poetry, 1865–1917.* Sorby observes that idealized child-figures dominated the climate of the period's poetry, which constantly featured "poets framed as children, children seen as poets, children posited as readers, children recruited as performers, and adults wishing themselves back into childhood" (2005, xvii). To the contrary, Piatt plays at de-infantilizing her readers and the child characters in the poems. In many cases, although the child remains the ostensible "pedagogical subject" and the "pedagogical object" of the poems, to use Sorby's terms, the poems' teachings do not complement what Sorby calls "the general cultural mania for childhood" of the late nineteenth century (xx). Although the poems "present" as pedagogical, child-centered texts, situated in those "social spaces, involving more than one person in the transmission of thoughts and feelings" (Sorby's criteria for the pedagogical text), Piatt's real concerns are to represent a stricken adult, melancholic subjectivity, whose blunt confessions often confound the practical goals of the pedagogical imperative (xxiii).

We may observe this tendency even further by identifying the types of texts that Piatt selects to occasion her mother-child dialogues. Whether offering a "dis-illusioning" feminist reading of Goethe's *The Sorrows of Young Werther* in her poem "The Sorrows of Charlotte" or glossing the most fatalistic moments of Shakespearean tragedy, Piatt's mothers hope to introduce their children (and hence their readers) to a bleak view of the world unpunctuated by regenerative tears. The poem "At the Playhouse," for example, finds a mother and child attending a performance of *Hamlet* with the child confused by the meaning of Hamlet's soliloquy.

> "What does he say?" What does he say?
> You ask it in a world where each
> Poor man you meet, in some poor way,
> Knows—my Lord Hamlet's famous speech.
>
> Your father does not know it, though?—
> He could not say a single word?
> One says that to one's self, you know.
> There are more things—than you have heard.
> (2001, 152)

Here the mother starts reciting Hamlet's lines from act 2, scene 1 ("There are more things in heaven and earth, Horatio, / Than are dreamt of in our philosophy") to suggest the sort of truths the child does not yet know. Unlike the boy's father, she is more than willing to voice the taboo thought of suicide that most adults would be inclined to repress, especially in the presence of children. Since Hamlet's condition is one that everyone must accept according to this mother, when her child asks if he must learn this "famous speech" for himself, she replies without hesitation,

> Yes, you must.—
> By heart, indeed. Nothing can save
> You from it—but a little dust,
> And rose-leaves for a child's sweet grave.
> (152)

Piatt alludes here to an acutely personal source of grief that Hamlet could not have known: in 1873 she lost a newborn child as well as her ten-year-old son Victor. Yet the scattering of "rose-leaves" rather than rose petals in the poem implies that the sentimental flower is not in the speaker's possession. The final lines of the poem abandon this off-hand gesture toward the sentimental, in favor of a joke that communicates only shortness. When the child expresses surprise and confusion at Hamlet's final words, asking "*He does not know the rest?*" the mother hushes her child by playing on Hamlet's own words: "Because—the rest is silence, child!" (2001, 152). Resembling the conclusion of "Questions of the Hour," when the mother sends her child to bed without answering any of her questions, "At the Playhouse" ends with a mother silencing her child, ostensibly so that she may remain engrossed by *Hamlet's* final scene, as the bodies fall to the boards.

Piatt included a child interlocutor in another poem with a theatrical setting, "At the Play," to similar ends. In this case, a mother has just returned from a performance at the theater—her allusion to "Shakespeare's Poor Player" implies the play is *Macbeth* (2001, 47).[4] The solemn cadences and end-stopped lines of the poem suggest that she is herself a version of life's "walking shadow." Just as the actors must play out their parts, this speaker attends the play with such regularity that she seems to be a ghost as well, doomed to haunt the theater without ever experiencing the communal release that tragedy is classically supposed to effect.

> I have been to the play, my child.
> Night after night I go.
> What if the weather be wild?—
> I am used to rain and snow.
>
> Shakespeare's Poor Player is there.
> The stage is wide and dim.
> The music is old, and rare
> Are the flowers I fling to him.
> (47)

Yet this motion of flinging flowers to the actors or musicians on stage is clearly an empty ceremony, for the speaker is not really moved by the performance. It is rather as if she—and all of the audience members—have been using the theater as a kind of opiate to distract themselves, albeit unsuccessfully, from the existential abyss of Macbeth's "signifying nothing."

> With jewels the boxes shine;
> Fierce eyes look out of the pit;
> All whisper: "The Play is fine,"
> And all are weary of it.
> (2001, 47)

The one truly arresting moment of the play seems to be the murderous "shadow-scene" when Macbeth "falls on his Brother's breast, / (His Brother is Death), I think" (47). But on the whole, the theatergoers, blankly watching the actors enact their ritual sound and fury, resemble unseeing "gods" who "stand by in stone" while "Christ clings to his cross / alone / In this bitter world, and dies" (47). Evidently there is no redemption to be found by observing the spectacles of suffering, despite the speaker's compulsion to return to them "Night after night." Piatt is not just dramatizing the subject position of the spectator. She is also performing a role in front of the child. This desire to stage the suffering of melancholia as well as its interpretation defines Piatt's consistently counter-pedagogical moves, designed to disabuse the children in the poems of their more innocent and optimistic expectations that late nineteenth-century readers were accustomed to bring to their readings of poetry.

PIATT AND THE QUESTION OF NOSTALGIA

Thus far, we have observed how the repercussions of loss correspond to what Freud calls "the criticizing faculty of the ego" suffering under conditions of unresolved mourning or melancholy ([1917] 1948, 159). Yet there exists the other side of Piattian melancholy, which corresponds to "the ego as altered by the identification" with the lost object (159). As I have previously argued, the strength of this latter identification is revealed in moments of poems that—so different from the poems we have just analyzed—brazenly embrace nostalgia and actively maintain the solvency of the introjected child and the sentimental ideals the child represents. To indicate how quickly this turn from skepticism to nostalgia can happen, there may be no more illuminating poem than "Another War," which begins with a troop of soldiers marching down the road, engaged in some sort of military exercise. When the son initially expresses admiration for the soldiers' "shining sport," for "the long sharp flash" of their swords, and "the fair silk flags above the line," the mother seems to be considering patiently how best to counter such dangerous enthusiasm (2001, 27). Having lived through the war herself, she knows that their uniforms were "made for skeletons to wear" (28). But before she has the chance to explain her knowledge, her son asks "Could we not have another war?" a question which prompts the troubled meditation that follows:

> Another war? Perhaps we could,
> Yet, child of mine with sunniest head,
> I sometimes wonder if I would
> Bear then to see the dead!
>
> But am I in a dream? For see,
> My pretty boy follows the men—
> Surely he did not speak to me,
> Who could have spoken, then?
>
> It was another child, less fair,
> Less young, less innocent, I know,
> Who lost the light gold from its hair
> Most bitter years ago!
>
> It was that restless, wavering child
> I call Myself. No other, dear.
> Perhaps you knew it when you smiled
> Because none else was near.
>
> Then not my boy, it seems, but I
> Would wage another war?—to see
> The shining sights, to hear the cry
> Of ghastly victory?

No—for another war could bring
No second bloom to wither'd flowers,
No second song to birds that sing,
Lost tunes in other hours!

But, friend, since time is full of pain,
Whether men fall by field or hearth,
I want the old war back again,
And nothing new on earth!
(28–29)

The mother's acknowledgment of her own childhood romanticization of war makes explicit what the more cynical mother-child poems might at first glance conceal: Piatt's mothers, for all their wariness, are still helplessly attached to the idealized figure of the child, and to the antebellum innocence which childhood often signified after the war. This attachment is associated at a complex level with a melancholic desire to return to the past, despite the obvious traumas of history. "Another War" effectively dramatizes the process by which this unconscious desire breaks through the surface of conscious reflection. Piatt's speaker knows, of course, that such attachments are problematic, even immoral: she describes her childhood self as "less young, less innocent" than her own son and hence, more culpable. Yet her melancholy is so intense, and her belief in the fatality of loss is so strong, that she is willing to accept a repetition of the past in exchange for the restoration of "Lost tunes in other hours." Although what "Another War" confesses to may be immoral, the poem is also ethical in the sense that it directly reflects upon a condition that might be repressed by a poet less open to contradiction. The speaker of "Another War" does not "uphold justice" by simply correcting the child's romantic love of war, as a responsible mother might; but neither does she promote the naïve nostalgia for childhood and the antebellum South that was prevalent in verse written by countless postbellum Southerners. Rather, "Another War" puts these two positions into relation with one another, in the form of an internal dialogue that represents two opposing truths—one a rational moral truth, the other emotional and wildly irrational.

This fantasy of returning to the past occurs in several other important poems that, as twenty-first century readers of Piatt, we might prefer to overlook. "There Was a Rose," for instance, features a woman mulling over a most Faustian bargain: to regain possession of "the rose" of youth and everything it symbolizes she agrees to a repetition of history (2001, 41–42).

"But a million marching men
From the North and the South would arise?
And the dead—would have to die again?
And the women's widowed cries
Would trouble anew the skies?

> "No matter. I would not care?
> Were it not better that this should be?
> The sorrow of many the many bear,—
> Mine is too heavy for me.
> And I want that rose, you see!"
> (42)

The poem "The Old Slave Music" illustrates this dilemma with unnerving clarity as well, by downplaying historical conditions in favor of the repugnant cliché that slaves were "free" whenever they sang (42–43).

> Were they slaves? They were not then;
> The music had made them free.
> They were happy women and men—
> What more do we care to be?
>
> There is blood and blackness and dust,
> There are terrible things to see,
> There are stories of swords that rust,
> Between that music and me.
>
> Dark ghosts with your ghostly tunes
> Come back till I laugh through tears;
> Dance under the sunken moons,
> Dance under the grassy years!
>
> Hush, hush—I know it, I say;
> Your armies were bright and brave,
> But the music they took away
> Was worth—whatever they gave.
> (43)

On a similar note, the poem "Over in Kentucky" is spoken by a mother who paints "fairy pictures from my fairy years" for her children before they go to sleep (2001, 37). This mother knows that her "phantom pencil" describes a "dewier" and "diviner" Kentucky than the real "Dark and Bloody Ground" governed by the "master's hold" that "kept the slave within" (37).[5] And yet, although the Ohio River that separates Ohio from Kentucky and the speaker's present from her past is figured as "a visible moan / Between two worlds," she cannot resist depicting Kentucky's "charmed side," glimmering with the "dim, dead dews of my lost romance" (37). In having the speaker do so, Piatt indulges her own nostalgia and knowingly feeds the idealism of the poem's young sons, whose "dimpled, pretty hands" now reach dangerously toward "unshaped steel, unfancied wars" (37).

To make better sense of Piatt's conflicting and conflicted stances toward the antebellum past, I want to turn to Svetlana Boym's scholarship on the historicity of nostalgia. In her book *The Future of Nostalgia* (2001), Boym discerns two different classes of nostalgia that will prove most useful for the Piatt reader. The first type of nostalgia Boym labels "restorative" because it "signifies a return to the original stasis, to the prelapsarian moment" of an imaginary past (49). Restorative nostalgia is dangerous because "it takes itself dead seriously" (49). At its most destructive, it leads to the *telos* of the "million marching men" that haunts so many of Piatt's poems (2001, 42). Yet Boym also describes a more creative, constructive form of nostalgia, which she considers "reflective." Reflective nostalgia "does not pretend to rebuild the mythical place called home," but instead acknowledges the irrevocability of loss, and uses creative means to work through one's feelings of alienation and dislocation (2001, 50). Whereas restorative nostalgia resists change, reflective nostalgia entertains various possibilities. As a serious form of creative play, it understands that "perhaps what is most missed during historical cataclysms and exile is not the past and the homeland exactly, but rather th[e] potential space of cultural experience that one has shared with one's friends and compatriots that is based neither on nation nor religion but on elective affinities" (53). This "potential space" is "not merely a homogenizing force" but rather "a space for individual play and creativity" that one associates with "the space of the play between the child and the mother" (53).

Piatt wrote a number of poems about the antebellum South that exemplify the playful and productive dimensions of reflective nostalgia. "A Child's Party" remembers a tea party thrown by the speaker when she was a young girl, only days after the death of her own mother (2001, 114–17). The success of this elaborate party, which involved the speaker and another child (crucially a slave) dressing up in adult clothing, is based upon the notion that this game of make-believe allows the child to deal effectively with her mother's loss.[6] A similar negotiation occurs in "Playing Beggars" in which two children imitate the "poor ragged soldier at the door" who frequently comes begging for food (2001, 11). These children take for granted what their father has said about such beggars—that they are mere impostors, asking for handouts that they don't really need. As a result, the children imagine that these hungry men are really "rich people" tramping around for the fun of it. In their version of this game of make-believe, then, the children end up performing a double theater: they play at being rich people who play at being beggars. For the children, the whole world is a theater. The aftershocks of war—actual impoverishment, homelessness, hunger—do not exist "for real." Everything is potentially true, but nothing is absolutely so. Identities are as fluid as imaginable, dependent on what kind of hat or dress you wear (as beggars, the children are more interested in their hats than in food).

Both "Playing Beggars" and "A Child's Party" narrate the creative negotiations of loss that are happening at the level of the *writing* of many of Piatt's poems. In an important sense, Piatt's question, "What if I tell, *in play*, the dreary truth," encompasses the full spectrum of her work, from the most cynical poems to the most nostalgic (2001, 32). It is worth noting how often the trope of the theater occurs across Piatt's work, along with the related activities of ventriloquism and dressing up. Even Piatt's most restorative-nostalgic poems, from this perspective, are but instances of *playing at* the idea of restoration, but in a reflective way. Reflective and restorative nostalgias are often operating simultaneously in Piatt's poems as she works out the arduous effects of melancholia.

This ongoing dialectic characterizes Piatt's mothers as educators of the complex sort that Adorno has imagined, since what they teach their readers is the psychological openness of the ethical orientation over the more settled confidence of the moral. If the results often appear to entertain deeply conflicted forms of subjectivity, these performances are relevant precisely because they represent what Adorno calls "the severity of what must be confronted" (1998, 193). Such confrontations are imperative not because they resolve anything in an illocutionary way, but because they illustrate what working through the past actually involves.

POSTSCRIPT: ON THE ROOTS OF AMERICAN MODERNITY

In fact, Piatt dramatizes something that we have come to accept as a basic truth of the modern relationship with history—that "working through the past" is by nature a fraught and fragmentary process, with ever inconclusive outcomes. One does not "work through" the past and come out the other end, for the past is never through with us. As Adorno suggests, in a very twentieth-century image, working through the past is not a matter of "clearing one's desk" of psychic clutter in order to be better adjusted to the more immediate, most realistic challenges of pragmatic life (1998, 101). The impulse toward normalization—in the individual's facile attempt to find a "substitute satisfaction in [her] identification with the whole," as Adorno puts it— is complicated whenever the subject of history is sufficiently self-conscious of the fact that the past is never healed, and that the whole with which one would like to identify is wholly fictive (96).

Haunted by this awareness of the perpetuity of loss, Piatt's poetry expresses a startlingly modern relationship with history. For her inability to believe in progress, whether psychological or national, is reflected by her poems' inability or unwillingness to transcend the sentimental discourse of so much nineteenth-century American poetry. By working within a discourse that could no longer fulfill its allotted function (of healing wounds and rejoining the individual to the communal whole) Piatt provides early signs of the sort of alienated subjectivity that would come to be one of the hallmarks of modernist verse.

This is to say, we do not necessarily need to wait for the stylistic revolutions of a twentieth-century modernist aesthetic sensibility to locate the roots of the modern in American poetry. As subjects of American history, it is normal to point to the Civil War as the decisive traumatic event that forced America into a more modern, more skeptical, more experienced relationship with history. Indeed, the most celebrated American Civil War poetry of Emily Dickinson or Walt Whitman's *Drum-Taps* or Herman Melville's *Battle-Pieces* offers considerable weight to this perspective. In the case of Sarah Piatt, however, we find a response to historical loss that grows more directly out of the sentimental style that defined the popular majority of nineteenth-century verse in America. Piatt was mourning the death of the utopian ideology that supported America's belief in itself, in social progress, and in moral perfectibility. Whereas modernist skepticism is most frequently explained in terms of the cataclysms of World War I, Piatt provides added evidence that, for Americans, the most material event in the development of a modern relationship with history was indeed the Civil War. To truly understand this development, we must adequately account for the changing status of sentimental poetics in the postbellum period. No poet represents these changes better than Sarah Piatt, in whom the impasses and the antinomies of modern melancholy coincide with the long and difficult death of antebellum sentimentality.

NOTES

1. Paula Bernat Bennett describes Piatt's resulting "borderland mentality" in her synopsis of the poet's life in the introduction to her edition, *Palace-Burner: The Selected Poetry of Sarah Piatt*, the text from which the majority of poems analyzed have been drawn (2001, xli).

2. Piatt shares the fate of the vast majority of nineteenth-century woman poets. With the exception of nominal inclusions in some anthologies of nineteenth-century poetry, and the occasional entry in a historical or literary encyclopedia, Piatt was absent from twentieth-century scholarship. In the 1980s and 1990s, however, she appeared as the subject of two doctoral dissertations and an undergraduate honors thesis. See Hanawalt (1981); Roberts (1997); Kincheloe (1997). Previous to the publication of Bennett's *Palace-Burner* edition in 2001, Piatt appeared in only two scholarly articles, one involving the late work from her years in Ireland (see Kincheloe, 1999), and the other by Bennett herself (1995).

3. Bennett makes this distinction as well in the introduction to *Palace-Burner* (2001, xxxii).

4. Piatt is naturally drawn to the most nihilistic moment in the play, Macbeth's famous statement in act 5, scene 5 that "Life's but a walking shadow, a poor player / That struts and frets his hour upon the stage / And then is heard no more."

5. The phrase "Dark and Bloody Ground" appears in "The Grave at Frankfort," a poem in which Piatt negotiates her relationship with Boone, "my old, rude kinsman" (2001, 27). Bennett's note to this poem recalls that the phrase refers to "a popular if inaccurate translation of the state's [Kentucky's] Shawnee name" (2001, 166).

6. For an excellent analysis of this poem's complex portrayal of race, see Janet Gray's (2004) chapter "Looking in the Glass: Sarah Piatt's Poetics of Play and Loss."

2

Reform and Sympathetic Identification

Chapter Four

"The Language of the Eye"

*Communication and Sentimental Benevolence in Lydia
Sigourney's Poems and Essays about the Deaf*

Elizabeth Petrino

"Cover your eyes for a short time, and you shut out this world of beauty. Close your ears, and you exclude this world of sound. Refrain from speaking, and you cease to hold communion with the world of intelligence."[1] Thus Lydia Sigourney asks the reader to imagine the deafness and blindness experienced by one of the students with whom she was acquainted at the Hartford Asylum for the Deaf and Dumb. The pupil was Julia Brace, who along with the deaf Alice Cogswell and another deaf and blind young woman, Laura Bridgman, became central figures in her poems and essays about the deaf. Sigourney analyzed Alice's powers of nonverbal communication while employed as a teacher in Hartford, Connecticut, from 1814 to 1817 and used her experience to explore in her poems and essays the inner, psychological workings of sentimentality and its limits and possibilities for interpersonal communication.

In her tribute volume to her students, *Letters to My Pupils* (1853b), Sigourney recalls teaching Alice Cogswell, whose enduring example stimulated her thinking about nonverbal expression and the communal learning that would become a model for her own benevolent learning narratives. Captivated by the power and eloquence of Alice's nonverbal expression, she drew from the girl's dramatic gestures, pantomime, and signing a basis for the rhetorical skills that would prepare her hearing pupils to persuade others, not least their future husbands, to support political causes. In particular, Sigourney promoted empathy for the disadvantaged through social scenes of reading and writing, often termed "literacy narratives" by today's scholars. As

Sarah Robbins explains, "home-based literacy events could become recurring literacy practices, managed by motherly domestic teachers to shape middle-class and, by extension, national values" (2004a, 57).

In this essay, I argue that Sigourney's observation of the nonverbal expression of the deaf became a central aspect of her sentimental benevolence and the basis for many of her poems. Extending the example Alice provided of the visual expression traditionally associated with the deaf—"the people of the eye," according to a recent apt phrase— in her sentimental poetry, Sigourney elevated the power of the gaze and of touch as means of expression surpassing verbal articulation.[2] In an image of an unidentified student and Sigourney from *Letters to My Pupils* (1851) (see figure 4.1), her intimate teaching method and her student's admiration for her are evident.

A brief survey of her conduct literature reveals that for her, the deaf could provide important lessons in promoting sympathy and moral behavior as well. Indeed, Sigourney's juvenile literature about deaf children exemplifies the structure of sentimental benevolence narratives in general: demonstrating empathy towards others, explicitly soliciting sympathetic feeling, and encouraging young readers to model their own behavior on that of deaf children.[3] While this literature stresses the acute difference between the physically challenged subject and presumably hearing readers, who need to mark their distance from the deaf in order to perform charitable actions, it also celebrates the deaf. In particular, it suggests the extent to which sentimentality can reach beyond the limits of human expression and allow the hearing to communicate with the physically disabled, who represent the otherness of all human beings. In the conclusion, I briefly gesture toward the evolution of nonverbal communication in Sigourney's later career and reflect on the influence of her work with the deaf on her theory of sentimental discourse.

SENTIMENTAL BENEVOLENCE AND TEACHING THE DEAF

Studies of sentimentalism claim that the cultivation of family bonds, such as those between mothers and children and husbands and wives, is essential to social advocacy and civic responsibility.[4] Scholars have not, however, explored how teaching the deaf—especially building relationships between teachers and pupils, such as Sigourney had with Alice Cogswell—could promote "sentimental benevolence."[5] While the term "benevolence" has a patronizing sound for most readers today, recent scholarship suggests that in the nineteenth century it indicated more than the conservative desire to spread Christianity and to lessen suffering.[6] A recent survey of critical positions on benevolence by Melissa J. Homestead shows that "benevolence"— also called "charity, philanthropy, poor relief, [and] social reform" (Homestead 2006, 176)—was a contested concept in the nineteenth century as well

Figure 4.1.   Picture of Lydia Huntley Sigourney, right, and an unidentified student. Facing title page, *Letters to My Pupils* (New York: Robert Carter and Brothers, 1851).

as today, insofar as it incorporates a set of attitudes and learned behaviors that reflect changing attitudes and divisions within the class and gender of its proponents. Susan Ryan contends that "the ubiquity of benevolent rhetoric signaled its instability; that is, antebellum Americans so often wrote about benevolence because they were engaged in ongoing and at times vitriolic conflicts over its meaning" (2003, 10).

Benevolence towards the deaf was subject to these same pressures. Although as a physical affliction deafness could strike anyone within the population, the similarities between the way in which the nineteenth-century deaf were treated and the treatment accorded racial minorities are striking. Like African Americans and Native Americans, the deaf lacked a voice in the larger culture; they too were considered savage, inhuman, and uneducable; and they had to struggle to be recognized for their intelligence and humanity (Krentz 2007, 9). As Christopher Krentz notes, the division between dominant and subaltern communities depends upon the majority culture's constructing binary oppositions with reductive labels like "deaf" and "dumb," which avoid recognition of the actual complexity of people's lives (Krentz 2007, 6). For the deaf as for African Americans and Native Americans, the prejudice instilled by such labeling was a major impediment to their full integration into mainstream society and impacted social attitudes towards benevolence as well when directed towards this minority population.

Critiqued in Sigourney's own day, sentimental benevolence is also critiqued today. A good part of the criticism of benevolence is based on what Ryan calls "the inevitable incompleteness of sympathetic identification" (Ryan 2003, 17). The benevolence narrative, like sentimental literature generally, relies on sympathetic identification in which the reader feels similarly to the suffering person; the reader needs to enter imaginatively into the body of another but also to recognize the impossibility of sustaining this identification between self and other. As Glenn Hendler explains, sentimentalism is limited by the boundaries—of class, gender, and race—that define individuals, and he argues that "the politics of sympathy is fatally flawed by its drive to turn all differences into equivalences, all analogies into coincidences" (Hendler 2001, 8, quoted. in Ryan 2003, 18). By identifying with others who are less fortunate, readers and listeners might be moved to action, but sentimental writers were also keenly aware that they (and their readers) relinquished, if only temporarily, their own distinctive qualities in order to identify with the oppressed.

Early in her literary career, Sigourney's experience teaching a deaf child afforded her an intimate understanding of the physical challenges of the deaf and affirmed her desire to become their social advocate. As the talented daughter of a gardener and estate keeper, she felt the same desire for social advancement and intellectual growth that she saw in her disadvantaged students. After the death of Mrs. Daniel Lathrop, who supported Sigourney's intellectual development, Sigourney travelled to Hartford for an extended stay with Mrs. Lathrop's relatives, Mrs. Jeremiah Wadsworth and her son, Daniel Wadsworth, who sought to relieve the grief that deprived Sigourney of speech for a short time (Haight 1930, 6). In light of her interest in the deaf, Sigourney's bout with temporary aphasia suggests a "real life" basis for her empathy with her deaf pupils.

After her marriage at twenty-eight, Sigourney left the teaching profession, but she pursued her interest in deaf students. As early as 1819–1820, she actively secured their tuition and began an ongoing relationship as a benefactor with the Hartford Asylum for the Deaf and Dumb, of which her husband Charles was a trustee (Sayers and Gates 2008, 385). Her affection for Alice extended to the young woman's family, including a brother, Mason Fitch Cogswell, whom Sigourney called "my dear Friend" and "my son," and the children of Alice's sisters, Mary and Elizabeth, whom she referred to as her "grandchildren" (Sayers and Gates 2008, 386). These epithets reflect an important aspect of sentimental benevolence: the traditional boundaries of the benefactor's family could be expanded to meet the needs of the recipients of their generosity. Even more important to our understanding of her evolving notions of sentimental benevolence, however, than her charitable acts and affectionate bonds were the insights in nonverbal communication that she gained from her intimacy with the Cogswells and from her determination to encourage hearing children and adults to think differently about their moral responsibility toward the deaf.

"THE LANGUAGE OF AFFECTIONS": THE EXAMPLE OF ALICE COGSWELL

In examining *Letters to My Pupils* (1851), one can see that Sigourney's objective was to showcase Alice's extraordinary talent and gain support for teaching deaf children. For Sigourney, teaching Alice provided firsthand knowledge of the need to develop creative methods for instructing deaf children while still maintaining a rigorous academic course of study and celebrating their achievements. At the suggestion of Daniel Wadsworth, who was impressed by Sigourney's increased eloquence and self-confidence when she returned to Hartford, she set up a school in his home in 1814 for a select group of fifteen girls. Between 1814 and 1817, the poet developed a strong bond with a precocious nine-year-old deaf child, Alice Cogswell, whom she taught to read, write, and finger spell. The daughter of Dr. Mason Cogswell, a prominent local physician and later benefactor of the Hartford Asylum for the Deaf and Dumb, Alice was accompanied by her two hearing sisters, Mary and Elizabeth, both handpicked by Wadsworth for Sigourney's instruction. As Sigourney tells us in *Letters to My Pupils*, Wadsworth "kept constantly in view similarity of attainments and station, so that all might be enabled in the prescribed studies to go on as one class," hoping to remove "those causes of disparity, which sometimes create suspicion, and check the growth of friendship" (1853b, 177–78). Edna Sayers and Diana Gates conclude that Wadsworth chose privileged students whose manners and values resembled Sigourney's in order to facilitate social contacts that would increase the number of sentimental benefactors (Sayers and Gates 2008, 374).

Perhaps because her students were wealthy, Sigourney sought to inculcate moral and intellectual preparation that would nurture their benevolence as adults. Rather than offer conventional "finishing" courses in painting, sewing, and embroidery, she required them to study reading, writing, penmanship, arithmetic, rhetoric, and grammar. To this standard fare, she added "Ancient and Modern Geography, [and] Natural and Moral Philosophy," with heavy doses of catechetical instruction (Haight 1930, 10). During her first experience teaching in Norwich, when she was sixteen years old, Sigourney insisted on maintaining discipline and beginning the day with her own extemporaneous prayer (Haight 1930, 9). The evangelical and intellectual focus was crucial to Sigourney's later attempts to aid the deaf. As Krentz argues, beginning in 1817 with the founding of the Hartford Asylum, deaf education was motivated largely "by some hearing peoples' desire to rescue deaf people's souls by teaching them the Gospel and, later, to convert them into assimilated American citizens" (Krentz 2007, 16). In order to encourage her students to perform charitable acts that would also foster their understanding of the importance of literacy, Sigourney had them routinely send packages of improving books, as well as useful objects, to local Native American tribes (Haight 1930, 26–27).

Critics have denigrated what they assume was Alice's subordinate position in Sigourney's school, but this accusation ignores both Sigourney's innovation in teaching Alice and her social advocacy.[7] One commentator calls Alice the school's "mascot" who begged for instruction and only wished to be treated like hearing children (Sayers and Gates 2008, 375). The opposite appears to have been the case. Praising Alice as a "child of genius" with a "fine intellect" and "vivid imagination," Sigourney lamented her own unfamiliarity with deaf education (1853b, 253). Despite "having no guide in this species of instruction," she learned to finger spell in order to communicate better with Alice. Because the "rapid manual alphabet" then in use in Europe had not yet arrived in the United States, Alice relied on "the tardy representation with both hands, of each letter constituting a word, and the few signs that [they] were able to invent, founded principally on visual resemblance" (250).[8] Admiring Alice's mental alacrity and tendency to "overleap every obstacle" to grasp factual knowledge quickly, she attributes Alice's success to her "histrionic talent," rather than to her own teaching. For Sigourney, her recognition through her pupil's example of the power of nonverbal cues was a watershed moment: "I was indebted to her for a new idea, that the hand and eye possessed an eloquence which had been heretofore claimed as the exclusive privilege of the tongue; that the language of the speechless might find an avenue to the soul, though all unaided by the melody of sound" (253–54).

As this revelation suggests, Sigourney's writing about the deaf raises questions about the interplay between body language and spoken words in sentimental literature. What are the connections between oral, written, and unspoken speech? How do oral and written forms of communication relate to unspoken language in her own writing? Alice learns to "speak" (finger spell, gesture, recite with others) and write (compose original thoughts in prose) with Sigourney's instruction in ways comparable to the communicative skills of other students. Clearly, as Sigourney's strategies for developing Alice's innate talent reveal, signing and writing were means through which the deaf could articulate their thoughts. But Alice also communicated through unspoken language that surpassed or perhaps supplemented written communication in ways that, for Sigourney, were fundamental to her understanding of nonverbal expression.

As scholars of sentimental literature have pointed out, the gaze is fundamental to the workings of sympathy and to the identification of the reader with the oppressed.[9] Like these scholars, I would argue that the gaze constitutes a formative moment in the construction of a reader's identification with the deaf child. Although Alice was not subject to physical or emotional abuse, her disability allowed Sigourney to use her and other hearing-impaired children as models for considering how sympathy might be elicited for oppressed subjects, especially through vision. As Sigourney explains about Alice, "Her peculiar misfortune—the deprivation of hearing and speech[—]opened for her new avenues to tenderness and sympathy. Though her tones might not reach the ear, from her eye flowed a resistless dialect, comprehended by all. The language of affections was eminently at her control. It found a response in every bosom" (1853, 249). Precisely because deaf children were unable to connect with the world through verbal language, their disability takes on a more abstract, intellectual quality and requires them to transcend their isolation through other senses. Nevertheless, despite Sigourney's celebration of this "language of affections," her writings on the deaf do not preclude the fear, especially in relation to the deaf and blind, that a connection with the world would never be made; this alarming revelation provoked a crisis in affective identification that she would struggle with for the rest of her career.

In order to allow Alice to keep up with her hearing and speaking classmates, Sigourney devised progressive methods that allowed her to recite, including enlarging the number of signs Alice used and organizing "a vocabulary of her scholastic gleanings" arranged alphabetically (Sigourney 1853, 251). During the weekly review of studies, in which each pupil presented her learning orally, Sigourney writes that Alice delivered her own lessons "joyfully, by the aid of this simple lexicon," in the same way her more advanced classmates did (251). Clearly, Sigourney realized that Alice could provide an important lesson in responsibility shared with her classmates: as Alice provided her own "definitions of words" and "gave them by signs," her fellow pupils interpreted them orally by turns, "exulting in every acquisition or commendation, as though it were their own" (Sigourney 1853, 251). Such collaborative scenes of instruction ensured that Alice's classmates had a stake in her success. Even at this early stage, Sigourney saw herself advocating literacy practices that were "collaborative activities whose outcomes could be noted in both individual and social terms" (Robbins 2004a, 61).

Following a tradition established in the Hartford Asylum's annual reports beginning in 1818, Sigourney also provides two excerpts of Alice's prose in *Letters to My Pupils* to document her growing development as a writer and narrator.[10] Rather than provide only the most proficient and polished efforts, she chose excerpts that demonstrated Alice's intellectual growth. The first, from 1815, discusses the illumination of houses and state buildings that took place to celebrate the end of the War of 1812 and displays something of what Alice was learning from her instruction in history and the Bible. This excerpt clearly reflects both the challenges Alice confronted and the mental capacity she possessed:

> "The world—all peace.—Now am I glad—Many candles in windows.—Shine bright on snow.—Houses most beautiful.—Friends at my home that night, and one baby. . . . Girls, fifteen in school.—You teach.—You write, and give letters.—Cleopatra I learn—great queen—face very handsome—say to maid,—bring basket—figs—asp bite arm—swell—die. . . .
> "You learn me text every morning.—I tell them you every night.—Oh, beautiful.—I love you.—To-day you teach, 'Beloved, follow not that which is evil, but that which is good. He that doeth good, is of God.'" (Sigourney 1853, 256–57)

Recounting her instruction, Alice reveals her remarkably independent observations of her surroundings and her desire to learn. Candles and stars, images of inner illumination and consciousness, often appear in Sigourney's literature about the deaf. These images are often mistaken for one another by uneducated deaf children, whose strikingly simple and poetic observations suggest that nature appears to be a magnificent but occasionally intrusive and hostile force. While Alice lacks mastery in standard written English—as witnessed by the omission of many conjugated verbs, the absence of indefinite articles, and the confusion of the verb "learn" for "teach"—she captures detail accurately and constructs a logical narrative in her story about Cleopatra. Her comment that Sigourney writes letters refers to the teacher's method of corresponding with her students to develop their writing skills, a fact referred to by Sigourney when she noted that Alice "rested not until she obtained permission also to become my correspondent" (1853, 254).

In the second excerpt, an anecdote from an unspecified year, Alice's intellectual growth and her intuitive moral perception become clear. Sigourney recalls an incident that Alice experienced in distributing alms among the poor in the company of other students who had formed a charitable society (1853, 252). Commenting that "the silent dialect of the hand and eye" conveyed more than actual speech could, Sigourney translated Alice's signed description of the event:

> "The father came in. He had in his hand a few pieces of pine. He had gathered them in the streets. He laid them on the fire. His wife spoke to him. Then he looked sorry. I asked my friends what she said. The words of the poor woman to her husband were, — 'Did you bring a candle?' He answered,—'No. I have no money to buy a candle.' Then there were tears on her cheeks, as she said,— 'Must we be in the dark, another long, cold night, with our sick child?'" (258–59)

By recounting a moment for benevolence seen through Alice's eyes, Sigourney reveals how Alice's friends inhabit her perspective, albeit momentarily, as they aid her in understanding what is going on. In contrast to Alice's earlier observation that the houses were lit by candles, this poor couple lacks even a single candle. Sigourney notes about Alice, "a tear of exquisite feeling glistened in her eye" (259). Alice's sympathetic response to the woman's tears gives the speaker-hearer a special opportunity to experience the world through the eyes of a physically challenged person. As Ryan contends, sentimental benevolence forces readers to recognize a paradox: their detachment from and compelling need to help others. The scene thus crystallizes Sigourney's belief that the deaf can model sentimental benevolence: through interpreting these events for Alice, the other children and Sigourney (and, of course, the reader) are transformed. As a result of Alice's example, these others not only understand their physical advantage; they also come to understand their class privilege.

In Sigourney's prose juvenile literature, deaf children manifest the principles of sentimental benevolence in ways that resemble other famous child exemplars. Eva St. Clare, the pious child in Harriet Beecher Stowe's *Uncle Tom's Cabin* (1851–1852), performs many of the acts of sentimental benevolence that Sigourney, like Stowe, believed would lead to the education and salvation of the world: she cultivates literacy and wishes to distribute books and other goods. In an 1837 article, "Do Your Duty to Your Brothers and Sisters," published in *Youth's Magazine*, Sigourney describes the deaf sisters, Phoebe and Frances Hammond, students in Hartford, who serve as models of filial piety and sisterly bonding. Phoebe, in particular, displays the motherly and evangelistic qualities that would be popularized in the otherworldly Eva. The older sister, Phoebe, is protective and tolerant, cultivating in her younger sibling piety and love, which she communicates through her glances and embraces of "utmost tenderness" (1837a, 232). Similarly, Stowe's Eva reaches out to others through touch, a method of contact that aligns her with Christ. Her father recalls that his saintly mother likewise emphasized the importance of physical contact in Christian evangelism: "'See there, Auguste,' she would say; 'the blind man was a beggar, poor and loathsome; therefore, he would not heal him *afar off!* He called him to him, and put *his hands on him!* Remember this, my boy'" (2010, 208). Despite their inability to speak, the Hammond sisters expressed affection physically, enhancing their communication through looks and gestures: "They were not able to speak because they were deaf and dumb, but they looked at each other with the sweetest smiles, and by the signs which they invented, and the tender language of the eyes, understood each other's wants and sorrows, and pleasures" (1837a, 231).

Like Eva, who divides her property among the slaves on her deathbed and vows that she would relinquish her mother's jewels to give them literacy—"I'd sell them, and buy a place in the free states, and take all our people there, and hire teachers, to teach them to read and write" (242)—the Hammond sisters were detached from worldly possessions and unified through love, as Sigourney notes: "If one received a gift, she divided it with the other; or if it could not be divided was considered as the property of both. . . . So entire was their love, that it seemed as if one heart animated both bodies" (231–32). After contracting tuberculosis in 1829, Phoebe evinced an evangelical fervor typical among literary child exemplars of the period: her final wish was to be carried alone into a room where she might pray for her sister, and, when asked if "she wished to be restored to health she replied, 'No, I would see Jesus'" (232). Sigourney concludes that the sisters might serve as an example to others of familial love and responsibility: "Let all, therefore who have brothers or sisters, perform their duty to them, and the God of love will bless them" (232).

THE "PRISON-ROBE" OF THE BODY: JULIA BRACE AND LAURA BRIDGMAN

Writing no fewer than forty-seven poems and stories relating to deafness during her career, Sigourney clearly believed that hearing-impaired children had a special role in literature. As Sayers and Gates sum up, her works "encourage readers first to pity but then, in the end, to share in the sublime that these children experience *because of* their sensory impairments" (Sayers and Gates 2008, 388). According to philosopher and aesthetic theorist Edmund Burke (1729–1797), the sublime is an aesthetic experience; feelings of fear and attraction occur when the subject confronts an imposing natural object or event much larger than the self. In contemplating the deaf child, the reader might have an experience similar to that of the viewer of Mont Blanc or Niagara Falls, one that raises awareness of his own physical and communicative limitations. Sigourney's writing about the deaf-blind presents a metaphysical conundrum akin to the problem of the sublime: while manifesting a childlike innocence and closeness to nature, deaf and blind children raise the specter of the incommunicability that haunts any human interaction.

While Alice offered an important lesson in nonverbal language, multiply-challenged Julia Brace (1807–1884) and Laura Bridgman (1829–1889) prompted Sigourney to begin interrogating the limits of human understanding and the very definition of personhood. In two poems, "The Deaf, Dumb, and Blind Girl of the American Asylum at Hartford" (in 1837b) and "Laura Bridgman, the Deaf, Dumb, and Blind Girl, Boston" (1838), Sigourney explored how the elevation of emotion and nonverbal cues, which were fundamental to sentimental discourse and originated in her teaching of Alice, might—or might not—succeed in reaching readers. Running counter to her era's tendency to romanticize and infantilize the deaf, Sigourney's poems reflect back to the reader presumptions, prejudices, and fears that existed among her generation, as when she claims that the deaf-blind's perceptual faculties outstripped those of hearing people. But her poems reject the prevailing notion that the deaf were meant to be restricted in the scope of their actions; furthermore, her actions as a sentimental benefactor illuminate her own role in widening the opportunities for the deaf through her social advocacy.

Published in *Youth's Intelligencer* for 1828, Sigourney's memorial essay, "The Deaf, Dumb, and Blind Girl," records Julia Brace's desire to learn and her other characteristics—such as orderliness, punctilious attention to ownership, and frugality—at least in part to inculcate the same virtues in her child readers. Not only was Sigourney's account of Julia's life widely circulated in children's periodicals, but narratives about Julia by other reporters were also copied and excerpted in children's literature and in newspapers and magazines, especially religious ones.[11] Despite Julia's origin in an "exceedingly poor family," Sigourney notes, she enjoyed a normal early childhood and progressed rapidly in reading, spelling, "plain sewing," and religious instruction. By the middle of her fifth year, however, she fell ill with typhus, which left her completely blind and deaf. After a difficult and lengthy period of recovery, during which she stopped speaking, Julia was supported "by some charitable individuals who paid the expenses of her board with an elderly matron, who kept a school for small children" ([1828] 2006, 9). Attempting to imitate other pupils, Julia would patiently hold a book before her and "would also spread a newspaper for her favorite kitten." When the kitten's lips did not move "like those of other scholars when reading, "[Julia] would shake the little animal, to express displeasure at its indolence and obstinacy" ([1828] 2006, 9). Julia's ill-tempered behavior undoubtedly reflects her frustrations at her own difficulties in learning to read. At the same time, Sigourney's observations humanize the deaf and portray the complexity of their emotional and intellectual lives.

Despite seemingly insurmountable obstacles, Sigourney sought to secure Julia's education as part of her advocacy of reform on behalf of the deaf. In 1825, perhaps through Sigourney's or her husband's efforts, Julia was enrolled at the Hartford Asylum as a boarder.[12] An official notation of the Hartford Asylum records that she "never received much instruction here"—as Gary Wait notes, "in light of our broader views of education . . . a masterpiece of understatement" (Wait 1992). When Samuel Gridley Howe, a prison reformer, an abolitionist, and the husband of Julia Ward Howe, visited the Hartford Asylum in 1841, he was encouraged by Lydia Huntley Sigourney to undertake Julia's education. Already famous for his success at using tactile signing and words printed with raised letters to educate his deaf pupil, Laura Bridgman, at the Perkins Institute for the Blind in Boston, Howe attempted to teach Julia, though with less optimism. Julia's advanced age, nearly thirty-five, made significant progress in reading and writing difficult; the Institute's efforts proved short-lived, and she returned to the Hartford Asylum. More tragic perhaps than Alice's brief life, Julia's personal history provides a backdrop that illuminates Sigourney's concerns regarding the efficacy of the language of emotion to reach its audience and, ultimately, redress the isolation that uneducated deaf children endured and sentimental literature tried to alleviate.

"The Deaf, Dumb, and Blind Girl of the American Asylum at Hartford" (in 1837b) implicitly challenges the view that the deaf are not educable by portraying them as fully thinking and emotionally sentient. Probing the deeper paradox that the deaf-blind raise, Sigourney also explores the definition of the human in her attempt to confront the question of whether a deaf and blind child's mind can be fully accessed by other human beings. Sentimental literature depends not only on empathy but also, as Joanne Dobson notes, on seeing "the self-in-relation; family (not necessarily in the biological sense), intimacy, community, and social responsibility are its primary relational modes" (1997, 267). Wrapped in "a moral night of deep despair" (in 1837b, 87, ll. 3–4), the deaf and blind child is isolated from these familial and social relations, yet the tactile or palpable pleasures of everyday life—sewing, joining others for meals, sleeping, embracing others—can provide her with a reason to continue living. In fact, touch becomes the means for the blind and deaf girl to transcend her limitations and unite with others: "With touch so exquisitely true / That vision stands astonish'd by, / To recognize with ardor due / Some friend or benefactor nigh" (88, ll. 17–20). Not only does Sigourney imagine that this girl's touch is more highly developed than the average hearing person's, but she portrays a heroic "benefactor" as raising the girl from inner desolation to awareness. Despite her lack of hearing and sight, smell and touch still connect her to the world, as the speaker notes that "fragrant buds" and the feel of a stranger's hand "[a]re pleasures left for her to feel" (88, ll. 22, 24).[13]

Nevertheless, Sigourney's poem is haunted by the possibility that the girl's reality may be inaccessible, a reality unlike our own. When the deaf-blind girl in a moment of reverie suddenly indulges in a "laugh of wildest glee" (in 1837b, 88, l. 26)—an observation she makes elsewhere about Julia herself[14] —Sigourney quickly transforms a behavior that might betoken lack of self-control into a sign of nature's desire to compensate her for her pain. Thus, she imagines the child's inner eye sees "gems" on "wit's fantastic drapery" (88, ll. 27–28) and concludes that "a mimic morning" arises in her mind to pacify "the chaos of her soul" (88, l. 31). Though the girl's mind is inaccessible to the reader, these images suggest that a "mimic" or imitation of reality might take the place of a true reality. In a series of rhetorical questions, Sigourney further asks whether or not the mind of the deaf and blind can be accessed by others:

> But who, with energy divine,
> May tread that undiscover'd maze,
> Where Nature, in her curtain'd shrine,
> The strange and new-born Thought arrays?
>
> Where quick perception shrinks to find
> One eye and ear the envious seal,
> And wild ideas throng the mind,
> Which palsied speech may ne'er reveal;
>
> Where instinct, like a robber bold,
> Steals sever'd links from Reason's chain,
> And leaping o'er her barrier cold
> Proclaims the proud precaution vain:
>
> Say, who shall with magician's wand
> That elemental mass compose,
> Where young affections pure and fond
> Sleep like the germ mid wintry snows?
>
> Who, in that undecipher'd scroll
> The mystic characters may see,
> Save Him who reads the secret soul,
> And holds of life and death the key?
>
> Then, on thy midnight journey roam,
> Poor wandering child of rayless gloom,
> And to thy last and narrow home
> Drop gently from this living tomb.
> (Sigourney, 1837b, 88–89, ll. 33–56)

The deaf and blind child presents an interpretive *cul de sac*: she cannot communicate with others, nor can others read her glance to grasp her intended meaning. Sigourney's imagery stresses the impenetrability of the child's mind—"undiscover'd maze," "undecipher'd scroll," and "mystic characters"—and compares her thoughts to writing that cannot be interpreted by human beings, though there exists a mystical "key."

For Sigourney, this problem was deeply metaphysical and religious: if one's purpose on earth is to know God and glorify his ways, how can a deaf and blind child reach such understanding without learning the Bible? Sigourney's answer was to leave to divine revelation the discernment of the child's thoughts. Since the observer cannot read them correctly nor can the child understand the purpose of her own actions, her prayers appear to be a sham, as she play-acts religious belief:

> Yes, uninterpreted and drear,
> Toil onward with benighted mind,
> Still kneel at prayers though canst not hear,
> And grope for truth thou may'st not find.
> (1837b, 89, ll. 57–60)

The ambiguity of the "benighted mind" is cutting: not only is the child blind, but she lacks access to knowledge, unless she is educated. As Sigourney presents it, only divine power can unlock the enclosure and grant release from the entrapment of the body. In another sense, the deaf-blind child exemplifies the means by which the physically challenged teach the reader to acknowledge not only the ambiguity of perception but also the metaphysical uncertainty whether or not divinity ("Him") exists.

In a tribute poem published in *Godey's Lady's Book* in 1838, "Laura Bridgman, the Deaf, Dumb, and Blind Girl, Boston," Sigourney implicitly draws public attention to Howe's benevolent acts by employing many of the characteristics of sentimental discourse. A deaf and blind young woman, Laura Bridgman became exemplary for readers of benevolent narratives. After visiting the Perkins Institute for the Blind in 1842, Charles Dickens wrote enthusiastically in his *American Notes* of Howe, whose success educating Bridgman became famous. Howe's own account of his methods in teaching Bridgman to read and write suggests that he took up her cause in a manner consistent with those detailed in other benevolent narratives. According to Cassandra Cleghorn, he adopted a chivalric stance and "staged for his audience gendered narrative patterns powerfully associated with sentimentalism: the passive, silent girl brought to civilization by her benevolent, all-powerful surrogate father" (1999, 164). As Sigourney had done with Alice Cogswell, Howe devised methods to allow Bridgman first to acquire language and then to communicate. Using tactile signing, he attached to objects pieces of paper on which printed raised letters spelled their names; eventually she progressed to learning the entire alphabet. Sigourney, unlike Howe, did not use her relationship with the physically challenged to raise her own literary market value, though she recognized the importance of such publications in raising awareness for their shared cause.[15] Bridgman's near total sensory impairment must have presented a conundrum for sentimental readers intent on relating to others through emotion: she is a sublime figure (uncommunicative and without affect), and she is imprisoned in her body. In the middle stanzas, Sigourney both captures her subject's sensory deprivation and alludes to the means by which she might overcome these obstacles:

> All is fled!—all gone!—not even the rose
> An odour left behind,
> Faintly, with broken reed to trace
> The tablet of the mind.
> That mind!—it struggles with its doom,
> The sleepless conflict, see!—
> As through Bastille bars, it seeks
> Communion with the free.
>
> Yet still its prison-robe it wears
> Without a prisoner's pain,
> For happy childhood's mimic sun
> Glows in each bounding vein,—
> And blest philosophy is near,
> Each labyrinth to scan,
> Through which the subtlest clue may bind,
> To Nature and to man.
> (Sigourney, *Lady's Book* ll. 9–24)

As Cleghorn observes, this poem deploys many conventions of gothic as well as sentimental discourse: Bridgman is confined by her body, a "prison-robe" with "Bastille bars," but she does not suffer physical pain. Her painlessness relieves the reader of concern that she might be tortured physically as a result of her limitations. But bodily imprisonment does not eliminate the "sleepless conflict" that readers are enjoined to imagine, though they might not see that kind of suffering in her expressionless face. "Bridgman," Cleghorn writes, "becomes the literal embodiment of gothic stories of enclosure, imprisonment, and enforced silence; and, in the next breath, of blessed release" (1999, 174). Scarlet fever at age five largely deprived Bridgman of smell and taste, preventing lasting sense impressions: like a "broken reed" on "the tablet of the mind," she is denied the scent of a rose and a permanent record of it on the mind.

Yet Sigourney promises a transformation that implies divine agency that can be accessed through a sentimental benefactor. Bridgman's figural imprisonment and interment are countered by the promise of religious salvation, a reminder that may offer only weak solace to Bridgman but would encourage benevolent-minded and especially religious citizens to support her:

> So, little daughter, lift thy head,

> For Christian love is nigh,
> To listen at the dungeon-grate,
> And every want supply.
> Say, lurks there not some beam from heaven,
> Amid thy bosom's night?
> Some echo from a better land,
> To make thy smile so bright?
> (Sigourney, *Godey's Lady's Book* ll. 33–40)

Infantilizing Bridgman by calling her "little daughter" and claiming that she lives in "happy childhood's mimic sun," she implies that the girl's escape from the "dungeon-grate" depends not only on faith but also on the spiritual beliefs of those charitable benefactors who would come to her aid. As Cleghorn argues, although Howe is not explicitly named, he might well be the material embodiment of the "beam from heaven" mentioned in the poem (1999, 175). Communion with others, beginning with her sentimental benefactor, was the means for Bridgman to access inner, spiritual light and escape from alienation and separation. While Sigourney envisions the work of the sentimental benefactor as crucial to educating deaf people, she also acknowledges through their example the impenetrability of all human beings.

More than ten years later, Sigourney returned to the theme of nonverbal communication in "Unspoken Language" (1849), a poem that was informed by her teaching of the deaf. Although this poem makes no explicit reference to deaf education, Sigourney's description of the acquisition of language echoes her experience teaching Alice Cogswell. "Language is slow," she begins, and "the mastery of wants doth teach it to the infant, drop by drop" (in 1854, 186, ll. 1–2). Words move slowly and laboriously, whereas the "language of the soul" immediately communicates itself through the gaze. The schoolboy spends "years of studious toil" to learn grammar and "Unfold its classic labyrinths," and the scholar and classical linguist (perhaps an allusion to Henry Wadsworth Longfellow) "who would acquire / The speech of many lands . . . must make the lamp / His friend at midnight" (ll. 4–5, 10–12). In contrast, the language of the soul is intuitive and natural. It is typified, though not exclusively, by the glance between mother and child, feelings "told through the eye" (l. 18). Besides mother and child, Sigourney identifies two other examples of relationships—lovers, and a dying friend and the speaker—that epitomize communication that surpasses speech. As Mary Louise Kete aptly observes, in this poem "Sigourney provides an excellent articulation of the theory of sentimental discourse" in which such close relationships become "the perfect epitome of [a] superior form of communication" (2000, 141).

Several aspects of "Unspoken Language" that reflect nonverbal communication are also noteworthy for their association with her experience as an educator of the deaf. First, intuitive language exists before spoken words and makes communication possible despite the absence of speech: "There's a lore, / Simple and sure, that asks no discipline / Of weary years" (1854, 185, ll. 15–17). Building on this innate knowledge or "lore," Sigourney elevates the immediacy with which glances can pass unobstructed from person to person, and one might hear the deaf child's attempts to speak in the poet's representation of physical impediments that prevent the flow of thought from speaker to listener: "Oft the stammering lip / Marreth the perfect thought, and the dull ear / Doth err its more tortuous embassy" (186, ll. 25–27). Second, the speed with which emotion is conveyed through the eyes is not physically impeded by language or signing, a fact perhaps suggested to Sigourney by Alice's rapid grasp of meaning despite the "tardy signs" of the American "old alphabet." For Sigourney, the immediate emotional connection between sender and receiver resembles the transfer of impulses through newly invented telegraph lines: "But the heart's lightning has no obstacle; / Quick glances, like the thrilling wires, transfuse / The telegraphic thought" (186, ll. 28–30). Like signing, Morse code can be translated into words, and the alliterative *t*'s and staccato rhythm of Sigourney's lines suggest that she attempted to convey the rhythm of sending a message across telegraph lines. Third, as Alice needed her classmates to interpret her signs, the glances between the viewer and receiver also need translation, a way of "being read," that afford the speaker and the reader an opportunity to observe the experience and vicariously enact it.

To take one example, Sigourney portrays a mother who communicates silently with her infant during a storm at sea. As the mother gazes at the child, her eyes "Fix'd with such deep intensity," his own gaze "Absorb'd their rays of thought, and seem'd to draw / The soul mature, . . . / Into his baby-bosom" (187, ll. 53–57). The difference in status between mother and child is disrupted, as the boy's eyes "absorb'd" the mother's "rays of thought." Witnessed by the speaker, the scene is interpreted and recalled later, despite the absence of words, as an unforgettable vision of "deep eloquence" (1854, 187, l. 65). Participating in the sublime through the child's gaze, the mother is drawn into the "wondrous knowledge" and "mysterious strength" that surpasses human understanding and partakes of the divine, as suggested by the speaker's contention that they exchange a silent "vow" (187, l. 61) Viewed in this way, the poem's speaker becomes a participant, rather than a bystander, translating the scene before her for the reader. While not supplanting verbal communication, the power of feeling and gesture that constitutes "unspoken language" in this poem is a driving factor in Sigourney's understanding and depiction of sentimental identification and benevolence.

CONCLUSION

Readers today who seek to understand sentimental benevolence might appreciate Sigourney's many individual acts of charity for the deaf. But even more important than her philanthropy were her development of a model of affective communication that she believed the deaf offered to the speaking community and the central role she attributed to it in her thinking about sentimentality. The nonverbal communication exhibited by the deaf, paradoxically, contributed to her own thinking about the importance of silence, emotion, and gesture in communicating with others in the hearing world. Deafness becomes in many of her poems a figure for the conflict between the culturally dominant and the minority. In "Indian Names" (1834), for instance, Sigourney attacks the unfeeling reader for ignoring the Indians' plight: "Think ye the Eternal's ear is deaf? / Think ye His sleepless vision dim? / Think ye the *soul's blood* may not cry / From that far land to him?" (Kelly [1834] 2008, 151). Answering her rhetorical questions with the "Yes" she solicits, readers can safely assume that Sigourney believed God can hear and will exact retribution after death for the injustice against the Indians. Her vision of social justice for the oppressed Native American echoes her belief, as an evangelical Christian, that after death the deaf would be no different from the hearing.

One can also see the impact of the deaf experience on poems such as "The Suttee" and "Niagara," whose speakers describe a moment of shared suffering or sublime beauty that eludes articulation. These moments of psychological blockage allow the reader emotional access to an event that, if not directly perceived or conveyed in language, can be imaginatively experienced. The speaker then translates the feeling of personal loss or threat to the self into a communal grief that will politically mobilize her readers. Perhaps critics are accurate that Sigourney idealized the deaf and knew she did so. But her portrayal of deafness clearly went beyond many nineteenth-century authors who "romanticize or demonize deafness, alternatively presenting it as a mark of purity and defectiveness, of innocence and corruption" (Krentz 2007, 15). Indeed, her commitment to the deaf remained constant, but her metaphysical concerns about the possibilities for communication with others deepened over the course of her career because of her attention to the deaf. Deafness offered an opportunity to contemplate how pre-lingual emotion could be conveyed outside of language. In her innovative teaching and sentimental writings about the deaf, she demonstrated her profound appreciation for what the sensory-impaired can teach her readers about the power of emotion and gesture. Not only did Sigourney advocate for the education of deaf students like Alice. She clearly believed that by bringing the hearing into their silence, the deaf encourage all her readers to listen more closely to them.

NOTES

1. My references to Sigourney's "The Deaf, Dumb, and Blind Girl" ([1828] 2006), come from *Textual Editing Project*, edited by Heather Lyda, pp. 8–16. This essay originally appeared in *Juvenile Miscellany* 4.2 (May 1828), 127–41, and was reprinted in *Religious Intelligencer* 13.11 (2 August 1828), 161–64.

2. I take the quoted phrase from the title of *The People of the Eye: Deaf Ethnicity and Ancestry* (Lane, Pillard, and Hedberg 2010).

3. A number of Sigourney's children's stories, such as "The Mute Boy" from *Tales and Essays for Children* (1835), are also based on her work with the deaf in Hartford and portray deaf children as models of juvenile behavior.

4. Much recent work on sentimentality has moved beyond scrutinizing the limited domestic sphere and toward understanding the broader effects of women's political action. See, for example, Kaplan (1998), Leland (2004), and Romero (1997).

5. Among several fine essays and books on the link between education and social advocacy are Wexler (1992); Robbins (2004a); and Levander (2006).

6. Critics have discussed the political implications of sentimental benevolence in equalizing political rights as well as its limitations in reaffirming class divisions. On sentimental benevolence in relation to individual authors, see Bergman and Bernardi (2005), Robbins (2004b), Ryan (2003), and Ginzberg (1992).

7. Unlike the notable achievements of Thomas Gallaudet, Abbé Sicard, Laurent Clerc, and Jean Massieu, Sigourney's support for deaf education has largely been ignored and her writing disparaged as sentimental. Lane (1984) gives a lively but unflattering psycho-biographical portrait of Sigourney as an egoist and narcissist, driven by "self-love" to combat her personal isolation through an alliance with the deaf: "[T]he poetess tried desperately to represent that isolation yielded richness of inner experience for Alice and for herself. The deaf and dumb, like the dead, commune directly with God, needing no language" (181). This view of Sigourney mischaracterizes many of her poems about the deaf that problematize their connection between the divine and human. Not only did she precede Gallaudet as Alice's teacher, but her subsequent publications both deepened her readers' sympathy for the deaf and portrayed significantly more complexity than had been previously acknowledged in literature. For other views that acknowledge Sigourney's social advocacy, see Sayers and Gates (2008), and Krentz (2007, 108–16).

8. Alice probably used the "indigenous American two-handed alphabet," a method we know was in use in 1815 when Thomas Hopkins Gallaudet, a neighbor of Sigourney's and founder of the American School for the Deaf in Hartford, mentions that he met a father and son who communicated with finger-spelling "using nearly our alphabet" (Sayers and Gates 2008, 378).

9. Noble (2000) argues that Sigourney's "The Suttee" invites readers to observe the mother's and child's loving gaze and identify vicariously with the pain of a woman's immolation. Through their gaze, the reader is "encouraged to feel the mother's suffering, and the air of erotic 'thrilling agony' in the poem is propped on that spectatorial suffering, making possible an experience of masochistic pleasure" (Noble 2000, 83). Sorisio (2000) refers to the "dynamics of spectatorship" in discussing the abolitionist writings of Frances Harper and Lydia Maria Child, in whose works scenes of physical torture and abuse of female slaves raise issues about how such violence might incite a perverse pleasure that would run counter to the evocation of sympathy (57).

10. According to the 20th issue of the *Report of the Directors of the Hartford Asylum for the Deaf and Blind,* "the specimens of original composition of the pupils, published annually in the Reports, have been offered as evidential of their ability to acquire the use of written language to a valuable extent, and in a few instances almost perfection" (21).

11. Wait notes that Lewis Weld included a lengthy description of Julia in the Annual Report for the Hartford Asylum for 1837, and the report contained reminiscences of Julia by the former matron at the school. Drawing upon these reports and her own observations, Sigourney wrote about Julia's virtues in her essay for children, but in her poems she stresses the more

metaphysically serious implications of Julia's deafness and blindness for communicating with others.

12. In Sigourney's era, deafness was mistakenly assumed to be a cause of muteness, leading to the popular term "deaf-mute" schools. Terms such as "asylum" and "institution" were replaced later in the nineteenth century by the more generic "school."

13. As Sigourney explains, witnesses noted Brace's acute senses of smell and touch, which helped her navigate through her environment. For example, when she moved to the Hartford Asylum, she smelled the individual thresholds in order to orient herself in the building, which she did with remarkable accuracy (Lyda 2006, 11).

14. Sigourney recalls about Julia that "sometimes, when apparently deep in thought, she is observed to burst into laughter" (Lyda 2006, 14).

15. Sigourney also corresponded with Howe regarding Charles Sanford, a blind boy whom she sent from Hartford to the Perkins School for the Blind in Boston, an institution that Howe founded, and she supported his education by paying for his clothing and miscellaneous expenses during his stay. In an 1835 letter to Howe, she praised his efforts and stated about Sanford, "I have written him a few lines that he may know there is one human being interested in his improvement" (Elliott 1904, 22).

Chapter Five

Lydia Maria Child's Use of Sentimentalism in *Letters from New-York*

Susan Toth Lord

Since the founding of the United States, many intellectuals have agreed that sympathy and compassion have played a vital role in the formation of our national consciousness. As Michael Bell observes, the notion that "most important thinking is imbued with feeling" is common in American culture (2000, 1). Elizabeth Barnes likewise affirms that "sympathy [is] crucial to the construction of American identity" (1997, 2). Indeed, as Kristin Boudreau notes, our nation's founders themselves, among them Thomas Jefferson, viewed a "uniformity of sentiments" as absolutely essential to the process of uniting diverse peoples (2002, 22). As a product of the Enlightenment, Jefferson would have been familiar with Adam Smith's *The Theory of Moral Sentiments* (1759), which argues that sympathy serves as the impetus to moral behavior, a view that scholars such as Robert Solomon and Travis Foster accept today as well. Thus, according to Solomon, sentimentality "provides the precondition for ethical engagement" (2004, 4), while Foster views sympathy as a learned response to others' suffering, "an urgent feeling that such suffering makes life less bearable for all" (2010, 2).

Today's critics disagree, however, on how effective sympathy is. Solomon contends that "compassion suggests that one somehow stands safely 'above' the misery of the other, affording one the luxury of commiseration" (2004, 58), a view that places the audience in a position superior to that of "the [unidentified] other," for whom they feel no true empathy. Barnes, on the other hand, argues that "[s]ympathy [is] a mediated experience in which selves come to be constituted in relation to . . . other imagined selves, while those other selves are simultaneously created through the projection of one's own sentiments" (1997, 5). To understand sympathy, therefore, one must focus on the collaborative relationship between the author, who creates imagined selves, and audience members, who project their sentiments onto these selves, thereby transforming them into familiar beings. Lydia Maria Child recognized the necessity of collaboration in sympathetic exchanges. In her first series of columns published in 1843 and collectively titled *Letters from New-York,* Child (1802–1880), a prominent abolitionist, prolific author, and editor of *The Juvenile Miscellany* and the *National Anti-Slavery Standard*, made seemingly private sentiments public, combining thought and emotion with the intention of informing and influencing her audience. In this work, she included many appeals to readers' sympathies, publishing what appear to be her unedited reactions to the people, places, and events she witnessed. Doing so, Child sought to evoke "a uniformity of sentiments," to use Jefferson's phrase, regarding the ways in which New York, and by extension the United States, departed from the utopian principles in which she believed and which asserted that all individuals were valued and regarded as equals.

As Glenn Hendler asserts, "'public sentiment' is something of an oxymoron. One can describe such sentiments, thereby potentially bringing them into public view, but the fact that such expression requires a publicizing act . . . only reinforces the commonsense idea that sentiments are, at their origin, nonpublic matters" (2001, 2). While Child claims to be revealing her private thoughts in *Letters from New-York*, she is in fact doing something entirely different: she is sharing with her readers carefully crafted expressions of thoughts that *seem* to be private in order to enlist their support for her ideas. Thus, in her persona as narrator, Child manipulates feeling in her audience by building on what Hendler calls a "fantasy of experiential equivalence [that] is at the root of [sentimentalism's] affective and political power" (7). Even Child's descriptions of nature are imbued with sentimentalism, a sentimentalism she used to heighten the spiritual awareness of her readers and to combine the familiar with the unfamiliar.

Child characterizes herself in the letters as an alert and contemplative observer of her surroundings. Her descriptions of New York City invite her readers to journey with her as she mediates between them and herself as their guide. Along the way, she treats them as companions and trusted confidantes, speaking familiarly with them as well as with the strangers she encounters. As she uses sentimentalism to make the unfamiliar seem familiar, Child's mediations minimize differences among people, creating a uniformity of sentiments, both between author and audience and between audience and subjects. As Bruce Mills, editor of the 1998 edition of *Letters from New-York,* explains, "Child's rendering of New York life survives as one of the period's telling attempts to mediate enduring cultural tensions through an inclusive literary and social vision" (1998, ix-x). Sentimentalism allowed

Child to succeed as a cultural mediator and put her in a position to collaborate with her audience on their reactions to her recorded observations.

In taking on the role of mediator, Child's decision to write letters rather than columns is crucial. According to Theresa Strouth Gaul and Sharon Harris, because "early newspaper editors filled their columns with the contributions of 'correspondents' . . . [,] one might go so far as to say that letters are the foundational genre of American journalism" (2009, 10). Elizabeth Hewitt points out that as early as the days immediately preceding the American Revolution, published letters were a means by which to influence public opinion; she notes, "[t]he letter . . . paradoxically emphasizes individual sovereignty (the capacity of the letter-writer to communicate his interests without restriction or coercion) at the same time as it stresses the need to coordinate citizens in the service of a common good" (2004, 7–8). Subsequently, "much abolitionist and proslavery propaganda took the form of epistolary writing" (2004, 116). Furthermore, as Herbert Ross Brown indicates, Child found a useful literary precedent in sentimental fiction, in which the letter, a commonly used device, offered "ample opportunities for didactic and sentimental appeal" (1959, 52), and Child likely chose this format for precisely this reason. Readers would have anticipated, even expected, just such appeals in her work. A letter, unlike a newspaper column, also *seems* personal, creating a sense of intimacy through its use of second-person pronouns, which address readers collectively as "you." As a result, consciously or subconsciously, her readers would have felt a personal connection both to the author of the letters and to her subjects. Readers could see what she was seeing in their minds' eyes, and consequently experience emotions in accordance with hers.

Child's first series of "Letters from New-York" appeared beginning on August 19, 1841, in the *National Anti-Slavery Standard*, which she edited from 1841 to 1843. In the fifty-eight columns that make up this series, Child includes multiple references to figures such as children, mothers, the elderly, and animals, commonly found in sentimental literature and therefore familiar to her readers. More importantly, in describing sights and narrating events, Child often assumes a childlike persona that conveys such reactions as wonder, joy, horror, and sadness with a wide-eyed innocence that she herself did not possess. As Roberts notes, Child's strategy was so successful that in her own time critics often overlooked her artfulness, "crediting the power of her letters to the spontaneous 'overflow' of her womanly heart rather than the success of her rhetorical and political strategies" (2004, 750). It is clear now that Child used her "womanly" emotional excesses, like her childlike persona, because she hoped that when her original audience recognized similarities between herself and them, they would not only be moved to compassion, but, like her, also be motivated to bring about reform.

As Roberts explains, "Child's narrative persona embodies the public heart, forging sympathetic connections with passing strangers and with her newspaper audience as a means of strengthening the communal bonds necessary to enable progressive social change" (755–56). Her sentimental accounts echo her own sympathy for and desire to aid casualties of American greed's dehumanization of the Other. However, while Roberts argues that Child is made emotionally vulnerable by the "morally disorienting labyrinth" of New York, which "render[s] porous her boundaries of selfhood" (766), what Child has actually done in making herself appear susceptible to the horrors she witnessed is part of her overall strategy. Modeling the kind of emotional reactions she hopes to inspire, she uses sentimentalism to awaken the consciences of her audience and to needle them to seek solutions to the social problems she exposes. As Barnes says of the relationship between the personal and the political in American sentimental literature in general, "[t]he conversion of the political into the personal, or the public into the private," becomes "a distinctive trait of sentimentalism" (1997, 2). In many of her columns, Child demonstrates a clear understanding of this connection by using statements of personal feeling to evoke similar feelings in her readers, her purposes being to mediate an understanding first between the audience and herself and then between the audience and the Other, with the ultimate goal of bringing about meaningful social change.

As a social critic, a writer, and "a visitor, a voyeur, as one of the tens of thousands flooding the area" (Mills 1998, xiv), Child was in a unique position to observe the city and to convey her observations to at least sixteen thousand readers in what she called her "'weekly portions of truth'" (Karcher 1994, 273). Since, as the wife of a lawyer-turned-farmer in rural Massachusetts, she was accustomed to natural surroundings, New York City was in many ways as strange to her as it would have been to much of her audience. She used this similarity to mediate between herself and her readers, negotiating an understanding based on common experience and shared feelings of disorientation and discomfort. In Letter XIV, for example, she laments, "[m]y spirit is weary for rural rambles. It is sad walking in the city," and asserts, "[w]herever are woods and fields I find a home" (1998, 59), a feeling that many of her readers no doubt understood. This tension between what Child sees on the city streets and the natural settings she can see only in memory prompts many of her jaunts in search of trees, flowers, and birds, or what she calls "the green sanctuary of nature" (106).

In a letter Child wrote to her brother Convers Francis in January 1841, she comments that in addition to her religious sentiments, "[a]nother means of keeping my soul fresh is my intense love of nature" (1882, 41). In New York City, as she confides to her readers, she rejoices in "the pretty parks, dotted about here and there; with the shaded alcoves of the various public gardens;

with blooming nooks, and 'sunny spots of greenery'" (1998, 10). Such sights refresh her after long days spent working on behalf of the abolition movement; in Letter I she asks that her audience "blame me not, if I turn wearily aside from the dusty road of reforming duty, to gather flowers" (12). After a visit to Ravenswood, a narrow strip of land bordering the East River, she comments in Letter IX, "I have placed the lovely landscape in the halls of memory, where I can look upon it whenever my soul needs the bounteous refreshings of nature" (42). As she traverses the city on foot, she takes her readers with her, in the process allowing them access to her spiritual musings.

To regard Child's accounts as the simple observations of a childlike *flâneur* is to ignore the spirituality that undergirds and informs her world-view and to miss what she intended readers to learn. Child wanted to teach as well as evoke an emotional response, and this dual purpose is reflected in her letters. As a Swedenborgian, her beliefs color her descriptions of nature, which are didactic but at the same time give the appearance of personal disclosure. As Child biographer Carolyn Karcher asserts, "[t]he seer's doctrine of 'correspondences,' which postulated that every aspect of the physical universe symbolized a spiritual truth, exerted an instant appeal" (1994, 14) that endured through much of Child's life, "furnish[ing] her with a refuge from worldly troubles" (358). For Child, her faith "'seemed a golden key to unlock the massive gate between the external and spiritual worlds'" (as quoted in Karcher 1994, 14). Like many Transcendentalists, including Emerson, who was likewise influenced by Swedenborg, Child "seized on a preexisting liberal tendency to poetize theology," as Emerson biographer Lawrence Buell explains (2003, 118). Mystic theologian Emmanuel Swedenborg (1688–1772) taught that "'the physical world is purely symbolical of the spiritual world'" (as quoted in Trobridge 1928, 60). "Nature," he stated, "in itself is dead, being created in order that the spiritual may be clothed by it with forms that may serve for use" (1913, 31). That is, for Swedenborg, nature's sole purpose was to enable spiritual instruction and enlightenment.

In Letter XXVI, Child shares with readers an original poem that expresses what Swedenborg called "correspondence" between the physical and spiritual worlds: "'There is a final *cause* for the aromatic gum, that congealeth the moss around a rose; / A *reason* for each blade of grass, that reareth its small spire'" (1998, 114). The church metaphor embedded in the word "spire" serves to strengthen the connection between nature and spiritual truth that Swedenborg and his followers, Child among them, embraced. For them, while nature is musical, it also has a distinct language. In Letter XVIII, Child explains that when one is surrounded by nature, "voices from the world of spirits" speak, and "the soul, in its quiet hour, listens intently to the friendly entreaty, and strives to guess its meaning. All round us, on hill and dale, the surging ocean and the evening cloud, they have spread open the illuminated

copy of their scriptures—revealing all things" (77). Flowers too, she explains, "have spoken to me more than I can tell in written words. They are the
hieroglyphs of angels" (112), and "their perpetually renewed beauty. . . a
symbol of the resurrection" (115). Each element of nature has its own distinct
connection to the Divine, and Child succeeds in instructing readers by uniting Swedenborgian tenets with the literary sentimentalism more familiar to
them.

Some of Child's descriptions of nature are more purely sentimental. For
example, in Letter XXV, she tells of a trip to Rockland Lake, where she "sat
all day long, too happy to talk. Never did I thus throw myself on the bosom
of nature, as it were on the heart of my dearest friend" (1998, 112). Even on
this trip, however, her joy in nature was not unmixed with sadness. She
laments "that man alone should be at discord with the harmony of nature"
and that "none but Him, who speaks through nature, can ever know what
heavenly things she whispered in my ear, that [same] happy summer's day"
(112). Child believed that although the language of nature is universal, its
message is untranslatable and therefore must be heard firsthand. Rather than
describe it in such a way that readers might try to hear and understand it
vicariously, she hopes that they will instead be inspired to follow her example. She admits, "I have spoken in a language which few understand, and
none can teach or learn. It writes itself in sunbeams, on flowers, gems, and an
infinity of forms. I know it at a glance; but I learned it in no school"
(114–15). Nature, she asserts, is the "great Missionary of the Most High"
(170). Contemplating it, moreover, helps make one's own "character. . .
beautiful" (15).

Child's self-revelation as part of her mediation between herself and her
audience is also evident in her observations of sights that delight her. In
conveying her enjoyment, she adopts, as noted earlier, a childlike persona,
looking at her surroundings with an innocence and wonder not typical of
adults. As Brown observes, in sentimental literature, "[t]he child, trailing
clouds of glory, was hailed as Heaven's most persuasive minister to man"
(1959, 302). Children's simplicity becomes an example for adults to emulate,
as in Letter XXIV, in which Child describes "a very little, ragged child
stooping over a small patch of stinted, dusty grass." Having found a white
clover, the girl responds with "a broad smile," and Child, obviously identifying with the child's joy and at the same time realizing that this little one's
pleasures would be severely limited in coming years, comments, "thou hast
taught my soul a lesson, which it will not soon forget." As the girl, poor,
neglected, and probably underfed, forgets her troubles in her delight with the
clover, Child reflects, "I thought of those who loved me, and every remembered kindness was a flower in my path. . . . Then it was revealed to me that
only the soul which gathers flowers by the dusty wayside can truly love the
fresh anemone by the running brook, or the trailing arbutus hiding its sweet

face among the fallen leaves" (1998, 103). Clearly, Child wants her audience to view her as one who resolves to "gather . . . flowers by the dusty wayside," seeking joy in simple blessings. She advises her readers, "[l]et us strive to be like little children," thus including them in her transformation from complicated adult to simple child (1998, 103).

Striving to be like a child would have been difficult for Child. When her first column in the *Anti-Slavery Standard* appeared in print, she was thirty-nine years old, married nearly thirteen years to David Lee Child, a lawyer who had struggled financially throughout their entire marriage and would continue to do so until his death. In constant financial difficulty, she had learned quickly to adapt to the limitations of her household budget, as her first domestic handbook, *The American Frugal Housewife* (1829), demonstrates. However, her public stance in favor of abolition cost her the editorship of her children's magazine, the *Juvenile Miscellany*, her library privileges at the Boston Athenaeum, and to some degree, her professional reputation. As Karcher asserts, Child had "outraged a public that had just canonized her as a paragon of feminine virtue" because of her traditionally feminine focus on domesticity (1994, 191). Her time as editor of the *National Anti-Slavery Standard* was also marked by controversy as she came under fire for pursuing a policy of excluding publication of extreme and potentially divisive points of view. Nonetheless, though Child was hardly naïve in many areas of adult experience, she expresses what we might consider an extreme delight in nature more appropriate for a child than a weary veteran of life's conflicts.

If Child's real thoughts were not as simple or as joyful as she led readers to believe, she appears not just to want to spark audience recognition but to follow her own advice to appreciate life's simple pleasures. Here an obvious influence was her Swedenborgian beliefs, which explain why she speaks so often of birds. According to Edward Madeley, author of *The Science of Correspondences Elucidated*, Swedenborg valued birds for "their astonishing quickness of sight" and for their ability to fly (1902, 190). Because of these attributes, he believed they corresponded to "the various kinds and degrees of thought, reason, intelligence, and the power of understanding . . . [f]or these faculties and their attainments impart to man intellectual acuteness and penetration, enabling him to fly, as it were, with wings, and disport himself in the atmosphere of knowledge" (190). Birds represented mental processes that provided an effective escape from the cares of daily life. Viewing the doves near the prison on Blackwell's Island as heavenly messengers, Child exclaims in Letter XX,

[t]here is nothing which makes me feel the imprisonment of a city, like the absence of birds. Blessings on the little warblers! Lovely types are they of all winged and graceful thoughts . . . more than the benediction of the flower,

more perhaps than even the mirth of childhood, is the clear, joyous note of the
bird, a refreshment to my soul. (1998, 86–87)

In the midst of negotiating a new life for herself in a strange new place,
where she faced new responsibilities and difficulties, birds provided a welcome reminder of the past, of more peaceful times, and certainly of the
higher reality that had initially motivated her to work for social justice. Child
tells a story about Alexandre Pétion, the first president of the Republic of
Haiti, who pointed out to his young daughter the similarity between a caged
bird and a slave: "'[w]hen this island was called St. Domingo, we were all
slaves. It makes me think of it to look at that bird, for *he* is a slave'" (1998,
87). Although Child makes no overt statement in favor of abolition here,
clearly she intends readers to make the connection for themselves, which
they, being readers of an abolitionist newspaper, no doubt did.

Child's single most significant description of birds, significant for what it
tells us about her own life, appears in this same letter when she remembers a
pair of barn swallows that performed "a beautiful little drama of domestic
love" in the woodshed on the family farm—a drama worthy of the happy
ending of a sentimental novel. Her account, which continues for some two
pages, paints a picture of a happy marriage, one in which the father and
mother take equal responsibility for their home and their offspring. In childlike fashion, Child assumes that the birds have human cognizance of the
responsibilities associated with their respective roles. They are, we might
say, "playing house," and Child describes them with all the joy of a little girl
reproducing a domestic scene in her dollhouse, referring often to the male
bird's devotion to duty which meant he "scarcely ever left the side of the
nest. There he was, all day long, twittering in tones that were most obviously
the outpourings of love" (1998, 89). When he returned with a feather to add
to the nest that he and his mate were constructing, he "offered it to his mate
with the most graceful and loving air imaginable; and when she put up her
mouth to take it, he poured forth *such* a gush of gladsome sound!" (1998,
89–90). The level of delight Child expresses in the bird's song seems excessive for an adult, even a Swedenborgian.

As her anthropomorphizing of the swallows continues, the male stays
with the nest, having "persuade[d] his patient mate to fly abroad for food."
Child comments that he "certainly performed the office with far less ease and
grace than she did; it was something in the style of an old bachelor tending a
babe; but nevertheless it showed that his heart was kind" (1998, 90). Like a
child left for the day with an unmarried uncle who knows little about meeting
children's needs, Child recognizes his well-meant, if bumbling, competence
as a nurturer.

In sentimentalizing the members of this avian family, Child transforms
them into a "beautiful family" that, in the devotion of parents to each other

and to their "children," might serve as a model for humans. When the birds finally departed the Childs' woodshed, she reports, she grieved, as one might mourn a deep personal loss: "[w]e had lived so friendly together, that I wanted to meet them in another world, if I could not in this; and I wept, as a child weeps at its first grief" (1998, 91).We might wonder if Child really misses the birds or the image of family that they obviously represented for her. Either way, she has disclosed much of her feeling about family life to her readers, feeling that helps characterize her as one like themselves.

At the same time, it seems likely that Child revealed more about herself and her personal life than she had intended. Being childless, she never had the opportunity to nurture babies, watch them grow, and experience the satisfaction of a job well done as they "left the nest." Nor was David Lee Child like the male bird she describes: he was not a good provider, and their marriage was not an equal partnership because his mate had to work hard to pay his debts and provide bare household necessities. As Karcher points out, early in their marriage Child realized that she "could no longer maintain her faith in [his] ability to succeed professionally" (198). Consequently, Child sometimes allowed David's needs to "dictate her professional priorities" (1994, 197). In an 1849 letter to her friend Louisa Loring, Child commented, "'It is curious how much of my life has been spent pumping into sieves'" (as quoted in Karcher 1994, 361). When she moved to New York City in 1841, David did not accompany her. Perhaps the sentimentalized memories of the swallows reflect her sorrow that a "beautiful family" was not possible for her.

Whether or not readers were aware of Child's own situation, her descriptions of familiar rural sights would have prompted recognition in many, especially those for whom urban life might have seemed foreign and threatening. In mediating between herself and her readers, Child established an understanding between them, a recognition on their part that she and they had much in common; they shared similar values and experiences. The second part of Child's strategy was to build on the understanding she established by mediating between her audience and the Other—the inhabitants of New York who were, figuratively or literally, foreign—and in so doing, invite collaboration with readers by seeking their identification with these strangers.

As Child shares her spiritual insights with her readers, she also attempts to evoke their sympathy for the poor, the imprisoned, and immigrants, often victims of gross inequities in this burgeoning metropolis. She complains in Letter XXVIII, "I wish I could walk abroad without having misery forced on my notice, which I have no power to relieve" (1998, 121). In her first letter, she refers to New York City as a "great Babylon," pointing to "[t]he din of crowded life, and the eager chase for gain" she witnessed there (9). In her attempts to gain readers' sympathy for those whose lives were adversely affected by such circumstances, Child often attaches descriptions of such familiar sights as flowers and birds to less familiar ones, such as poverty-stricken city dwellers and the residents of New York's orphanages and prisons. This juxtaposition softens the impressions she creates of these social outcasts by demonstrating ways in which they, like her more fortunate audience, would benefit from "the Beauty, that is ever around us, 'a perpetual benediction'" (170). Child insists, "[l]et science, literature, music, flowers, all things that tend to cultivate the intellect, or humanize the heart, be open to 'Tom, Dick and Harry;' and thus, in process of time, they will become Mr. Thomas, Richard, and Henry" (12).

Similarly, in the account of her visit to the prison on Blackwell's Island (in the East River between Manhattan and Queens, now called Roosevelt Island), she describes the doves she sees, musing, "what blessed little messengers of heaven they would appear to me, if I were in prison." In considering the convicts, she explains that if "doves do not speak to *their* souls, as they would to *mine,*" this is because "[s]ociety with its unequal distribution, its perverted education, its manifold injustice, its cold neglect, its biting mockery, has taken from them the gifts of God" (1998, 125). Rather than blame convicts for their crimes, Child blames society. As a result of poverty and desperation that lead many to illegal actions, prisoners "are placed here, in the midst of green hills, and flowing streams, and cooing doves, after the heart is petrified against the genial influences of all such sights and sounds" (125). Having identified herself with convicts and thus having encouraged reader identification with them, Child now seems to be asking her audience to consider carefully the responsibility that they bear as members of a society that produces such victims.

While Child minimizes differences between her audience and the convicts, she often highlights contrasts between the wealthy and the poor, the fortunate and the unfortunate, commenting wryly, "[w]ealth dozes on French couches, thrice piled, and canopied with damask, while poverty camps on the dirty pavement, or sleeps off its wretchedness in the watch-house" (1998, 9). In Letter XII, she describes the "splendid" windows of the stores, where "[a]ll that Parisian taste, or English skill could furnish, was spread out to tempt the eye" (54). Such a display stands in sharp contrast to Five Points, a squalid Manhattan neighborhood and a center for prostitution, of which Charles Dickens, who visited New York in 1842, stated, "'[a]ll that is loathsome, drooping, and decayed is here'" (as quoted in Burrows and Wallace 1999, 698). At Five Points, Child explains, "you will see nearly every form of human misery, every sign of human degradation," as well as "[t]he leer of the licentious, the dull sensualism of the drunkard, [and] the sly glance of the thief" (1998, 17). Because Child has motivated her audience to identify with her, they are likewise horrified, and she is able to use those collective emotions to evoke sympathy for the residents of this frightening place.

Child also uses sentimental appeals on behalf of alcoholics, for whom her readers might have felt little sympathy. During the early to mid-nineteenth century, the number of alcoholics in the United States increased dramatically. Historians Burrows and Wallace report that a combination of increased grain production, better distillation techniques, and more efficient transportation resulted by the mid-1820s in a large supply of alcohol in New York City (1999, 532). Indeed, as historian Sally McMillen indicates, at the time Child was writing her "Letters from New-York," "the nation seemed awash in liquor." With average annual consumption of alcohol ranging from five to seven gallons per person, drinking had become "a threat to civility and good health." As a result, McMillen explains, "[o]f all the antebellum reform efforts, the temperance movement attracted the widest support" (2008, 52). Brown notes that at the second convention of the American Temperance Union, held in 1836, "four hundred delegates from nineteen states and territories . . . met to renew their attack upon ardent spirits and to extend their hostility to include all intoxicating beverages" (1959, 201). Other temperance organizations proliferated as well, including the American Society for the Promotion of Temperance and The Washington Temperance Society.

Such widespread efforts indicate the extent to which drunkenness was recognized as a national problem. In a nation that actively promoted independence and self-reliance, excessive consumption of alcohol was linked to unemployment, poverty, domestic violence, neglected children, and crime. Proponents of temperance, many of them women, struggled to protect the innocent victims and urge the guilty to reform or, as was said at the time, to "take the pledge." Child, while demonstrating sympathy for the wives and children of alcoholic men, also expressed sympathy for the alcoholics themselves, using her influence on behalf of the movement while humanizing those whom the movement sometimes demonized. Brown states that at the time, "[i]ntemperance was represented as the parent stock from which all other sins sprouted" (1959, 205). If alcoholics were considered sinners, according to Christian doctrine, sinners could repent, and it was repentance, not sin, on which Child focused.

Child describes a temperance parade that she witnessed, stressing the procession's sentimental appeals, which include one banner on which "a wife [knelt] in gratitude for a husband restored to her and himself," and another depicting "a group of children . . . joyfully embracing the knees of a reformed father" (1998, 13). However, for Child such banners were not enough, and she laments that "there should have been carts drawn by garlanded oxen, filled with women and little children, bearing a banner, on which was inscribed, WE ARE HAPPY NOW!" If such sentimental figures are lacking in the event itself, she explains, "the absent ones were present to my mind" (14). As a result of her suggestion, they are now present in readers' minds as well. By including them here, she has effectively altered what they as vicarious witnesses to the parade have "seen" and connected the vanquishing of the scourge of alcoholism to the familiar social value of domesticity.

In the same way that Child sentimentalized the plight of alcoholics and their families, she used sentimentalism in her attempts to evoke sympathy for New York's many immigrants. Roberts notes, "[o]ne of the defining traits of Child's Christian cosmopolitanism is precisely its determined acknowledgement of the presence of others on the city streets, in all their diverse subjectivities" (2004, 755). At the time Child was a resident of New York, Europeans, many of them desperately poor, were beginning to swarm to the United States by the thousands in search of better employment opportunities and living conditions; according to Burrows and Wallace, by 1825, more than 25 percent of the city's population were immigrants (1999, 478). In the face of such sweeping social change, Child tried to reassure her readers that these newcomers, despite differences in appearance, customs, and religion, were not very different from themselves. Unfortunately, her task was made much harder by public attitudes toward the poor, which were often unsympathetic and judgmental.

According to Burrows and Wallace, the public believed that "[p]auperism . . . stemmed from laziness, fraud, and assorted moral degeneracies, and it called for chastisement and correction, not charity" (1999, 493). The Society for the Prevention of Pauperism, founded in 1817, blamed paupers for their own misfortunes, proclaiming that the causes of their poverty were "ignorance, idleness, intemperance, extravagance, imprudent marriages, and deficient childrearing practices." In line with these attitudes, it recommended that paupers receive no public assistance. Instead, the group's solution was to "inculcate the undeserving poor with the values that would make them useful and productive members of society: sobriety, cleanliness, industriousness, frugality, punctuality, good manners, and the like" (Burrows and Wallace 1999, 494–95).Unemployed or underemployed immigrants who were hungry and/or sick and whose families lacked basic necessities could not count, therefore, on public assistance or even private charity. As a result, many of the most desperate turned to crime or beggary to obtain money or to alcohol to deaden their pain. Child, who did not share the xenophobic and judgmental attitudes of many Americans at the time, did not feel threatened by such people; nor did she condemn them. Instead, she demonstrated sympathy for them. By sentimentalizing their plight, she gave her audience a chance to see the human faces behind the labels, thus negotiating a greater understanding of them.

As part of her efforts to increase sympathy for the immigrants, Child describes a cemetery in which many were buried. She notes its neglected appearance and the presence of grave markers inscribed in German and French, commenting in Letter XIV:

[t]he predominance of foreign epitaphs affected me deeply. Who could now tell with what high hopes those departed ones had left the heart-homes of Germany, the sunny hills of Spain, the laughing skies of Italy, or the wild beauty of Switzerland? Would not the friends they had left in their childhood's home, weep scalding tears to find them in a pauper's grave, with their initials rudely carved on a fragile shingle? Some had not even these frail memorials. It seemed that there was none to care whether they lived or died. (1998, 63)

Given the degree to which sentimental culture dwelt on death, including making cemeteries traditional settings for sentimental musings and tears, Child is again tapping into her audience's expectations as readers of sentimental fiction. For the unfortunate immigrants whom she describes, hopes and plans for the future will remain forever unrealized. Many of Child's readers, in considering their own dreams for the future, might have been able to see themselves, perhaps with an uncomfortable degree of clarity, in these eternally unrewarded dreamers. Taking her examples from various foreign cultures, moreover, Child succeeds in making them seem less foreign. They are no longer menacing or even frightening figures who dress oddly, worship differently, and speak strange languages. Instead, she demonstrates that they possess strength, courage, determination, and tenacity, everything that Americans regarded as their own best qualities. They face the same hazards, illnesses, and ultimate end as do all Americans.

In addition to her descriptions of adult immigrants, Child included accounts of the difficulties faced by immigrants' children. Since sentimental literature abounds with the trials, tribulations, and tears of unfortunate children, these examples, familiar in their emotional appeal, would have had a powerful effect on Child's audience. In Letter XIV, Child recalls several immigrant children whose faces, she tells readers, "haunt me in my sleep . . . begging the comfort and hope I have no power to give." One was "a ragged urchin, about four years old," who was selling newspapers. His "sweet voice was prematurely cracked into shrillness, by screaming street cries, at the top of his lungs; and he looked blue, cold, and disconsolate." Child is moved both by the child's evident poverty and by the hardships she imagines he must endure. In true sentimental fashion, she exclaims, "[m]ay the angels guard him! How I wanted to warm him in my heart" (1998, 60).

Nor does Child stop there. As the boy walks away, Child follows him in her imagination to "the miserable cellar where he probably slept on dirty straw." She imagines him being beaten by cruel, alcoholic parents. Such treatment would lead him to steal, she predicts, "to avoid the dreaded beating." Years later, having been taught "no clear distinction between right and wrong," he would be arrested and end his life as a convicted criminal (1998, 60). When he finds himself in the police station for the first time, Child speculates that

one tone from a mother's voice might have wholly changed his earthly destiny; one kind word of friendly counsel might have saved him—as if an angel,
standing in the genial sunlight, had thrown to him one end of a garland, and
gently diminishing the distance between them had drawn him safely out of the
deep and tangled labyrinth, where false echoes and winding paths conspired to
make him lose his way. (1998, 60)

Since he has no one to save him, the neglected and exploited boy cannot
escape his fate. Child concludes, "God grant the little shivering carrier-boy a
brighter destiny than I have foreseen for him" (61). For this child, as for so
many others living in New York in the 1840s, the New World holds little
promise; no angel, no mother will save him. In a society that placed great
value on the influence of parents, especially that of mothers, a nation in
which popular handbooks for women emphasized the tremendous importance of their guidance and the innocence and malleability of their children,
such an account would have evoked pity, perhaps even shame, in her audience.

In the same letter, Child tells of "two young boys fighting furiously for
some coppers." Because of their "black hair, large, lustrous eyes, and . . .
olive complexions[s]," she infers that they are either Italian or Spanish. Nearby is their mother, a "ragged, emaciated" woman seemingly so demoralized
by the struggle for survival that she pays little attention to her sons' battle for
a paltry sum. Overcome by this family's plight and her own helplessness in
the face of such abject poverty and hopeless misery, Child exclaims, "[p]oor,
forlorn wanderer! would I could place thee and thy beautiful boys under
shelter of sun-ripened vines, surrounded by the music of thy mother-land!"
This mother, who, Child notes, "did not understand my language," can only
look mournfully at the sympathetic but helpless Child, who notices that the
windows behind the woman's "weather-beaten head" reveal "large vases of
gold and silver, curiously wrought," that provide further proof of the gross
inequities in her society: "the sad contrasts in this disordered world" (1998,
61). The vases themselves, as well as the wealth and self-indulgence they
represent, prompt Child's reflection that in a just society, one in which Love
plays a role, "no homeless outcast would sit shivering beneath their glittering
mockery. All would be richer, and no man the poorer." Pondering the future
of humankind and the possibility of economic equality, she is not comforted;
instead, the "huge stone structures of commercial wealth . . . gave an answer
that chilled my heart" (1998, 61). Unfortunately, her prediction that nothing
would change proved all too accurate.

In *Letters from New-York*, Lydia Maria Child uses sentimentalism to mediate
two understandings, one between herself and her readers, and one between
her readers and her human subjects, the Other, those who were foreign to her

audience. In doing so, she attempted to make the poor, the desperate, and the merely unfamiliar seem less strange and less threatening, following a practice common among writers at the time of using the epistolary form "to relay honest knowledge and sentiment across a terrain of differences," as Hewitt explains (2004, 118). In these foreign and unknown surroundings, she became her readers' eyes and ears, using sentimental images that they recognized in order to evoke sympathy in hopes of inspiring their collective social action. In a nation that was becoming increasingly divided into proslavery and antislavery factions, Child, whose feet were planted firmly on the side of the abolitionists, attempted to increase a sense of unity among Americans by mediating between rural dwellers and urban dwellers, rich and poor, those born in the United States and their "alien" neighbors. As Solomon points out, "[c]ompassion and its kindred emotions . . . are above all *motives*: they move us to act" (2004, 59). Child's use of sentimentalism, which renders the unknown familiar and thus no longer foreign, fostered recognition, understanding, and sympathy—audience reactions that she hoped would lead to social change.

Chapter Six

Sympathetic Jo

Tomboyism, Poverty, and Race in Louisa May Alcott's
Little Women

Kristen Proehl

In the opening paragraphs of Louisa May Alcott's *Little Women* (1868), tomboy protagonist Jo March and her sisters lament the Civil War's negative impact upon their holiday celebration. "Christmas won't be Christmas without any presents," Jo declares, to which her elder sister, Meg, replies, "it's so dreadful to be poor" (2004a, 11). Clearly, the March daughters—and Jo, in particular—have a lot to learn about *both* poverty *and* religion. They not only reflexively associate the Christmas holiday with the pleasures of commercialism, but they are also unappreciative of the comforts of their own middle-class status. Their opening dialogue signals that issues of class rather than race will structure the novel's sentimental lessons about sacrifice, community, and the Civil War era.

Like most nineteenth-century sentimental texts, *Little Women* is fundamentally instructional. By portraying the March family's sympathetic relations with impoverished members of their community, Alcott not only teaches readers how to cope with the emotional and economic trauma of war but also how to respond to the suffering of others.[1] Yet, considering Alcott's personal involvement in the antislavery movement—her close relationships with abolitionist leaders, expressed opinions about slavery, and short stories about interracial relationships and the Fugitive Slave Law—her decision to emphasize issues of poverty rather than racial oppression seems inconsistent with her abolitionist views. Alcott's avoidance of mid-nineteenth century racial issues in *Little Women* sets her work apart from earlier sentimental novelists—in particular, from those authors who shared her antislavery sympathies such as Harriet Beecher Stowe and Lydia Maria Child. As Caroline Levander notes in *Cradle of Liberty*, both these latter novelists sought to "solicit consent to governance among their readers by representing race as an integral element of social affiliation and civic selfhood" (2006, 108). But Alcott does not move onto this broader social stage. Not only are there no black characters in the novel, with the exception of a brief mention at the end of a "quadroon" child who joins Jo and Professor Bhaer's Plumfield School, but by focusing on Jo's growth toward sympathy as a matter of gender identification, Alcott contains the political ramifications of sympathy itself, making her novel more acceptable for young readers.

Taking this apparent contradiction in Alcott's thinking into account, the principal focus of this essay will be on the way in which Alcott makes the subversion of gender norms in *Little Women* directly disproportional to Jo's expressions of sympathy across class (rather than racial) divisions. More specifically, as Jo's sympathy increases for those who are marginalized due to class oppression, her tomboy traits gradually subside. Sentimental authors such as Stowe and Maria S. Cummins often highlighted the female child's sympathy for others across racial and class differences, closely associating sympathy with femininity as a result. By emphasizing Jo's initial *lack* of sympathy for underprivileged individuals and groups, Alcott distinguishes her from earlier sentimental protagonists. Alcott's reflexive manipulation—and, in this respect, inversion—of sentimental conventions thus opens up an imaginative space for the tomboy protagonist. But while the novel's emphasis on the intersections of tomboyism, poverty, and sympathy, to the exclusion of race, was crucial to its cross-regional popularity in the post-Civil War era, its ultimate portrayal of the tomboy's trajectory to normative womanhood unravels its more liberatory visions of social equality.

Over the past fifteen years, we have witnessed a renewed interest in Alcott's life and writings, particularly in fields such as the history of childhood and sentimentalism, gender, and sexuality studies. Often using Alcott's fiction as a starting point, scholars such as Marianne Noble, Richard Brodhead, Cindy Weinstein, and Elizabeth Barnes have expanded earlier conceptualizations of sentimentalism, exploring key themes of repression and aggression, discipline and love, and the subversion of gender and sexual norms. In spite of this recent surge of scholarly and popular interest in Alcott's work, the complex interplay between poverty, sympathy, and tomboyism in *Little Women* remains under-examined.[2] By exploring the ties between sympathy and gender subversion in this novel, as well as the related role of "disciplinary intimacy" (Brodhead 1993, 17–18), we gain new insights into the relationship between literary sentimentalism and the emergence of the tomboy narrative in early American fiction.[3]

While sentimental literature originates in the novels of mid-eighteenth century England, the tomboy narrative is indebted to mid-nineteenth-century American sentimental fiction such as Susan Warner's *The Wide, Wide World* (1850), Stowe's *Uncle Tom's Cabin* (1852), and Cummins's *The Lamplighter* (1854). The first American tomboy figure, Cap Black, emerges in E.D.E.N. Southworth's highly popular sentimental novel, *The Hidden Hand* (1859). In later years, the tomboy narrative continued to draw upon many of the key themes and conventions of literary sentimentalism, including its emphasis upon personal and collective loss, disciplinary intimacy, moral suasion, and sympathetic identification.[4] Like many sentimental novels, the tomboy narrative is an incarnation of the bildungsroman: a coming-of-age narrative that charts the spiritual, emotional, and psychological development of a young protagonist. Typically marketed to an audience of young women readers, tomboy narratives feature pre-adolescent girls who exhibit behavior that is stereotypically associated with young boys. In this sense, they differ from the more conventional female protagonists of Warner's and Cummins's novels. Like most tomboy figures, Jo subverts gender norms in a myriad of ways but primarily through "boyish" clothing, outdoor activity, aggressive outbursts, and even physical violence. On a larger scale, tomboy figures often witness social upheaval and historical change, such as wars or economic depressions. Jo, for instance, endures both the emotional and material sacrifices of the Civil War.

To the historically informed reader, it may seem counterintuitive that nineteenth-century sentimental culture produced our first recognizable tomboy figures. In contrast to the rambunctious, gender-bending tomboy, the proto-typical female protagonist of the sentimental novel is more commonly associated with the indoctrination of conventional femininity in young girls and women. Consequently, I would suggest, scholars of literature and history have overlooked and, thus far, failed to trace the precise constitutive relationship between literary sentimentalism and the tomboy narrative. Like many tomboys, Jo is caught between two competing models of nineteenth-century girlhood: one that encouraged Christian submission and another that promoted pioneering independence. As a result, cultural anxieties tied to gender and sexuality always hover over Jo, particularly when adult authority figures discipline her to conform to gender norms. These disciplinary measures emerge from conscious *and* subconscious fears that the tomboy figure is destined to lesbianism, spinsterhood, or some other nonhetero-normative future.

It is, however, Jo's lack of sympathy for marginalized community members that distinguishes her most from earlier sentimental protagonists such as Little Eva of *Uncle Tom's Cabin*. In contrast to Little Eva, or even the more classically sentimental March daughters, Meg and Beth, Jo initially fails to display a capacity for "sympathetic identification": "the act of imagining oneself in another's position" (Barnes 1997, ix). In recent years, many literary critics have argued that identification is at the core of sympathy: to quote Glenn Hendler, "to feel compassion, as opposed to mere pity, one must be able to imagine oneself, at least to some extent, in another's position" (2001, 3). Jo's frequent inability to do so underscores her tomboy traits, especially when one compares her to her more conventionally feminine sisters, Beth and Meg, who readily display sympathetic identification. Through the presence of these other sisters and through Jo's own ultimate transformation, *Little Women* upholds the pervasive nineteenth-century belief that femininity and sympathy are inextricably intertwined. Through her struggles with sympathy, Jo models to other characters—and, by extension, to the readers of *Little Women*—new potential avenues of response to the often paradoxical gendered expectations for women in the nineteenth-century United States.

Larger trends in literary scholarship may help to explain the general lack of critical attention to the theme of poverty in *Little Women*. As Karen Sánchez-Eppler notes in "Playing at Class," both childhood and class have been "highly visible yet often under-theorized features of nineteenth-century American identity" (2000, 819). They have been neglected, she suggests, for similar reasons: "national ideologies of class promise that in the United States poverty, like childhood, is merely a stage to be outgrown" (819). *Little Women* persistently engages with the *question* of whether or not poverty can be outgrown. In the novel's early chapters, the March daughters, under their mother's guidance, offer their Christmas breakfast to their impoverished German immigrant neighbors, the Hummel family. By emphasizing here the March family's attention to the symptoms rather than the root causes of the Hummel family's poverty, Alcott endows their class status with a sense of long-term inevitability. But in the novel's conclusion, Jo and her husband establish a school for impoverished young boys, suggesting that poverty can, in fact, be overcome or, quite literally, "outgrown" (819). By sympathetically targeting the young and poor, Alcott posits that educational intervention may reverse the effects of poverty upon childhood development.

Considering Alcott's familial history, her emphasis upon class reform through education is perhaps unsurprising. Her father, Bronson Alcott, a Transcendentalist philosopher, was not only known for his commitment to social reform, particularly through education, but also for his anti-materialist philosophies and practices. Alcott's letters and journals reveal, however, that his involvement in reform activities often placed great financial strain upon the Alcott family. Young Louisa's journals indicate that she learned a great deal simply by watching her mother, Abba, *respond* to her father's inability to financially support the family. As Saxton notes, Abba and Bronson viewed their union as a "mission to cooperate in doing good," although Bronson's sense of "goodness" had "somewhat of a more ethereal cast than Abba's, whose idea of goodness was warm clothes for the poor" (1995, 135). Abba was often the family's sole financial provider during difficult times; through her example, the Alcott girls were persistently "schooled" to respect their father's decision to sacrifice the family's economic stability for his philanthropic principles.

Abba remained dedicated to the underprivileged—so dedicated, in fact, that she often alienated herself from other reformers. In particular, she accused fellow philanthropists of merely sympathizing with the effects of poverty rather than working to combat its causes (Saxton 1995, 180). As she said, "And for myself I feel that I have much to do to prevent myself from yielding to a false sympathy with the symptoms, rather than making a stringent effort to overcome the necessity for so much begging and Almsgiving" (as quoted by Saxton, 180). Her sentiments about philanthropy and poverty parallel the narrative trajectory of *Little Women*. At the start of the novel, the March family could be accused of merely expressing sympathy with the effects of poverty: they strive to meet the Hummel family's immediate needs but do little to help them escape their position. Jo and Professor Bhaer's school for boys thus signals a different kind of philanthropy—one that will combat poverty's origins.

During her childhood, Alcott did not view her own family as "poor," as the March girls do at the start of *Little Women:* she even recorded a resolution to "be kind to poor people" in her journal (Alcott 1997, 45). By the time she entered young adulthood, however, Alcott was more cognizant of her family's financial burdens and referenced their poverty in her journals (Sterne 1997, 16). She increasingly assumed her family's financial responsibilities and described herself as "driven by the prospect of bills which must be paid" (Alcott 1997, 154). She worked tirelessly to pay off their debts and eventually grew proud of her ability to earn money through her publications. "I am very well and very happy," she wrote to her father in an 1856 letter; "Things go smoothly, and I think I shall come out right, and prove that though an *Alcott* I *can* support myself. I like the independent feeling; and though it may not be an easy life, it is a free one, and I enjoy it" (Alcott 1890, 89).

With the phenomenal success of *Little Women*, the Alcott family's financial difficulties began to subside. In a journal entry in 1869, Louisa remarked, perhaps snidely, that with the debts paid she could at last "die in peace" (Alcott 1997, 171). The American reading public displayed interest in this positive turn of events for the Alcott family. As Pendleton King, a reviewer for *Lippincott's Magazine*, wrote: Mr. Alcott "is, as you know, the father of Miss Alcott, whose popularity pleases us all, especially as the father's income is limited" ([1884] 2003, 129). King's words reveal that Bronson's self-imposed poverty, as well as Louisa's role as the family's financial provider, interested readers of the novel. In the immediate aftermath of the Civil War, as the North and South struggled to recover from the material and emotional losses of the war, the subject of poverty had cross-sectional appeal.

Of course, literary representations of antislavery politics and the ideological causes of the Civil War would have been a very different matter. As David Blight and others have noted, "for many whites, especially veterans and their family members, healing from the war was simply not the same proposition as doing justice to the four million emancipated slaves and their descendents" (2001, 3). Tellingly, while Alcott offers semi-biographical representations of the March family's struggles with poverty and philanthropy, she diverges from her familial history as she avoids discussion of their views on abolitionism. Alcott's imaginative repression of her family's involvement in the antislavery movement becomes a reflection of the reconciliationist moment of the novel's publication. Its popularity is inextricably intertwined with the politics of memory—and, in particular, the postbellum American public's repression of the cultural memory of slavery and its association with the ideological causes of the Civil War.[5]

In spite of the Alcott family's financial constraints, their rich cultural and intellectual relationships in New England led them to the inner circles of the antislavery movement. Abba and Bronson were not the most prominent figures within the antislavery movement, but over time they gained the support and respect of the abolitionist community. They did not hesitate to enlist their daughters' support in racial reform activities; for instance, when Abba was dissatisfied about the absence of a good school for blacks in Boston, she and her daughters offered reading lessons to black children in the city (Saxton 1995, 176). The Alcott family also welcomed fugitive slaves into their own home, teaching them how to read and write (Alcott 2004b, 431). In 1838, Bronson Alcott admitted a biracial female student to his already controversial and struggling Temple School. This decision led to a further decline in enrollment and Bronson, almost bankrupt at this point, was forced to close the school shortly thereafter. Famously, in 1854, Bronson publicly displayed his antislavery fervor when he demonstrated his opposition to the imprisonment of Anthony Burns, a runaway slave captured under the Fugitive Slave Law.

Alcott herself claimed that her antislavery sentiments were strong even in her early childhood years. In her autobiographical sketch titled "Recollections of My Childhood," she describes a formative encounter with a young African American child: "when running after my hoop I fell into Frog Pond and was rescued by a black boy, becoming a friend to the colored race then and there, though my mother always declared that I was an abolitionist at the age of three" (2004b, 428). By the age of twenty, she had started to attend antislavery meetings and felt moved to action. In response to hearing Wendell Phillips and Ellery Channing speak at an antislavery meeting in 1851, she claims that she "felt ready to do anything,—fight or work, hoot or cry"

(1997, 26). In 1861, she drafted a song for the Concord School Exhibition that generated controversy due to its allusions to John Brown. When some individuals complained that it was too controversial for public presentation, the Alcott family's friend, Ralph Waldo Emerson, offered to present it for her (Matteson 2007, 263). This turn of events delighted Alcott, as she described in a letter to her sister:

> Emerson spoke, & my song was sung after a little flurry beforehand. It has one verse in it about John Brown, Phillips, & Co. & some of the old fogies thought it better be left out. But Mr Emerson said, 'No, no, that is the best. It must be sung, & not only sung but read. *I* will read it,' & he did, to my great surprise & pride. Concord will never dare say a word now. What a queer narrow minded set many of the people are. (1995, 62–63)

Concerning the Concord abolitionists, Alcott wrote, "my greatest pride is in the fact that I have lived to know the brave men and women who did so much for the cause, and that I had a very small share in the war which put an end to a great wrong" (Alcott 2004b, 429). After nearly dying from typhoid while serving as a nurse in the Union army, Alcott wrote to her abolitionist friend Thomas Wentworth Higginson: "I should like of all things to go South & help the blacks as I am no longer allowed us to nurse the whites. The former seemed the greater work, & would be the most interesting to me" (1995, 96). The antislavery movement put young Louisa in contact with some of the major writers of her era and also brought her early public recognition.

In 1863, Alcott did publish material that addressed the issue of slavery, including two short stories, "My Contraband" and "M.L.," but the process of publication was a struggle. She expressed frustration toward major publishers, whom she perceived as reluctant to print literature on controversial racial topics. In particular, *The Atlantic Monthly* refused to print "M.L.," which focused on a romantic relationship between a white woman and a former slave. Alcott attributed the rejection to racial politics and corresponding sectional tensions. *The Atlantic Monthly*, she told a friend, "won't have M.L. as it is antislavery and the dear South must not be offended" (1997, 98). As her own words reveal, then, even before she attempted to publish *Little Women*, she was wary that sectional politics and racism might negatively affect her publication opportunities. Even though the characters in *Little Women* rarely discuss their abolitionist or Union sentiments, Southern reviewers still reacted negatively to the war's presence in the novel. As one reviewer noted in *The Southern Review* in April 1869:

> This is a simple book for girls, and is a simple, natural picture of home life. . . . It is, it seems to us, an unmistakable sign of returning health in the taste of the juvenile American, that simple stories like this are in such demand . . . but why 'the inevitable soldier,' or scraps of the late war, in a book about 'little wom-

en.' If it had only been about *little men*, then, indeed, might an abundant
supply of appropriate characters have been found among the heroes of the late
war. (69)

Tellingly, this reviewer complains that *Little Women* is *overly* focused on the
Civil War. As a Southern reader, he illustrates a heightened sensitivity to *any*
invocation of Union soldiers, suggesting a desire to move beyond traumatic
memory of the conflict. He uses a gendered line of argument to critique
Alcott, implying that discussion of warfare is inappropriate for a text about
"little women." It may seem rather ironic that he views the popularity of
Alcott's work—and, in particular, the appeal of her "simple," "natural" depictions of Northern domestic life—as a sign of the returning health of the
postwar nation. Nevertheless, his words reflect the role of sentimentalism
combined with a repression of racial politics in the national movement toward sectional reconciliation (69).

Alcott describes the modest furnishings of the March family's home before she mentions Mr. March's involvement in the Union army. Her brief
reference to his blue army sock is the only initial indication of the March
family's Union affiliation; they do not engage in any ideological discussions
about the meaning of the Civil War, nor do they discuss antislavery politics
or states' rights. Instead, they understand the war in terms of material and
emotional sacrifices. Rather than focusing on what is missing from their
lives, Beth encourages her sisters to appreciate their current blessings:
"'we've got father and mother, and each other, anyhow,' Beth says content-
edly from a corner" (2004a, 11). Meg then offers a similar, but perhaps less
convincing, speech about sacrifice. Taking on her mother's role in an "altered tone," she tells her sisters:

> You know the reason mother proposed not having any presents this Christmas,
> was because it's going to be a hard winter for every one; and she thinks we
> ought not to spend money for pleasure, when our men are suffering so in the
> army. We can't do much, but we can make our little sacrifices, and ought to do
> it gladly. But I am afraid I don't. (11)

Her honesty about the challenges of sacrifice—specifically, her admission
that she does not "do it gladly"—facilitates the novel's "cultural work"
(Tompkins 1985, xv). Instead of preaching to readers about sacrifice, Alcott's characters are often torn between personal desires and a higher duty.
As a result, the novel may have appealed to readers across the post-Civil War
North and South, many of whom made exceptional sacrifices during this era
but may have likewise struggled to "do it gladly" (11).

Jo and Amy, even more than their sisters, struggle intensely with the
gendered expectations and implications of personal sacrifice. More precisely,
when Jo *does* offer to make sacrifices, they not only run counter to nine-

teenth-century gender norms but barely qualify as sacrifices since they are things she really wants. For instance, while her mother and sisters emphasize emotional sacrifices, Jo wants to be more physically involved in the conflict. As she says, "I can't get over my disappointment in not being a boy; and it's worse than ever now, for I'm dying to go fight with papa, and I can only stay home and knit, like a poky old woman" (2004a, 6). Initially, Jo's desire to help with the war effort is largely self-interested: she wants to serve in the war because it appeals to her sense of adventure. Her interest in the battle-front is also markedly divorced from the war's most prominent ideological issues: she does not appear concerned about emancipation, the preservation of the Union, or even abstract democratic principles. She is, however, keenly aware of the gendered limitations of the nineteenth-century battlefield. Jo's willingness to engage in physical sacrifice displays a new vision of Yankee womanhood—one that is infused with independence and physical power. Her tomboyism offers a pointed contrast to the stereotypical image of the delicate Southern female slaveholder. But it also highlights the limitations of her willingness to make sacrifices for others.

Although *Little Women* idealizes the March family's middle-class poverty, which demands only that they relinquish unnecessary material possessions, it presents a less romantic vision of the Hummel family's unchosen poverty. With their mother's encouragement, the March daughters visit the Hummel household on Christmas, where they encounter a disturbing domestic interior: "A poor, bare, miserable room it was, with broken windows, no fire, ragged bed-clothes, a sick mother, wailing baby, and a group of pale, hungry children cuddled under one old quilt, trying to keep warm. How the big eyes stared, and the blue lips smiled, as the girls went in!" (2004a, 21). In response to their generosity, the Hummel children refer to them as "angels." With their "blue lips," sickness, and saucer eyes, the Hummels appear thoroughly alien in contrast to the March family.

Alcott's depiction of the Hummel family's poverty exposes the nuances of her portrayal of philanthropy and is therefore central to the novel's expression of sympathy. The Hummels appear rather one-dimensional and, at times, almost inhuman; they lack the depth and interiority of Alcott's other characters. Like other impoverished characters in *Little Women*, they do not develop meaningful relationships with the March daughters as a result, since such relationships would demand a high degree of interpersonal identification. Instead, they serve to facilitate the March daughters'—and, especially Jo's—spiritual growth. But, in spite of the Marches' assistance, the Hummels do not change over the course of the novel; consequently, the novel's early chapters imply that poverty is a natural and perhaps even unalterable state for this immigrant family. As Alcott portrays the March family's initial philanthropic efforts, she pointedly illustrates the very type of philanthropy that Abba so abhorred. That is, the March girls work to alleviate the Hummel family's suffering but do little to understand or combat the origins of the family's poverty. By portraying the good intentions but limited effectiveness of the Marchs' philanthropy, Alcott thus sets the stage for Jo's later decision to open a school for boys. In the novel's final chapters, Jo models a different form of philanthropic sympathy, suggesting that educational intervention during childhood development may combat the long-term effects of poverty.

Little Women not only associates Jo's lack of sympathy for the poor with her tomboy identity but also shows that it may have dangerous consequences. Jo fails to care for the Hummels because she wants to play with her wealthy neighbor and sibling-like friend, Laurie. This is partly a consequence of her tomboy identity: she longs to play outdoors, asserts independence from her nuclear family unit, and is often impetuously oblivious to the consequences of her actions. Jo's relationship with Laurie also highlights her conflicted relationship with wealth at this point in the novel: she relishes Laurie's company partly because it allows her to vicariously experience his upper-class status. When Jo fails to take her rightful turn caring for the Hummels, Beth goes in her place and contracts scarlet fever: the illness that eventually leads to her death. With this sequence of events, the novel offers a contradictory set of moral lessons, for it seems that *both* caring for the poor and *not* caring for them may have dangerous consequences. Disease further stigmatizes the Hummels, who inadvertently bring illness into the March family's otherwise healthy domestic space. The spread of the disease is partly a function of the Hummels' lower-class status because they lack the appropriate medical care and scientific knowledge to halt its progression. To cope with her remorse, Jo devotes herself to Beth's care "day and night" and, gradually, develops into a more sympathetic figure. While in this care-giving role, Jo's tomboy traits begin to subside and she begins to embody a model of normative womanhood.

As biographer Martha Saxton has noted, Alcott's fictional portrayal of the events leading up to Beth's illness invoke and, ultimately, revise a painful episode from her family's history. After working with a sick family, Abba unintentionally exposed her daughter, Lizzie, to the illness that eventually led to her death. Part of the reason Lizzie failed to recover from the illness is that she, like the Hummels, did not receive appropriate medical care. Abba reportedly claimed, "I dare not dwell on the fever which I carried to my home, which devoured the freshness of her life" (as quoted by Saxton 1995, 217). But while Abba's philanthropic work with the poor led, albeit unintentionally, to her daughter's illness, Alcott transforms this tragic incident into a more productive moral lesson for her readers. She portrays the disastrous effects of Jo's *failure* to engage in philanthropic work with the poor: Beth dutifully goes in Jo's place, becomes sick as a result, and then dies. As readers, we can understand that Jo should not be held accountable for Beth's illness, but her unintentional contribution to this tragedy proves crucial to her spiritual development. Jo's heightened sense of guilt because her actions led, albeit indirectly, to Beth's illness expands her own capacity for sympathy.

Alcott's contradictory messages about poverty resonate with those of other antebellum-era reform writers, such as her friend and literary contemporary Henry David Thoreau. In "Poverty and the Limits of Literary Criticism," Gavin Jones summarizes Thoreau's perspective on poverty: "when chosen freely as a way of life . . . poverty defines a state of philosophical wisdom and heightened aesthetic appreciation that focuses on the vital essence of existence" (2003, 772). However, when Thoreau encounters an Irish immigrant "who appears trapped in his suffering and want," Jones notes, "Thoreau recoils in horror, blaming poverty on cultural patterns that seem biological in their power to transmit degeneration. *Walden* perfectly illustrates the ethical dilemmas of applying aesthetic notions to low-status social groups" (772–73). Jones's critique of Thoreau's limited vision of class reform could likewise be extended to *Little Women* and the Marches' perspective on philanthropy. On the one hand, the sparse domestic interior of the March family household, a product of their self-selected poverty, is described in rather affectionate terms. The March daughters, on the other hand, like Thoreau, recoil in horror at the sight of the immigrant Hummel family's unchosen poverty. In spite of their philanthropic efforts, they maintain distance from them, never fostering close relationships or emotional intimacy.

While Alcott's characters' references to poverty often seem to displace serious discussion of antislavery politics, a brief exchange between Marmee and Jo suggests a parallel relationship between these two issues. The March daughters do not hold ideological discussions about slavery within their home, but Jo does quote memorized passages from *Uncle Tom's Cabin*: the Civil War era's most famous antislavery text. In so doing, she connects the novel's discourse on poverty to race, demonstrating a close familiarity, if not affinity, with the antislavery movement. As Michele Abate has noted, Alcott was an "avid devotee of Stowe's writing" and had listed *Uncle Tom's Cabin* as one of her favorite books (2008, 60). "In addition to possessing a professional admiration for the popular abolitionist author," Abate explains, "Alcott also forged a personal connection with her" (60). As daughters of New England intellectuals, Stowe's and Alcott's lives overlapped in numerous ways, including their shared familial connections to and personal involvement in the antislavery reform community.[6] Tellingly, Jo invokes *Uncle Tom's Cabin* immediately *after* Marmee shares a story about young girls who find happiness in spite of poverty. "'We needed that lesson," Jo assures her mother, "and we won't forget it. If we do, you can just say to us as Old Chloe did in Uncle Tom['s Cabin]—'Tink ob yer marcies, chillen, tink of yer mercies'" (2004a, 43). Alcott adds that Jo "could not for the life of her help getting a morsel of fun out of the little sermon, though she took it to heart as much as any of them" (43). Even as Alcott links the novel's theme of poverty to slavery, she uses humor to undercut this connection, subtly encouraging readers to not take the reference too seriously. Nevertheless, it is significant that Jo can quote from the abolitionist text with ease as it affirms that the March daughters share an implicit sympathy and familiarity with the anti-slavery cause. Jo's invocation of Stowe's novel thus perfectly epitomizes the complex, if all but entirely subtextual, interplay between poverty and race in *Little Women.*

Although Alcott's emphasis upon the March daughters' responses to poverty often displaces serious discussion of racial inequality in the Civil War era, Jo and Professor Bhaer's Plumfield school does bring these two issues together in the novel's final chapters. Like Bronson Alcott's asceticism, Bhaer's poverty is largely self-imposed and tied to his own philanthropic philosophies. Describing Jo's observations about Bhaer, Alcott writes: "He was poor, yet always appeared to be giving something away,—a stranger, yet every one was his friend. . . ." (2004a, 276). Jo thus learns new information about herself through her relationship with Professor Bhaer, discovering, for instance, that she has a "most feminine respect for intellect" (276). In contrast to Laurie's repeated expressions of self-interest, Bhaer's philanthropy tends to bring out Jo's sympathy and feminine traits. His self-selected poverty, therefore, plays a key role in Jo's progression from tomboyism to normative womanhood.

Laurie emerges as the voice of practicality, asking rather un-altruistic questions about how they will support the school. Earlier in the novel, Laurie may have unintentionally tempted Jo away from caring for the Hummel family, but this time he deliberately interferes with her efforts to aid poor students. He questions her level of commitment, teasing that it will be challenging for her to support the school financially if she only admits the "little ragamuffins." Ironically, Jo's efforts to dismiss Laurie's criticism actually reveal the extent to which she is still limited by her own desires. As she replies:

> Now don't be a wet-blanket, Teddy. Of course, I shall have rich pupils, also,—perhaps begin with such altogether; then, when I've got a start, I can take a ragamuffin or two, just for relish. Rich people's children often need care and comfort, as well as poor. I've seen unfortunate, little creatures left to servants, or backward ones pushed forward, when it's a real cruelty. Some are naughty through mismanagement or neglect, and some lose their mothers. Besides, the best have to get through the hobbledehoy age, and that's the very time they need the most patience and kindness. (2004a, 375)

By stating that she intends to admit a "ragamuffin or two, just for relish," Jo not only dehumanizes her impoverished students but also transforms them into objects of pleasure for her personal consumption. Taking the same attitude, she describes a poor child that Mr. Laurence has recommended for the school as the "style of boy in which she most delighted" (2004a, 376). The novel's conclusion thus exposes the limits of Jo's sympathetic transformation: Jo may dedicate herself to serving the underprivileged, but she nevertheless emphasizes how they will provide *her* with "relish" and delight. Far from being altruistic, Jo's use of language suggests that although her philanthropic impulses may have evolved throughout the novel, they still remain riddled with self-interest.

By surrounding herself with schoolboys, Jo maintains some ties to her tomboy identity, but there is, nevertheless, a conservative undercurrent to her transformation. She starts to relinquish some of her tomboy traits and behave in more feminine ways—for instance, she speaks in a "maternal way of all mankind" (2004a, 379). She ceases to feel positive about her tomboy identity: she perceives her earlier life as "selfish, lonely and cold" and is glad to have learned to derive pleasure from self-sacrifice, as would a conventional sentimental heroine. The novel's conclusion thus suggests that self-sacrifice is inextricably linked to a more normative feminine gender identity. Although Jo's role in the school environment is somewhat empowering and represents a logical progression from her tomboy childhood, she remains in the shadow of Professor Bhaer. Once again reimagining her familial history, Alcott revises the failures of her father's Temple School through her portrayal of Jo and Professor Bhaer's more successful model.

In the final chapters of *Little Women*, Jo's sympathetic attention turns more explicitly to children of color within her community. Alcott emphasizes the diversity of Jo's Plumfield students: "There were slow boys and bashful boys, feeble boys and riotous boys," she writes, "boys that lisped and boys that stuttered, one or two lame ones, and a merry little quadroon, who could not be taken in elsewhere, but who was welcome to the 'Bhaer-garten,' though some people predicted that his admission would ruin the school" (2004a, 377). This detail offers a fictional portrayal of Bronson Alcott's decision to admit a black child into his Temple School—a decision that decimated his enrollment. As we consider Alcott's authorial decisions, it may be helpful to consider that *Little Women* was originally published in two volumes: Volume I was published in 1868 and Volume II in 1869. Perhaps due to the success of Part I and the surety of publication, Alcott felt more comfortable including direct references to African Americans in Part II. It would have been riskier to identify the March family's support for racial equality at an earlier point in the novel, whereas readers across the North and South finishing the serial publication would likely have already been fans of *Little Women*.

Alcott's phrasing of Jo's eventual interest in the "ragamuffin poor" and "merry little quadroon" reflects the blind spots in the novel's vision of social reform. Jo simultaneously idealizes and infantilizes her impoverished and African American students, reinforcing the categories she seeks to transcend.

She not only objectifies both her black and poor students, but she also falls into a sympathetic trap of her own making: she derives pleasure from her marginalized students because they allow her to continue her own philanthropic work. By admitting a black student into her school, Jo hints at a commitment to racial equality, but she fails to offer any concrete insights into how former slaves and their children, for instance, might be integrated into the school—and, in a larger sense, into postwar Northern society. In contrast to her more extensive treatment of class and gender issues, Alcott's inclusion of African Americans at this late moment in the novel reads like a footnote targeted to highlight Jo's sympathetic transformation. Although Alcott affirms the worth of racial integration through Jo's privately funded school, she fails to articulate a broader vision of equality beyond the classroom walls for late nineteenth-century Americans.

While *Little Women* suggests that education may indeed help "ragamuffin" children to outgrow the effects of poverty, it also demands, rather problematically, their removal from a home environment and community. Alcott fails to consider the personal costs of their isolation from family and home communities. Moreover, Jo's philanthropic approach leaves many questions about racial equality in the United States unresolved. If poverty and tomboyism can be "outgrown," what about racial identity? Do Jo and the "ragamuffin" poor have more potential for transformation—and, thus, upward mobility—than the "merry quadroon"? And, what is ultimately lost and gained through these transformations?

Although Alcott's focus on poverty throughout most of *Little Women* displaces serious attention to racial oppression in the mid-nineteenth century, the novel's conclusion *does* briefly integrate these themes, suggesting a parallel relationship between racial and economic inequality. This is not to say that racial politics are ever entirely *absent* from the novel's earlier chapters; rather, it is through the process of developing sympathy for the poor that Jo acquires sympathy for the biracial Plumfield student. In the world of *Little Women*, then, philanthropy for the underprivileged, a virtue established in the novel's opening chapters when the March daughters donate their Christmas breakfast to the Hummel family, eventually translates into cross-racial sympathetic identification. In her vision of the Plumfield school, Alcott thus progresses a step beyond her more ambiguous portrayal of the March family's racial politics at the start of the novel. While there are certainly limits to her vision, Alcott suggests that educational reform and integration are viable ways to combat racial and class oppression. Moreover, the novel suggests that Jo's personal growth and development are inextricably tied to her capacity for sympathy across differences in race, physical ability, and class. More problematic, I would suggest, is the novel's implication that female independence and assertiveness run counter to sympathetic relationships with members of several marginalized groups. As Alcott juxtaposes the decline of Jo's tomboyism with her increased sympathy for those marginalized due to poverty, race, and disability, she returns to the conventions of literary sentimentalism and especially its pervasive pairing of sympathy and normative femininity. Ultimately, *Little Women* concludes with a somewhat more inclusive—but, nevertheless still deeply troubled—vision of social reform.

NOTES

1. Hendler (2001) and Barnes (1997) offer descriptions of the relationship between "sentimentalism" and "sympathy" that reflect my own usage of these terms. As Barnes explains, "sympathy complements the work of sentiment, for each can be defined as a set of registered impulses psychologically connecting an individual to things and people outside of him and her" (23).

2. One notable exception is Foote (2005). But even Foote's article devotes most of its attention to the intersection of gender issues and upper/middle-class tensions in *Little Women*, thus failing to address the roles of poverty, race and tomboyism in the novel.

3. Dobson (1997) provides a detailed overview of "literary sentimentalism" that reflects my usage of the term in this essay. Dobson writes that sentimentalism "is premised on an emotional and philosophical ethos that celebrates human connection, both personal and communal, and acknowledges the shared devastation of affectional loss. It is not a discrete literary category, as the term *genre* might imply, but rather an imaginative orientation characterized by certain themes, stylistic features and figurative conventions" (1997, 266).

4. For a more extensive discussion of this topic, see Proehl (2011).

5. For more discussion of race and sectional reconciliation, see Blight (2001) and Silber (1993).

6. For more discussion see Elbert (1988), Abate (2008), and Saxton (1995).

Loss, Death, Mourning, and Grief

Chapter Seven

Desired and Imagined Loss as Sympathetic Identification

Donald Grant Mitchell's Reveries of a Bachelor

Maglina Lubovich

I writ of melancholy, by being busy to avoid melancholy. There is no greater cause of melancholy than idleness, no better cure than business.—Burton, *Anatomy of Melancholy* ([1621] 1927, 16)

Often in course of my journeying have I remained for hours in a half melancholy mood picturing to myself . . . the probable employments and situations of my friends . . . I have heard the social laugh. I have seen the smile of affection beaming on each countenance—I have awakened from my reverie and found myself alone, wandering about the earth perhaps forgotten by those very persons on whom attachments I grounded my hopes of happiness—perhaps remembered but as a sick spiritless fellow whose dull society was irksome. . . . What has a poor devil like myself to do with love. —Washington Irving, letter to Alexander Beebee in Rust [1805] 1978, 200–1

For the past thirty years, scholars of nineteenth-century American literature have made sentimentalism in all its forms a principal vector for their criticism, defining it as a mode of literary and cultural discourse that evokes a language of sympathy, elicits an exchange of feelings, attempts to teach others how to care and, finally, invites them into community. This essay examines a specific subset of sentimentalism unique to bachelor men—what I call bachelor melancholia. Through the study of this subset, this chapter explores the limits of sentimentalism, expanding its definition and calling attention to its multiple uses in antebellum culture. As I shall argue, bachelor men, such as Donald Grant Mitchell, utilized the basic structure of sentimentality for their own purposes. Objects of suspicion for many, bachelors found in melancholia a means of identification in a culture that left them outside the national conversation on family and mourning that sentimentality afforded. For them, bachelor melancholia was an unfinished language of *imagined* loss and grief, which allowed them the opportunity to fold the self into community and into marriage, the markers of right citizenship in early America. As single men, they imagined their lives as they were not; and dreaming (the very thing bachelors were often criticized for) became the vehicle through which they managed this transformatory process. This chapter, that is, will look beyond sentimentalism to something more deeply rooted in the hearts of bachelor men.

THE BACHELOR IN SCHOLARSHIP AND HISTORY

The scholarship that most immediately informs my discussion of bachelor melancholia begins with the essays collected in Mary Chapman and Glenn Hendler's *Sentimental Men* (1999), a landmark text that explicitly challenged earlier assumptions about sentimentalism's gender-specific character. For my purposes here, Mary Louise Kete's gender-neutral *Sentimental Collaborations* (2000) is the most important study of sentimentality since Chapman and Hendler. Kete focuses on collaborative mourning and discusses sentimentalism as a way of bringing people into belonging. Kete defines sentimentalism as a "system of exchange in which evidence of one's affection is given in such a way as to elicit not only a return donation of affection but also a continued circulation of affection among an increasing circle of association" (53). Kete's discussion is useful in that it allows us an avenue into analyzing what exactly differentiates bachelor melancholia from sentimentality per se. What her work suggests is that while writers like Mitchell may have familiarized themselves with the mode of discourse that sentimentality afforded, they tailored it to fit their own means and ends.

Among texts by male sentimentalists, Mitchell's *Reveries of a Bachelor* (1850)—published under the name Ik Marvel—is still relatively understudied despite the book's enormous popularity in its own day.[1] Those scholars who have recognized *Reveries'* cultural value have largely located it in the text's offering of alternative forms of gender and sexuality. Vincent Bertolini, for example, reads Mitchell's "sentimental revery" as a euphemism for the single man's "masturbatory fantasy" (1999, 27).[2] According to Bertolini, who doubts the bachelor's overall sincerity, "Marvel is pleading to be allowed to bring his unmarried and excited penis into contact with his feeling and properly ordered heart, to unify sentiment and sexuality in a socially validated practical identity." For Bertolini, such sentimentalism "opens itself up to reveal the faint outlines of alternative sexual subjectivity" (27). Katherine Snyder similarly locates the "sentimental commerce" between Mitchell and his readers as the space where dream life "contributes to an alternative economy of meaning" (1999, 62). "Implicit in the alternative ontology and the alternative economy of this text is an alternative model of manhood," she claims (62). Examining letters from *actual* readers, Linda Spiro (2003) argues that by reading Mitchell's book, fans "were able to peer across the boundaries of identity in bourgeois America, so that women could shape more daring dream selves and men, too, could imagine themselves as leisured dreamers" (87).

As the work of these scholars makes clear, alternative forms of manhood are a significant aspect of the bachelor's story and his identification process.[3] They do not, however, account for everything. In particular, although these scholars make a strong case for gender issues in Mitchell's text, save for Bertolini, they do not consider the motivation behind the bachelor's use of sentimentality. This is to say, they do not consider *why* such a language of loss, lack, longing, and desire seems so fitting for the bachelor in the first place and why it is more appropriate therefore to call his condition melancholic rather than sentimental. The fact is that melancholia as a kind of unfinished, unavoidable *and* desired grief is not peculiar to Mitchell. It has a long history among literary bachelors, going back to the mathematician and philosopher, Robert Burton (1577–1640), author of *Anatomy of Melancholy* (1621). And it gained widespread popularity in the century in which Mitchell lived.[4] As I hope to show, taking this history into account radically alters how the bachelor's sentimentality can be viewed.

Critics have missed an important intertwining detail in Mitchell's *Reveries of a Bachelor* (1850) with two of the most famous bachelor books preceding his own—Robert Burton's *Anatomy of Melancholy* and Washington Irving's *The Sketch Book* (1819–20). Both Irving and Mitchell evoke the memory of Burton, drawing epigraphs from him for their own texts. *The Sketch Book* begins with Burton's claim, "I have no wife nor children, good or bad, to provide for. A mere spectator in other men's fortunes and adventures, and how they play their parts, which, methinks, are diversely presented unto me, as from a common theatre or scene" (Burton 1621, 14). Mitchell likewise begins by quoting Burton: "—It is worth the labor—saith Plotinus—to consider well of Love, whether it be a God, or a divell, or passion of the minde, or partly God, partly divell, partly passion" (1621, 618). Even before their narratives begin, Irving and Mitchell thus use Burton to establish themselves and their bachelor figures as "spectators" of the lives of others. Moreover, by circling back to Burton, who was also a bachelor, they reiterate his image of the melancholic male.[5] Centuries after Burton, Irving and Mitchell work together to continue the bachelor conversation he began, a desire Mitchell makes even more evident in his "dedicatory letter" to Irving that begins his 1851 book, *Dream Life*:

I know not to what writer of the English language, I am more indebted, than to you. And if I have shown a truthfulness of feeling, that is not lighted by any counterfeit of passion, but rather, by a close watchfulness of nature, and a cordial sympathy with human suffering—I know not to what man's heart, that truthfulness will come home sooner, than to your's. (1893, iv)

For Mitchell, Irving was a model for the kind of literature he wished to write, one based not on *false* feeling, but rather on a genuine "sympathy" for the suffering of others, bachelors included.

With his precursors in place, Mitchell, using the guise of idle "dreamer" or mere bystander, sets *Reveries* up as a bachelor's collection of observations about marriage, an experience he never actually had. His little book, he says, is "neither more nor less than it pretends to be"—"a collection of those floating Reveries which have, from time to time, drifted across my brain" (1850, 5). If the reader finds offense, Mitchell slyly offers, "let him remember,—that I am dreaming" (7). And it is *this* act, which he claims is innate to bachelors (and which Irving, too, exemplifies in the quotation used at the beginning of this chapter), that gives *Reveries* its bachelor-specific nature for, Mitchell writes, he has "never yet met with [one] who had not his share of just such floating visions" (5). The only difference between Mitchell and these other dreamers is, he claims, that he has "tossed [his visions]" from himself "in the shape of a book" (5),[6] a claim refuted by the other bachelor-authored texts written at the same time, wherein one finds just the same kind of dreamy fantasizing about "lost" goods.

That Mitchell was familiar with this literature is suggested by his decision to publish the first chapter of *Reveries of a Bachelor* in *The Southern Literary Messenger*, the year before the full text came out. Perhaps more than any other periodical, *The Messenger* was overwhelmingly concerned with bachelor identity.[7] Some of the single men figuring in these texts are confirmed bachelors who celebrate their unattached lives, but others indulge in the same kind of melancholia that I am exploring here. In the 1838 poem "Lament of an Old Bachelor," for example, the speaker tells the reader his "tale of earthly wo," refers to himself as a "sad relic of departed days" and, quite literally, *laments*:

> And now, the dreams of fancy gone,
> By friend and foe, and love forgot
> I'm left to weep my fate alone,
> In this poor shattered cot.
> No cherub lisps a father's name;
> No fair one smiles to find me near;
> No anguished heart is here to claim
> The tribute of a tear.
>
> . . .
>
> No "ladye-love" is there to soothe

The anguish nature's laws impose
Nor make the bed of sickness smooth,
Nor sympathy disclose.
(523–24)

As depicted here, the bachelor is a man plagued by a specific kind of grief. His dreaming is coming to an end; he is left alone, anguished and nostalgic. He mourns those objects he has "lost," though he never actually possessed them in the first place: his role as father, a wife (i.e., no "fair one" or "'ladye-love'"), a comforter's sympathy, and a home that is greater than his "poor shattered cot." These are the fantasized "lacks" that serve as key components of the bachelor's melancholia, something we will see in Mitchell's narrator in *Reveries* as well. But why is such an imaginary, melancholic, and remorseful identity so appealing and even desirable for the bachelor?[8] Taking Mitchell at his word, (i.e., that he is a "sincere" recorder of his bachelor dreams) I will now turn to look at what I see as the cultural and historical effects surrounding the antebellum single man who expresses a deep sense of loss and longing in a heterosexual context, focusing in particular on what motivated him to do so.

MITCHELL'S *REVERIES OF A BACHELOR*

Each of Mitchell's four chapters in *Reveries of a Bachelor* represents several dream sequences that serve as possible scenarios for the bachelor, or rather, for the bachelor turned lover or husband. The narrator—popularly known as Ik Marvel—begins as a confirmed bachelor in the first reverie, "Smoke, Flame and Ashes," and takes us to his own version of the bachelor's abode: a quiet country farmhouse that happens to be the "only place in the world of which [he is] *bona-fide* owner" (1850, 12). Such home ownership grants him the right to make a bold claim: "I have a vast deal of comfort in treating it just as I choose." This bachelor, we come to find out, is a careless and unrestrained owner of domestic space: "I manage to break some article of furniture, almost every time I pay it a visit; and if I cannot open the window readily of a morning to breathe the fresh air, I knock out a pane or two of glass with my boot" (12). Like other bachelors before him, Irving included, Mitchell illuminates the stereotype of the bachelor as the man who stands in conflict with the domestic by asserting his freedom and self-will upon the sanctity of "home."

Mitchell's sense of play with his readers is obvious here, for surely they must laugh at the image of a man who would truly bring such intentional and physical havoc upon his home merely to get a breath of fresh morning air. This initial portrait of the bachelor also identifies his freedom as antithetical to the domestic and the proper care of this space. Instead of *keeping* house, as many domestic manuals of the day advised, the bachelor destroys it at his leisure, and no one is there to tell him to do otherwise. He admits, however, that his actions would "make a prim housewife fret herself into a raging fever" (1850, 12), a possibility that he seems to enjoy contemplating. He is his own man; he sits back in his chair and has a laugh out loud that even the thought of this "prim housewife" does not scare him. The narrator here is literally a home *wrecker*, one who advances his individualism, his right to self and his property. He is the independent man who can do what he wants with his home and with his time. We must ask, however, why play with readers in this way? Why reproduce the very problem society finds with the bachelor?[9] For Robert Burton idleness and solitariness are both causes and symptoms of melancholia, and the best way to avoid the condition is to stay busy enough not to succumb to it: "I writ of melancholy, by being busy to avoid melancholy. There is no greater cause of melancholy than idleness, no better cure than business" ([1621] 1927, 16). Mitchell writes his bachelor into the very behaviors that lead to melancholia—idleness, solitariness, and dreaming.

Before he sits down to his fire for an evening of bachelor musing, Mitchell's narrator is aware of his privilege of being able to spend his time in "such sober, and thoughtful quietude" that "very few of [his] fellowmen have the good fortune to enjoy" (1850, 13). This country scene of bachelorhood equated with freedom is contrasted with the tenant in the adjacent room who gives a rather different picture of manhood—the husband and father. As the bachelor settles down to his evening fire, the tenant attempts to put his two children down to sleep, a task the bachelor approximates to take about an hour. He cannot be sure of the exact duration of time because, in true bachelor fashion, he never feels the need to carry a watch in the country. Instead, he measures the passage of time by the flames of his fire. Mitchell sets the bachelor up here as a man who stands outside the confines and rules of society, including manhood and marriage, reiterating the initial juxtaposition of married men and/against single men. But it is precisely this divide that the bachelor will slowly close as his reveries move forward.

Beginning in the first reverie, Marvel's identity as a confirmed bachelor begins to undergo a shift. What, he wonders, if he desired or even had a wife? After fearing the thought that has entered his mind (perhaps, he says, it was prompted by hearing the baby cry in the next room or even the "home-looking blaze" of his fire), "something . . . had suggested . . . the thought of—Marriage" (1850, 14). His trepidation at the thought is obvious both in the narrator's use of dashes and in his hesitation at complying with such a foreign notion. Then the bachelor begins to situate himself in that space between thinking of marriage and remaining in his single state. He expresses fear as he piles wood on his fire: "and now, said I, bracing myself courageously between the arms of the chair,—I'll not flinch; I'll pursue the thought wherever it leads, though it leads me to the d—(I am apt to be hasty,)—at least—continued I, softening—until my fire is out" (14). But Marvel does not stop here; he cannot hold back his continual desire to dream, to go into a world of fantasy that is in fact both the symptom and the cause of his melancholia.

At this moment, as the first reverie begins, Marvel transfers himself into the dream life, and we more clearly recognize his melancholic discourse, attachments, and identifications. In the first reverie, he traces a bachelor's indecision about marriage by implementing the metaphor of a fire. As the fire moves from smoke, to blaze, to ashes, his thoughts about marriage move from doubt, to cheer, to "desolation." "A wife!—thought I—yes, a wife! And why?" (1850,15). His doubt makes clear his own defense of single life and his recognition of what a bachelor gives up when he becomes a husband— namely independence and comfort, trading them for "the die of absorbing, unchanging, relentless marriage" (15). Part of the attack against marriage used here emphasizes its repetition, its claustrophobia, its boring stability, and its predictability. All these qualities contrast sharply with the way the bachelor lives his life. While the bachelor can escape and has the freedom of mobility, the husband is tied to the home, his wife, and children.

The bachelor takes us through a series of contemplations regarding whether or not he should move out of bachelorhood (at least in his dreams), by repeating the word "Shall." That is, "*Shall* a man who has been free to chase his fancies over the wide world, without let or hindrance, shut himself up in the marriage-ship, within four walls called Home, that are to claim him, his time, his trouble, and his tears?" (1850,15). The "marriage-ship" might "shut [him] up" and enclose him within the walls of "home," but the bachelor also calls forward the connotation of the antebellum home, a place that while it might "claim" him, also claims his time, trouble, and tears. Mitchell, as Washington Irving had done several decades earlier, reiterates and highlights the bachelor stereotype of mid-century America: "Shall this brain of mine, careless-working, never tied with idleness, feeding on long vagaries, and high, gigantic castles, dreaming out beatitudes hour by hour—turn itself at length to such dull task-work, as thinking out a livelihood for wife and children?" (16). Based on the divide between married and single, Mitchell's presentation of his bachelor here matches how his readers presumably imagined the single man to be—as a man who could never *possibly* tire of his own idleness and dreaming.

But Mitchell does so only to make this binary less permanent and stable. That is, by playing into these stereotypes, Mitchell seeks to change his readers' minds about the bachelor and fold a new kind of man into the role as husband. The role this idle bachelor will next perform is his move into "husband," and in so doing, the line separating married and single begins to blur. Mitchell's bachelor makes his transition from single man towards an identity as husband, but not without first pointing out the absurdity in having to search for a wife: "And where on earth, then, shall a poor devil look for a wife?" (1850, 17). Where else, but in his dreams? Once the "poor devil" of a bachelor has found the imagined wife, "Peggy," he foresees everything that could go wrong with this marriage. There are "the plaguey wife's relations," including the "maiden aunts" who will spend months in his home drinking tea, the "twisted-headed brothers," the mother-in-law who will be in his domestic affairs, the "little bevy of dirty-nosed nephews who will come to spend the holydays and eat up your East India sweetmeats," and finally, the "fidgety old uncle" whom the bachelor/husband must tolerate if only because he might one day give his fortune to Peggy (18–19).

In such lines, Mitchell presents the very worst of the bachelor identity (selfish, solitary, idle) and its negative perspective on marriage. His narrator thinks about the wealth Peggy might inherit and draws attention to the bachelor's known avarice. He is also deeply troubled by the potential lovelessness of marriage, which makes of it for some a necessary evil and an ordeal to endure. The newly appointed "husband" is not at home with Peggy; he merely maintains a front of domestic bliss with his "shrewish" wife, who does not after all, "care a fig" for him (1850, 22). All of these things the bachelor fears. This, then, is Mitchell's rhetorical strategy: by painting the bachelor in such a negative light *first,* by calling forward everything the reader already believes to be true about him, he can then turn this picture around to reveal what apparently are the "true" inner thoughts of the bachelor—his dreams about marriage, loss, sympathy, the domestic, a wife, children. [10]

As the blaze of his fire grows cold, this would-be husband seeks instead a reverie that will afford him true love. As his fire starts again, "blaze— signifying cheer"—leads him to now reconsider his solitary position. The empty chair beside him takes on new significance, as he wonders:

> —If now in that chair yonder . . . were seated a sweet-faced girl, with a pretty little foot lying out upon the hearth . . . the hair parted to a charm over a forehead fair as any of your dreams;—and if you could reach an arm around that chair back . . . and if you could clasp with your other hand those little white, taper fingers of hers, which lie so temptingly within reach,—and so, talk softly and low in presence of the blaze, with the hours slip away without knowledge . . . if, *in short, you were no bachelor, but the husband of some such sweet image*—(dream, call it rather,) would it not be far pleasanter than this cold single night-sitting—counting the sticks—reckoning the length of the blaze, and the height of the falling snow? (1850, 25–26, emphasis added)

Idle bachelors, we learn, keep busy by counting sticks, watching fires, and keeping an eye on the falling snow. In this dream within a dream, the bachelor realizes the error of his former ways and transforms those faults of the single man into an image of domestic respectability and reciprocity. In so doing, he gives his wayward and useless life meaning through performing the domestic husband and by showing a desire to become the man whom antebellum culture has clearly identified as the proper version of manhood—the married man. He goes on to ask whether "[b]enevolence" would "ripen with such monitor to task it"; would selfishness "grow faint and dull" while "guile" would "shiver, and grow weak before that girl-brow, and eye of innocence!" The boy who is the bachelor can now finally become the man who is the husband: "How would not all that boyhood prized of enthusiasm, and quick blood, and life, renew itself in such presence!" (27).

The bachelor appears to fully and finally realize that marriage is, after all, what is needed to normalize his wayward and useless ways. His "wife" fulfills all her domestic duties and provides the very kind of sympathy in times of loss that bachelors lack (as we find in the bachelor who "laments" in "Lament of an Old Bachelor" as well). When death comes to the imagined husband's friend, then his sister, and then his mother, "*she* is there" (Mitchell 1850, 28). When the bachelor/husband imagines that the mother's death would render him "alone and homeless," he quickly reconsiders: "But you are not homeless; you are not alone; *she* is here;—her tears softening yours, her smile lighting yours, her grief killing yours; and you live again, to assuage that kind sorrow of hers" (29).[11]

Marriage for Mitchell becomes tied to a specific communion of suffering and sorrow in which the single man simply is barred from participating. The fluidity of identity and the circular movement of grief in Mitchell's description make it virtually impossible to distinguish the sufferer from the alleviator of that suffering; she cries and grieves *for* him as he lives essentially only to lessen her own sorrow. Moreover, in this kind of domestic sympathy, the wife feels his pain so intimately that she can fulfill more familial roles than just one: "Your sister, sweet one, is dead—buried . . . *she,* she says, will be a sister . . . God has sent this angel surely!" (1850, 28). Mitchell ends this section by emerging from his reverie and returning again to his bachelor identity. He concludes by making a repeated reference to the bachelor's isolation and loneliness; as the fire goes out he ends the scene, "I was alone, with only dog for company" (31). There is little exchange of sympathy to be had here—"it is not enough, after all," Marvel tells us earlier, "to like a dog" (25).

SYMPATHY, CITIZENSHIP AND BACHELOR IDENTITY

Marriage, we begin to see, affords one a life of connection, built upon a sentiment akin to what Elizabeth Barnes and others define as "sympathetic identification," "the act of imagining oneself in another's position" (1997, ix). When the bachelor is conceived of as *outside* the bonds of marriage, he is excluded from attachments, including those of citizenship. For example, when Mitchell's bachelor-turned-husband contemplates the pain he has endured, he thinks, "To a lone man it comes not near; for how can trial take hold where there is nothing by which to try" (Mitchell 1850, 39). As he imagines the bachelor, he is alone, without human connection, and suffers from a want of both company and sympathy; and it is here that the stakes in Mitchell's bachelor text become apparent.

Republican marriage played a principal role in the "making" of Americans up to the 1850s, but it is also closely related to another important facet of national ideology—sympathy and sympathetic exchange. As Kristin Boudreau argues, "To fully understand the nineteenth-century culture of sympathy, one must return to the conscious efforts to recruit sympathy into the service of national identity" (2002, 21). Most scholars of sentiment and sympathy return to Adam Smith's *The Theory of Moral Sentiment* (1759), which "represents sympathy as the foundation of any moral society" (Noble 2000, 63). Barnes appropriately questions the sympathetic allegiance to democracy, but my interest here is in the use of sympathy as a means of identification and union.

What does sympathy (the fellow feeling of sentimentality) accomplish, then, and how is it relevant to the bachelor? The act of imagining oneself in another's position, as Marianne Noble explains, brings separate individuals together: "In that it brings people together through sympathetic extensions into each others' experiences, the sentimental project is one of unification" (2000, 64). The bachelor's melancholy works for his own unification and identification process by effectively bringing himself into the status of useful, respectable citizen. Moreover, he can *imagine* a life built around suffering, and suffering, we have learned, unites. While sympathy focuses on the sufferer's pain revealed to the observer, which brings about a coming together over the lost object of one's mourning, Mitchell's bachelor alters this traditional structure. It is through this revision that the bachelor's melancholic identification becomes more complicated.

Earlier I discussed melancholy's attachment to "lost" objects; that is, the melancholic, like the sentimentalist, mourns those objects which have become "lost" to the sufferer. But what if the mourned objects never belonged to the subject in the first place? What does it mean if one *desires* to live in a world where he merely *imagines* that these objects are "lost" to him? What is the point in mourning, in forming melancholic attachments to the domestic fantasy—to a life that is not, that may or may not ever be, to a wife one never had, to a husband one never was, to a marriage one never participated in as lived experience? Mitchell's use of this illusionary and assumed loss resembles instead what Slavoj Zizek aptly terms *lack*. In "Melancholy and the

Act," Zizek writes that "what melancholy obfuscates is that the object is lacking from the very beginning, that its emergence coincides with its lack, that this object is *nothing but* the positivization of void or lack, a purely anamorphic entity that does not exist in itself" (2000, 660).[12] Sentimentality has long suffered from the critic's accusation that it is "false in sentiment and/or unskilled in expression," as Joanne Dobson (1997, 263) explains, but Mitchell offers a version of sentimental literature that includes a mourner who desires and seeks out suffering in order to belong to the "culture of sentiment"[13] that is thriving around him. The bachelor in the texts we have been discussing imagines a *reason* to feel sentiment—not exactly the sentiment itself. And as the Adam Smith-based scholars point out, cognition precedes feeling (including sympathy).

I find Zizek's distinction between loss and lack useful because it helps to define the specific kind of affect in which bachelors like Mitchell's participate. Moreover, it also situates him in opposition to the way we usually think of structures of sentimentality and sympathy, as Mitchell presents us with a new and paradoxical way to utilize these modes of discourse. The bachelor wants to, and *has to,* really, bring himself into the national project of sympathetic identification and can only do so through imagining the family and dreaming of its pain. Mitchell's project is not necessarily the same kind of sympathy that is evoked in what studies of sentimentality use as its classic example, that is, the sympathy required of Harriet Beecher Stowe's readers in *Uncle Tom's Cabin*. Stowe invites us as readers/mothers to *feel* the way Eliza feels through the grief of losing a child, and asks that we imagine ourselves as Eliza, essentially to feel her pain. Stowe's narrator addresses us directly: "If it were *your* Harry, mother, or *your* Willie, that were going to be torn from you by a brutal trader, tomorrow morning . . . How many miles could you make in those few brief hours?" (1852, 48). As readers of Mitchell, we must ask, what kind of sentimentality or sympathy can be built upon, not the expression of one's loss, but the *desire* for loss? The feeling, such as readers experience it, would connect him to other people.

The bachelor's yearning for pain and suffering creates a world in which the subject imagines *himself* in the role of sufferer. Attaching such a sense of pleasure (or desire) to suffering and loss draws our attention to Marianne Noble's claim in *The Masochistic Pleasures of Sentimental Literature* that "[l]ike masochism, sentimentalism can be read, broadly, as a quest for a state of union, or plentitude. And like masochism, sentimentalism describes a world in which pain is an avenue toward achieving that desired state of oneness" (2000, 62). Noble is here linking the theories of Calvinism to sentimental discourse and is obviously not describing the bachelor's "desire" for marriage. However, the bachelor's melancholic identification works along similar lines as Noble's theory of the masochistic pleasures of sentimentality. The bachelor dreams not only of marriage but also of the pain that comes with the loss dreaming engenders. His transcendence of the married/single binary becomes ever the more crucial because, by leaving bachelorhood, the single man (even if he is "just dreaming") transforms himself into the right kind of citizen. Now, he is the husband, the one who feels pain and participates in the sympathetic identification used by and required of families and nations. This bachelor tests the boundaries of marriage and manhood.

In the first reverie, as the bachelor moves into "heart desolation," he becomes overwhelmed with the melancholy and loss entailed in marriage. In this version of the domestic, poverty strikes his family. He mourns the thought and questions, "Will it solace you to find her parting the poor treasure of food you have stolen for her, with begging, foodless children?" (Mitchell 1850, 36). But beyond his loss of economic stability, his favorite child, Bessy, is dying. As Karen Sánchez-Eppler notes in her study of nineteenth-century affect and its commodification of the dead and dying child, "Dying is what children do most and do best in the literary and cultural imagination of nineteenth-century America" (1999, 64). Mitchell's melancholic bachelor recites the scene all too common to both the lives and literature of his readers:

> 'Dear Bessy'—and your tones tremble; you feel that she is on the edge of the grave. Can you pluck her back? Can endearments stay her? Business is heavy, away from the loved child; home, you go, to fondle while yet time is left—but *this* time you are too late. She is gone. She cannot hear you: she cannot thank you for the violets you put within her stiff white hand.
> And then—the grassy mound—the cold shadow of head-stone!
> (1850, 36)

Mitchell picks up here on the rhetoric used in a culture accustomed to mourning the dead and in particular, the dead child; it is an object of loss with which his readers can easily identify. As Barnes explains, the goal of sympathy is not only to make others *feel* what you do, but to make them identify with the lost object and with your loss as though it were their own (1997, 5).

While the thought of the dead child moves Mitchell's imagined husband/father to tears, it simultaneously pushes him away from this melancholic thought and we observe the bachelor's reverie as a movement of retraction/attraction. He pulls away from it and thanks God that he is "no such mourner" (1850, 36). In other words, the narrator is both drawn to the thought of the sentimental sufferer and the mourning father, and repelled by it. Mitchell seems to make the argument that marriage, by the nature of human connections and sympathies, already anticipates the sorrow of suffering. One cannot escape it—except by remaining a bachelor. Luckily for him, he can return to his solitary life free from such loss; however, this particular bachelor is not quite ready to give up on his melancholic fantasies.

Marvel returns again to his imaginary family, the one that is quickly being eradicated. Here I wish to emphasize again the connection between marriage and sympathetic identification, two sites of potential connection from which the bachelor has been exiled. Before his wife dies, the narrator reiterates the parental loss of the child by turning death upon his son. As Sánchez-Eppler writes, "[t]his sense of the dead child" is the "most powerful sign of *right sentiment*—for the family and the individual" (1999, 66, emphasis added). The bachelor now—as the suffering father—can experience the "right senti-ment" as that which folds the individual into the family. He is no longer on the outside. On his own, the bachelor lacks such identification; he lacks "right sentiment" because he has no one to turn his suffering upon and no one with whom to suffer.

When the "father" finds that his son is no longer breathing, he employs the sentimental product of affect, tears: "Oh, the tears—the tears; what blessed things are tears! Never fear now to let them fall on his forehead, or his lip, lest you waken him!—Clasp him—clasp him harder—you cannot hurt, you cannot awaken him! Lay him down, gently or not; it is the same, he is stiff; he is stark and cold" (Mitchell 1850, 38). Bertolini reads this passage of "sentimental inhabitation of the role of loving husband and father" as a means to bring the bachelor "into being through mutual constitution with dominant masculinity" (1999, 78). I wish to add to this claim by focusing as well on what the bachelor's version of sympathy (i.e., his melancholic iden-tification) affords him.

If, as scholars of sentimental literature claim, the family is the site where nineteenth-century sentiment occurs, then the bachelor must posit himself as a man who can also feel and be part of this relationship. Following Adam Smith, Elizabeth Barnes explains that "familial feeling" has been understood as the foundation of sympathy and, while she ultimately questions the effect of such feeling, she nevertheless still places sympathy in relation to the family. Barnes also explains the idea of republican marriage under such an ideology, whereby marriage "stands as a figure for social relations" and as a way for early Americans not only to imagine and emulate democratic citizen-ship, but also to build structures of feeling around a family's connections to each other (1997, 66). When Mary Louise Kete discusses the common and necessary features of most sentimental texts, she writes that "Home and family are, indisputably, among the signal topoi of the sentimental home. . . . However, it is more precise to say that two of the three fundamental subjects of sentiment are homes and families under the condition of loss" (2000, 31–32). If bonds between individuals are forged through "familial feeling"— which includes sympathy—then the bachelor can only *imagine* himself as part of this exchange. He dreams of himself as this right kind of citizen, if part of what it means to be an "American" depends upon marriage and the exchange of sympathies.

CONCLUSION

Although Mitchell associates himself with Burton and a trajectory of melancholia, he himself obviously does not use the phrase "bachelor melancholia"
to describe his own project. As others have done, he makes an argument that
his own work participates in and elicits "sympathy." The second chapter of
Reveries begins by discussing the wealth of letters he received from readers
after the first reverie appeared in *The Southern Literary Messenger* the previous year. Mitchell explains the content of this growing packet of letters he
has been compiling: "not letters of cold praise, saying it was well done,
artfully executed, prettily imagined—no such thing: but letters of *sympathy*"
(1850, 48). Mitchell receives letters from a mother who has recently lost a
child of her own and from a father who "has laid down the book in tears"
(50–51). In Mitchell's estimation, his readers have "seen a heart in the Reverie" and have found it to be true. He asks what difference it makes if
"literally" there was no wife or child, for "Is not feeling, feeling; and heart,
heart?" (1893, 49). What difference does it make, he asks, if there were no
wife, no dead child, no "coffin in the house" (48–49)? With these questions,
he challenges how we think sympathy should be both executed and received.
He questions the *experience* as well as the exclusiveness of marriage as the
source of sympathy. That is, the idle, solitary bachelor can in fact, through
the act of dreaming, be a "husband" and expose conflicts in courtship and
marriage.

A year later, in his 1851 *Dream Life,* Mitchell remarks on the public
doubt surrounding *Reveries:*

> [A] little book that I had the whim to publish a year since, has been set down
> by many as an arrant piece of imposture. Claiming sympathy as a Bachelor, I
> have been recklessly set down as a cold, undeserving man of family! My story
> of troubles and loves has been sneered at, as the sheerest gammon. . . . The
> trouble has been, that those who have believed one passage have discredited
> another; and those who have sympathized with me in trifles, have deserted me
> when affairs grew earnest. *I have had sympathy enough with my married
> griefs; but when it came to the perplexing torments of my single life—not a
> weeper could I find!* (1893, 27, 28, emphasis added)

Sympathy, then, is precisely what Mitchell hoped to achieve with the earlier
novel; however, his plan to gain *bachelor* sympathy in fact backfires, at least
in part. According to the above passage, what he actually gained was sympathy for his "married griefs" (which were imagined) and not for the "perplex-
ing torments of [his] single life" (which were real). Instead, readers focused
on the true identity of the author and doubted that a *real* bachelor could know
so many intimate details about husbands, marriage, and love. What Mitchell
does not realize is that his overall project in *Reveries,* to make dreams as real

as reality, succeeds. This is such a crucial point because it in fact shows that he has bridged the binary between married and single. It does not matter whether he is a bachelor; actual husbands have no more claim than their single counterparts to partake in familial feeling and connection. Would "such objectors sympathize more," he asks, if there really was a (dead) wife and child, "if there was actual, material truth superadded to [the] Reverie?" (1893, 49).

What, then, are the implications of these reveries? Mitchell's bachelor purposefully and carefully creates an identity based on loss/lack to assert his position in the larger community, as if to say: *I can feel, too. I know what it must feel like to lose a child, a wife, to be poor, to be lost.* Melancholic identification allows him a place within humanity, including bachelors past and marriage/domesticity as the site of attachment (even if it is imagined); he is no longer separate from such spaces, but included within them. The bachelor is less threatening, and has devised a way to be more like a "man," more like a husband who offers a new kind of domestic manhood.

At the same time, as a literary businessman, Mitchell must also have known who constituted the primary readership of the mid-century marketplace—women. By making his principal theme marriage, Mitchell not only appeals to a literary trope commonly associated with "women's fiction," but also forces a reconsideration of the subject deemed antithetical to bachelors and manhood. He can both write his way into marriage and, at the same time, appeal for bachelor sympathy from his readers. Arguments against the bachelor are countered with this plea: Don't blame us that we are single, for we want to be married, too. We regret that we are not; we are not selfish, greedy, or disruptive citizens, but merely melancholic men for whom circumstances have prevented our entering into the stability of the domestic sphere.

In this chapter, I have attempted to show that while Mitchell might very well want to make others *feel* how he feels (whether it is in a state of loss or merely absence) and to make readers sympathize with his reveries, he simultaneously uses this discourse to carve out for himself a space within national identity and citizenship. Melancholia becomes an unfinished language of mourning among dreaming bachelors wherein the *imaginary* and *desired* world of loss brings about a place where he, too, can test American manhood and experience belonging. He brings the wandering bachelor home and folds him into marriage; his reveries create a dream world in which the divide between married and single is closed, where naming himself as the solitary, melancholic bachelor also provides him a distinct identification process. As Lauren Berlant explains, mourning "supplies the subject the definitional perfection of being no longer in flux" (2001, 127). Bachelor melancholia provides the bachelor an identity, a place of stability and belonging, even amidst mourning and the chaos of imagined loss.

NOTES

1. Spiro (2003) notes that *Reveries* sold more than a million copies by the end of the nineteenth century and that it was "so influential" that one late nineteenth-century critic compared it to *Uncle Tom's Cabin* (61). See as well Spiro's online edition and commentary (1999) on "Smoke, Flames and Ashes," the first chapter in *Reveries*. She here discusses the revised editions of *Reveries* that came after 1850; Mitchell revised and reissued the title in 1863 and again in 1883.

2. Otter (1999) makes this point too, reminding us that "reverie" was "commonly, and negatively" associated with masturbation (223).

3. Although I have no wish to avoid the issue of homosexuality, this essay is not about queering the bachelor. Rather, it looks at the bachelor in terms of heterosexual marriage and where the single man fits in during a century when being married was a national and civic duty. Many bachelors exhibit what I would call a kind of "queer heterosexuality," but it is misleading to make the single man homosexual simply because he "lacks" the signifying marker of heterosexuality—a family. For discussions of the bachelor and homosexuality, especially at the turn of the century, see Chudacoff (1999) and Sedgwick (1990), especially her chapter on Henry James and the urban bachelor.

4. Any mention of "mourning and melancholia" requires a reference to Sigmund Freud's (1963) distinction between the two in his 1917 essay by the same name. My intention here is not to make the bachelor pathological but to argue that these men relied upon a discourse of melancholia both to construct an identity and self and to establish their status as citizens in good standing. That said, for Freud mourning is the "reaction to loss" of an object, whether it be a person or an abstraction, but is a response that assumes an end point. That is, when the subject has finished its period of mourning, "the ego becomes free and uninhabited again" (166). Melancholia, on the other hand, is what Freud and those after him, including Judith Butler, label the "unfinished process of grieving" wherein the lost object of one's mourning is not fully grieved (Butler 1997, 132). Instead, the lost object is subsumed in one's ego formation and in this way one's identity (or character formation, as Freud calls it) develops from this attachment to loss. As Freud puts it, "Thus the shadow of the object fell upon the ego" (1963, 170).

5. As far back as Aristotle, melancholia has been gendered male and has been aligned with the solitary man of genius. See Schiesari (1992). In this study of melancholia in Renaissance literature, she explains Aristotle's definition of the condition as an "unfortunate malady that invariably affected 'all' great men" (1992, 6). "The great melancholic of yesteryear," Schiesari writes, "would have been a tortured but creative male genius" (1992, 16).

6. Irving's most famous bachelor, Ichabod Crane, in "The Legend of Sleepy Hollow" (1819–20) is a notorious dreamer as well—about the Van Tassel estate, about his life as Katrina's husband, and about the status such a dream turned reality would afford him.

7. We should note that bachelors are melancholic in a way that husbands, wives, and spinsters in the nineteenth century are not. In fact, some of our most telling observations about marriage from this period come from those who were assumed to be on the "outside." While we surely have husbands in American literature up to the postbellum period, we do not necessarily have husbands who explore their identities as such or critique marriage and the domestic in their narratives.

8. Although the bachelor figured prominently in *The Southern Literary Messenger* it was not alone in its attention to him in antebellum America. *The Colored American, Godey's Lady's Book*, and *Harper's New Monthly* also published stories and poems concerning this peculiar figure of the unmarried man. See also Spiro's online edition of Mitchell's "Smoke, Flame and Ashes" (1999) wherein she includes a bibliography of "Bachelor Fiction" throughout the nineteenth century. Snyder (1999) as well provides a useful list of bachelor texts that may have been influenced by Mitchell's *Reveries* (48).

9. For an example of the way bachelors were condemned in antebellum literature and popular press, see temperance and moral crusader, Arthur (1845). Arthur expresses a sentiment common to his historical time: marriage is a "state essential to the perseveration of the human race" and, moreover, it is a "state for which everyone is created" (32). The bachelor of his tale

dies alone, "No wife—no child—no friend. For him no one feels a movement of sympathy. He has lived for himself, and dies without being thought of or cared for" (1845, 151). One state (i.e. marriage) provides a man with compassion and "sympathy," the other (i.e. bachelorhood) with selfishness, loneliness, and lack of human connection.

10. At the same time, this reversal of stereotypes makes the bachelor difficult to pin down. Mitchell's bachelor also dreams of coquettes, flirts, and of various lovers. It is the coquette scene that Bertolini (1999) reads as a "masturbatory fantasy."

11. Otter (1999), Snyder (1999), Kete (2000), and Spiro (2003) each point out Mitchell's use of the "I/you" rhetoric in *Reveries* as a means to "establish bonds with . . . readers" (Spiro 2003, 65). Mitchell makes his readers part of the reveries by imagining them as the protagonists. The divide between "I" and "you" becomes blurred; the "I" of the narrator also becomes the "you" of the reader, as we see in the passage described here, "you are not alone" (Mitchell 1850, 28). Kete explores the "I/you" in her discussion of Robin Warhol's *Gendered Interventions* (Kete 2000, 40).

12. Zizek's essay is about queer and postcolonial studies and their use of melancholy. He critiques what he finds to be problematic about this kind of nostalgia. Nevertheless, I still find the distinction between loss and lack fruitful for my discussion of the bachelor's similar "dream of a world [he] never had" (Zizek 2000, 659). Sentimentality, on the other hand, does not typically include *imagined* sufferers, except in that fiction itself invites us to weep real tears for imaginary characters.

13. I borrow the term "the culture of sentiment" from Samuels (1992). She defines sentimentality as "a set of cultural practices designed to evoke a certain form of emotional response, usually empathy, in the reader or viewer" (1992, 4).

Chapter Eight

The Collaborative Construction of a Death-Defying Cryptext

Walt Whitman's Leaves of Grass

Adam Bradford

In March of 1837 a resident of Dover, Vermont, Lois Gould, presented to her new sister-in-law, Harriet Lazell Gould, a small book, rather plain in design, filled with blank sheets of paper. While the book could have been used for anything (keeping notes, addresses, accounts, even a diary), Lois gifted it to Harriet with a specific purpose in mind. In the epigraph, Lois wrote:

> Should dearest friends some kind memento trace,
> Along the unwritten columns of this book
> When distance or the grave hides form and face
> Into this volume sweet t'will be to look.
> Each fond remembrance oft will speak to you
> In language which may never be forgot
> Of those who ever constant were and true
> And gently whisper O forget me not.
> (as quoted in Kete 2000, 187)

Thanks to the inscription Lois penned in the volume, we now know that her gift to her new sister-in-law was an invitation to Harriet to participate in one of the many rituals central to what I am calling nineteenth-century America's culture of mourning and memorializing. This was a culture that championed the use of objects like ornate hair-weavings, memorial quilts, mourning portraits, and in this instance a memorial volume to be filled with sentimental poetry, to preserve a "trace" of those loved ones whose "form and face" were inevitably hidden by distance or "the grave." Harriet quickly accepted the invitation, writing in the volume herself and diligently circulating her book among friends who "trace[d]" their own sentimental "mementos" onto its pages. Within roughly ten years, Harriet had filled the book with page after page of sentimental verse memorializing loved ones, some poems written in her hand, some in the hands of her friends. By the end of the 1840s, she was adding folded sheets of paper. Accepting her sister-in-law's invitation, Harriet had created a textual collection by virtue of which she would always be able to hear what Lois characterized as the faint, if not uncanny, "gentl[e] whisper[s]" of the absent or deceased (as quoted in Kete 2000, 187).

As Lois implies in her inscription to Harriet, part of the power and promise of sentimental poetry is that it is capable of granting its writer a sense of presence despite his or her physical death and dissolution. Even if only in "gentl[e] whisper[s]," such poems nevertheless allow the reader imaginative access to the voice of the poet to such a degree that the affective ties that have bound reader and poet in the past can be perpetuated in spite of the poet's bodily absence. Such recuperative poetics made sentimental mourning poetry a potentially powerful tool for those who employed it as Harriet's burgeoning album complete with addenda suggests. It certainly was a tool widely used, with people living in bustling New England cities, the genteel enclaves of the South, and even the frontier towns of the West, all creating memorial albums not unlike Gould's. Given the proliferation of this type of poetry throughout America's social landscape, it is perhaps not surprising to find professional writers of sentimental verse like Lydia Sigourney and Alice and Phoebe Cary making use of a similar poetics in their work as well. More surprising, however, is that a fundamentally similar poetics lay at the heart of Walt Whitman's *Leaves of Grass*, a work that, on its surface, appears to be radically different, both stylistically and topically, from the work of a sentimental poet like Harriet Gould. Indeed, while critics have long admired *Leaves of Grass* for its remarkably frank and open embrace of sexuality, its fervent championing of democratic ideals, and its expansive rhetoric of inclusion, few have explored the way in which Whitman's 1855 text grew out of the sentimental literary practices surrounding death, mourning, and memorializing that proliferated throughout nineteenth-century America. Nevertheless, as this essay discloses, Whitman drew heavily on his early experience as a writer of sentimental poetry and tales to create *Leaves of Grass*. Using the very same literary devices that Gould and other writers of mourning poetry employed, and designing his physical text to resemble the popular memorial albums of the time period, Whitman tied his otherwise radical text to the relatively conventional literary practices associated with mourning during the period.[1] He did so, I argue, not only to acknowledge his indebtedness to this culture and literature, but also to signal to his readership that his text, like the albums from which it borrowed, was a repository for a vibrant and accessible, if otherwise "disembodied," entity, namely, the poet himself.

THE "SENTIMENTAL BITS"

Whitman's relationship to the sentimental literature and literary practices that were central to the culture of mourning and memorializing began with what he called the "sentimental bits" that he produced long before the 1855 publication of *Leaves of Grass*. These early writings constitute a corpus of sentimental literature that, in the ungenerous words of one critic, resembles the work of "the innumerable horde of fourth-rate and unoriginal versifiers who occasionally found, as did Mrs. Lydia Sigourney, a following" (Brasher 1963, xv–xvi). For all its mean-spiritedness, such a comparison has some justice. Sigourney's *oeuvre* is a good deal more complex that Brasher suggests. She was, for example, the first author to make the fate of native Indian peoples the substance of a national epic, the book-length*Traits of the Aborigines of America: A Poem*. But she also treated death as the principal subject of many sentimental and moralistic poems and tales—as did Whitman. Indeed, of the fifty or so pieces of literature published prior to *Leaves of Grass* (including Whitman's temperance novel *Franklin Evans*), death features prominently in at least half. Among these are *memento mori* poems dedicated to reminding the reader that regardless of fame, ambition, or personal accolades, he or she too must die, and standard mourning pieces that either memorialize an individual or seek to console a reader about the nature and purpose of death. Perhaps the most overt examples of Whitman's preoccupation with death are the poems he wrote in response to the death of MacDonald Clarke, called the "Mad Poet of Broadway," who died March 5, 1842.

Clarke, a Byronesque figure known for his eccentric behavior, was frequently the butt of ridicule and abuse as he wandered around Manhattan, suffering "acts of cruelty" that, according to Whitman, "completely broke down what was left of his mind" and threw him into the aggrieved state of "mortification and frenzy" that ultimately claimed his life (as quoted in Hollis 1964, 200). Touched by the fate of the poet and by the public's failure to mourn and memorialize him properly, Whitman, writing in New York's *Aurora*, sought to rectify these injustices by publishing two thoughtful eulogies and an elegy for him. The first of these appeared on March 8 (only three days after Clarke's death), a eulogy in which Whitman stated that "although it was not our fortune to be acquainted with the Poor Poet . . . we feel grieved at the news. He seems to have been a simple, kindly creature—a being whose soul, though marked by little that the crowd admire, was totally free from any taint of vice, or selfishness, or evil passion" (1842a, 2). Following this sentimental start, Whitman went on to sketch the tenor of Clarke's character as well as his literary work. As he did so, Whitman repeatedly called upon readers to join with him not only in remembering Clarke, but also in imagining him as a now exalted figure, reminding them that "he is in that place which we are fond of believing to be peopled by joy never ceasing, and by resplendent innocence and beauty" (2). In closing, Whitman apostrophized the dead poet: "Peace to thy memory. . . . In 'the sphere which keeps the disembodied spirits of the dead,' may the love of angels, and the ravishing splendor of the Country Beautiful, and the communion of gentle spirits, and sweet draughts from the Fountain of all Poetry, blot out every scar of what thou hast suffered here below!" (2).

Unquestionably conventional and sentimentalized as it is, this last apostrophic moment nevertheless accomplishes important work. Considering that Whitman's entire column has been an attempt to memorialize Clarke, and considering that he places such emphasis on the fact that Clarke now enjoys a transcendent existence, this use of apostrophe has the effect of confirming for readers the "facts" that Whitman has been asserting all along. As Barbara Johnson has stated, such an apostrophe or "direct address of an absent, dead, or inanimate being by a first person speaker" makes "the absent, dead, or inanimate entity addressed . . . present, animate, and anthropomorphic" (1986, 30). In addressing the dead poet directly, Whitman reinforces the idea of Clarke's continued existence by tacitly asserting that he is an entity *capable* of being the recipient of such address. In the words of Jonathan Culler, it is a moment that is "not the representation of an event; if it works, it produces a fictive, discursive event." The "event" to which Culler refers occurs in the "now" of reading and makes the addressee into a still vital, reachable entity with whom one might discourse and commune despite the material facts of his current (in)existence (1981, 153).

Apostrophic styles of address were a staple of Whitman's early literary career, and he used such modes of address prolifically when writing about Clarke. In using them, Whitman sought to invoke a sense of "presence" and interpersonal communication between himself and the dead poet, and between himself and his reader. The latter can be clearly seen in another tribute to Clarke that Whitman penned only four days later, and again in an elegy he published a few days after that.[2] The elegy, entitled "The Death and Burial of McDonald Clarke" (1842b), sought to heighten the sense of the speaker's presence in such a way that his "communion" with "you [the reader]" might carry a sense of urgency, vitality, and directness that would spur "you" to greater action. In the elegy's first section, Whitman details the circumstances surrounding Clarke's death and burial. Here he works to invoke a reader's sentiments by lamenting the lack of appropriate obsequies. There was no one to extend the "sympathy" that would have "pardon'd his madness," "no mother or friend [to hold] his dying head," no one to issue a "sigh...[or] tear" on his behalf, no one, once death had claimed him, to wind his body in a shroud of "purple or linen," no one to see to it that a "polish'd coffin enclosed his breast," and finally no one to "weep o'er the poet's sacred bier" (1842b, 1). It is at this moment, however, that the poem takes a decided turn, directly addressing, if not indicting, those who have only belatedly recognized the injustices Clarke suffered and have since come to pay homage to the poet they once ridiculed:

> Ye hypocrites! stain not his grave with a tear,
> Nor blast the fresh planted willow
> That weeps o'er his grave; for while he was here,
> Darkly and sadly his spirit has fled,
> But his name will long linger in story;
> He needs not a stone to hallow his bed;
> He's in Heaven, encircled with glory. (Whitman 1842b, 1)

Much as in his earlier elegy for Clarke, Whitman uses an apostrophic style of address to create a sense of "presence" that lends the poem a feeling of intimate interpersonal communication. Only here, the communication is between an anxious speaker and "you" the reader instead of between Whitman and Clarke. By speaking directly to his readers, employing the (archaic) second person plural and condemning them as "Ye, hipocrites," Whitman's voice takes on an added sense of presence as what had seemed a narrative of the circumstances of Clarke's death shifts into a moment of atemporal personal address. Whitman is no longer describing Clarke's death and the lack of respect shown him, as he did throughout the first half of the poem. Rather he is speaking directly to "you" and is doing so *now*, condemning "you" for both your duplicity and for uncharitably "refus[ing] [Clarke] a crumb and a pillow" (1842b, 1). In this moment, Whitman's apostrophic direct address becomes a mode of invoking a sense of the speaker as an entity "present, animate, and anthropomorphic" (Johnson 1986, 3). It is a challenge to "you," the reader, to behave and feel properly, and it gains traction and power as the poem shifts from a narrative to a "discursive event" of intimate, if not heated, interpersonal communication (Culler 1981, 153).

In both his eulogy for Clarke and his other writing on him, Whitman made use of apostrophic styles of address in order to heighten a sense of immediate "presence" and of "discursive" communication between speaker and addressee (whether that addressee was Clarke or "you" the reader). By 1842, when both of these pieces were written, Whitman was clearly comfortable making use of the device, as well he should have been since he had been employing it in his writings about death for some time. Indeed, even in Whitman's earliest extant piece of published literature, "Our Future Lot," which appeared in 1838 when Whitman was only nineteen, he relied on apostrophe to make an otherwise absent entity present. The poem is a meditation on death with its speaker seeking consolation and respite from the grief associated with his realization that he is mortal. The first section describes him as being in a state of "flashing hope and gloomy fear" as he contemplates the ultimate state of "[t]his curious frame of human mould," whose "troubled heart and wondrous form must both alike decay" (Whitman 1963, 28). Hoping to temper the "gloomy fear" and bolster his "flashing hope[s]," he reaches out to "Nature."

> But where, O Nature! Where will be my mind's abiding place?
> Will it ev'n live? For though its light must shine till from the body torn;
> Then when the oil of life is spent, still shall the taper burn?
> O, powerless is this struggling brain to pierce the mighty mystery;
> In dark, uncertain awe it waits the common doom—to die!
> (1963, 28)

This apostrophe might seem merely a rhetorical one, for certainly in appealing to "Nature" one cannot really expect a reply. However, a reply is precisely what is found in the poem. The speaker's voice ceases, and "Nature" voices the lines that follow:

> Mortal! And can thy swelling soul live with the thought that all its life
> Is centered in this earthly cage of care, and tears, and strife?
> Not so; that sorrowing heart of thine ere long will find a house of rest;
> Thy form, repurified, shall rise, in robes of beauty drest.
> The flickering taper's glow shall change to bright and starlike majesty,
> Radiant with pure and piercing light from the Eternal's eye!
> (28–29)

Nature's response is remarkable because the picture Whitman paints with it not only accords nicely with contemporary sentimental images of heaven and the afterlife, but because the words Nature utters, and the way in which this utterance is structured (as a direct address to the speaker), work together to confirm the validity of its message. Because the speaker's apostrophic address to Nature is answered with a direct address back to the speaker, the poem becomes a "discursive event" in which speaker/reader communes with a now "present, animate, and anthropomorphic" (not to mention apparently omniscient) Nature capable of dispensing emphatic knowledge regarding the speaker's certain "change to bright and starlike majesty" at death. Moreover, the fact that the "mortal" speaker/reader finds himself or herself able to commune with "immortal" and divine Nature confirms the idea that the "immortality" of which Nature speaks (and which it embodies) certainly exists, and therefore remains a possibility to be enjoyed by everyone. Thus apostrophe becomes a key device through which a sense of presence and communion can be "effected," a sense of presence and communion that itself confirms the assertions of immortality that are topically the concern of the poem.

Apostrophe and direct address, as one might infer based upon their role in the elegy to MacDonald Clarke and in "Our Future Lot," were mainstays of Whitman's early literary writing, and he generally employed them to encourage a sense of proximity between speaker and some other entity—such as Nature, or a reader. Certainly such is the case in Whitman's 1840 poem "We

All Shall Rest At Last." Penned two years after "Our Future Lot," it uses direct address to establish a remarkable sense of presence, this time between speaker and reader. The poem begins with the speaker proclaiming his understanding of the fact that "On earth are many sights of woe, / And many sounds of agony," which he then goes on to detail before ending with "All, all know grief; and at the close, / All lie earth's spreading arms within." After delineating the sources of woe that cause most individuals pain—a list that culminates with death—Whitman then begins to direct an otherwise personal meditation on the nature of death toward the reader, whom he queries: "O, foolish, then, with pain to shrink / From the sure doom we each must meet. / Is earth so fair—or heaven so dark—/ Or life so passing sweet?" (1863, 16). Whitman continues with this direct address, employing the archaic second person pronoun, "ye" (earlier used in his elegy for Clarke), to heighten the sense that he is "present(ly)" speaking to "you," the reader: "No; dread ye not the fearful hour— / The coffin, and the pall's dark gloom, / For there's a calm to throbbing hearts, / And rest, down in the tomb" (16).

In thus making his reader the object of his address, Whitman moves the poem away from being a meditation on the nature of death and towards something much more akin to a dialogue, one in which the reader's (assumed) skepticism is overtly addressed by a speaker interested in helping him or her understand the real nature of death and immortal individual identity. Whitman then expands on this concept when he tells the reader that after death

> Our long journey will be o'er,
> And throwing off this load of woes,
> The pallid brow, the feebled limbs,
> Will sink in soft repose.
> Nor only this: for wise men say
> That when we leave our land of care,
> We float to a mysterious shore,
> Peaceful, and pure, and fair.
> (1963, 17)

And this address is followed, perhaps fittingly, with yet one more direct address in which Whitman exhorts the reader to "welcome death! Whene'er the time / That the dread summons must be met," not only pressing his points regarding the nature of death as something to "welcome," not fear, but also furthering the sense that this speaker is capable of directly exhorting, speaking, or communing with "you," the reader, in the moment of reading (1963, 17). Such communion, facilitated through these apostrophic styles of address, thus allows the speaker to seem "present," and capable of speaking to *you* (or "*ye*," as the case may be) "now," in every moment of reading. The resulting sense of proximity complements the text's assertion that individual identity and interpersonal communication are not integrally tied to the corporeal presence of those involved, thus asserting the potential for continued association with otherwise "absent" entities such as the beloved deceased.[3]

SENTIMENTAL ADDRESSES TO THE DEAD

In every instance where Whitman chose to employ apostrophic styles of address, he was working to heighten the sense of "presence" and proximity enjoyed by speaker and addressee. Whether with Clarke (directly addressed in Whitman's eulogy), or the reader, as in "We All Shall Rest At Last" and "Our Future Lot," Whitman relied on apostrophe to "produce a fictive, discursive event in which an otherwise "absent, dead, or inanimate entity [is made] . . . present, animate, [and] anthropomorphic" (Culler 1981, 153; Johnson 1986, 30). This use of apostrophic styles of address to counter the otherwise deleterious effects of death was, of course, not unique to Whitman. Indeed, the sentimental literature of the antebellum period, especially that of writers like Lydia Sigourney, was replete with apostrophes and direct address because these literary devices worked, in the words of Mary Louise Kete, to "create the site in which the important utopian promise of sentimentality—of nonviolated community, of restored losses, of healed wounds—" could be realized. In this site, "both the . . . self of the present and the past [or 'passed'] subject" could be "called together . . . in such a way that the absent or deceased seem a presence still vibrant, vital, and capable of being reached" (2000, 47).

Sigourney's poem "On the Death of a Friend" serves as a good example. Its opening stanza sketches out the benevolent character of a lost "friend," claiming that "hers was the unwavering mind, / The untiring hand of duty. Firm of soul / And pure in purpose, on the eternal Rock, / Of Christian trust her energies reposed, / And sought no tribute from a shadowy world" (1837b, 208). Most of this stanza continues in this vein, ending with the assertion that due to the departed friend's goodness, "He" (meaning God or perhaps Christ) surely "remember[d] her" in her final hours of pain and death. At this point the poem breaks its descriptive, narrative, and temporal flow as the speaker directly addresses the departed loved one:

> Oh thou whom grieving love
> Would blindly pinion in this vale of tears,
> Farewell! It is a glorious flight for faith
> To trace thy upward path, above this clime
> Of change and storm. We will remember thee
> At thy turf-bed—and 'mid the twilight hour
> Of solemn musing, when the buried friend
> Comes back so visibly, and seems to fill
> The vacant chair, our speech shall be of thee.
> (1837, 208)

This final stanza, which begins with the apostrophe to the dead, brings the memorialized friend back into intimate association with the speaker and, given the collective pronoun "we," apparently with the reader as well. Doing so, it establishes a powerful sense of the potential for continued interpersonal association between speaker and subject, even going so far as to forecast many more such moments in the future. Indeed, the poem suggests that the communion that is being carried out "now," that is, in the moment of reading, is a communion that can be repeatedly enjoyed whenever the "buried friend" is spoken of, since in such moments, if apostrophic address is employed, the deceased "[c]omes back so visibly, [she] seems to fill / The vacant chair" (1837b, 208).

For any (mournful) reader who finds Sigourney's description of the deceased person apt, the poem is thus primed to become a powerful means of reentering into a sphere of association with the deceased. The reader is allowed not only to "see" the loved one once more in her "unwavering mind," her "firm . . . soul," etc., but is encouraged by the inclusive "we" to share in the speaker's assertions. Thus, the reader, as much as the speaker, addresses the dead directly and is assured that interpersonal contact will continue. Moreover, because Sigourney's poem is a mass-produced poetic object, the "thin" description she chooses to employ when speaking of her "friend" (refraining from mentioning such details as her name and appearance) makes of the poem a versatile image that is capable of being "impressed" with almost any specific identity of the reader's choosing. As such, it allows the conditions of mass production to facilitate the poem's ability to establish a sense of the continued "presence" of any number of deceased women so long as they in some way fit the description above—at least in the reader's mind.

While Sigourney's use of apostrophic styles of address and "thin" descriptions primed her poetry to be a means of brokering connections between large numbers of readers and their lost loved ones, other poets made use of such styles of address in poems much more topical and intimately personal. Harriet Gould wrote on the loss of her young son in "Lines on the Death of Warren S. Gould who died April 6th 1843." Like Sigourney's "On the Death of a Friend," Gould's poem takes as its goal establishing a sense of continued "presence" and "communion" with the lost loved one, and the means of achieving this goal are basically the same in the nonpublic, nonprofessional literary practice of individuals such as Gould as they are for a professional writer like Sigourney.

In her 1844 poem, written a year after Warren's death, Gould relies upon apostrophe to create a kind of communal space in which she, her reader, and her deceased son "interact" with one another, making them all, as it were, active, vital, and "present." She does this by speaking directly to her son but in such a way as to make clear that the poem is immediately concerned with

inviting others into a sphere of mourning where they can commune together
and aid her in her bereavement.

> Oh can it be a year has fled
> Its scenes of grief and joy
> Since we were bending o'er the bed
> Of thou my sainted boy?
> Since almost with a broken heart
> I watched each faint drawn breath
> And felt I could not with thee part
> To meet the embrace of death.
> (as quoted in Kete 2000, 213)

Gould's apostrophe, like Whitman's to "Nature" in "Our Future Lot," works
from its very first sentence to invoke a space in which author, son, and reader
are all present by remembering (or inviting the reader to imagine remembering) the presence of all three at the moment of the boy's death. For the first
three lines of the poem, the address seems intimate and personal between the
speaker and the reader—they are the "we" who were "bending o'er the bed"
where the boy lies dying.

However, as soon as Gould invites her reader into this shared space—a
space created by their shared experience, she moves into directly addressing
"thou," "my sainted boy"—an act that shifts the reader's sense of being
addressed to a sense of being "with" the speaker as she addresses the boy
herself. A company of author, reader, and deceased boy are now together and
the speaker serves as mouthpiece for both herself and the reader. With reader, speaker, and deceased boy all made "present, animate and anthropomorphic" what was materially only "human mould" (to borrow from Whitman)
becomes, at least imaginatively, a discrete individual, capable of being
"reached" and "communed" with through the poem. And having established
such "community" between speaker, reader, and deceased boy, Gould then
moves to facilitate increasingly intimate exchanges between them, from describing what his death was like to fostering a sense of perpetual connection
with him. This occurs, once again, as she directly addresses her son, with the
reader seemingly there to bear witness to all that she proclaims:

> Alas my boy, though sundered far
> Beyond those orbs that shine,
> I look above those twinkling stars
> And claim thee still as mine . . .
> Oh it shall be a source of joy
> That earth so near to heaven
> That love can go and clasp my boy
> And feel a welcome given.
> (as quoted in Kete 2000, 214)

In these lines, the speaker, with the reader looking on, again reasserts the eternality of her relationship with her son, joyfully reminding him that though death separates them, "earth [is] so near to heaven" that love can bridge the difference. Not only can she "go and clasp" him, but she can "feel [his] welcome given" in return.

This sense of her son's presence is invoked so powerfully that the poem not only ends with a remarkable vision of the much longed for scene of heavenly reunion, where "my Warren at the opening door / . . . wave[s] his little hand," but also with Warren himself speaking to us. We (both speaker and reader) "hear" him "cry[ing]" to us and encouraging us to "fear not the threshold crossed," since here, he says, "you'll find no thrill but joy"—the joy of being reunited with "the better one you lost . . . now an angel boy" (as quoted in Kete 2000, 215). Gould's final apostrophe, the culminating moment of this poem, arguably achieves what she has sought all along, namely the continued association with her deceased son, and taken together, these moments of apostrophic direct address generate a powerful "discursive event," an instance of communion between a variety of individuals, living and dead, despite material absence. Like Whitman's early poetry and tales and Sigourney's works, Gould's sentimental verses thus function to create a community *of* and communion *between* individuals as intimate personal bonds are generated and strengthened.

WHATEVER ELSE, A DEATH-DEFYING CRYPTEXT

There can be no question that Whitman's later poetry—beginning with *Leaves of Grass* in 1855—made extensive use of similar apostrophic styles of address in order to create a sense of intimate communion and community between himself and his reader. Indeed, scholars have found it virtually impossible to write about *Leaves of Grass* without grappling at some point with the infamous direct address, the radical "you," which Whitman famously made such provocative and liberal use of throughout the volume. Some scholars have sought to account for this style of address by focusing on Whitman's journalistic background, while others have focused on the address's oratorical and/or performative nature, categorizing it as a kind of virtuosic moment without precedent, "the most successful metonymic trick in poetic history," as Hollis described it (1964, 252).[4] Still others have seen the address as Whitman's mode of opening up otherwise foreclosed (socio)sexual possibilities and fostering the "intimate relation with a man that he yearns for," or they have seen it as springing from Whitman's political sensibilities, a stylistic means of evoking a kind of radical "democratic collectivism" (Vendler 2005, 4; Bertolini 2002, 1051).

But if Whitman's direct address in *Leaves of Grass* performs a kind of expansion of sexual and/or democratic possibilities, it does so, just as certainly, by invoking a sense of intimate interpersonal communion and individual "presence" that he had already created in the sentimental literature that he produced in the two decades prior to writing *Leaves of Grass*. By continuing to make styles of apostrophic direct address and the sense of communion they foster central to his later poetic work, Whitman not only displays his indebtedness to and appreciation of the literary conventions of nineteenth-century sentimental mourning literature. He also ensures that *Leaves of Grass* is always also engaged in asserting something close to the rituals of mourning and memorializing that lay at the heart of sentimental culture. This potentially alters the way we might read, say, even the most overtly sexual passages of the text, such as the following:

> I mind how we lay in June, such a transparent summer morning;
> You settled your head athwart my hips and gently turned over upon me,
> And parted the shirt from my bosom-bone, and plunged your tongue to my
> barestript heart,
> And reached till you felt my beard, and reached till you held my feet.
> (Whitman 1996, 30)

The use of direct address in a passage such as this creates an undeniable sense of "presence" for the speaker/poet, as he fosters what appears to be an intimate sexual communion with the reader. As the reader answers the hail of the "you" and "writes" himself or herself in as the partner involved in the actions depicted, the scene constructs a memory of a sexual experience that didn't happen but nevertheless *is* happening. Despite Whitman's material absence—indeed, regardless of whether or not Whitman is even still living—the scene's mode of address makes him into an active, living entity with whom it is possible to "commune" (in mind, memory, and body) on even the most intimate of levels. The reader "now" has a memory of the feel of "his hips," the spread of his chest, and the prominence of his "bosom-bone," the taste and feel of plunging his or her "tongue to [Whitman's] barestript heart," etc. In directing his address to the reader and in providing the details necessary to imagine such an intimate physical encounter, Whitman makes himself into a discrete individual "presence" who is active, vital, and present in the reader's temporal moment. Even if dead, the poet, through his words, becomes an entity, one capable of being "reached" and even "held" as if he were with the reader "now."

Whitman's embodiment and "present-ing" of self in a passage that reads overtly about sex tropes to a significant extent on the work of sentimental mourning and memorial literature.

Just as Harriet Gould's poem helped her ignite "the beacons of [her son's] memory" to the point where she believed she could once more "clasp" him (as quoted in Kete 2000, 214), so Whitman's text, in this moment, works to make his "self"—his physical body and individual identity/character/ "soul"—"present" in the reader's mind. So powerful is such writing that readers experience him as a vital, living, approachable entity capable of being "reached," "held," and loved despite his absence or even (in)existence. Whatever else he appears to be, Whitman, no less than his partner, is "present, animate, [and] anthropomorphic" in such a passage (Johnson 1986, 30).

Whitman's attempts to invite his reader to collaborate with him in creating this remarkable sense of presence and communion—where both reader and speaker share intimate space and experience each other—suggest that the fundamental eros which undergirds Whitman's text is arguably the same that undergirds all mourning and memorial literature and objects (hair weavings, memorial portraits, etc.). It is the drive to "extend" the self beyond the bounds of physicality and temporality, "ceaselessly," as Freud put it, so that that self can always be available for contact or communion. Consider that even the most erotic moments between Whitman's speaker and "you" only gain efficacy in direct proportion to how "real," "vital," and "alive" the speaker appears to be. If, as Freud argues, sexual activity is largely the overt articulation of a more fundamental eros that drives us in a "ceaseless trend towards extension," then the text that approaches its reader in a sexually erotic way is always already dependent on the speaker's desire to extend himself (Freud 1989, 77). Without the speaker's uncanny and intimate sense of being present, Whitman's erotics would seem, at best, coolly distant, impotent, flaccid even. Understood thus, Whitman's most erotic moments are arguably not the overtly sexual ones, but, like the mourning and memorializing objects his work parallels, emerge when his "procreant urge" spurs him to extend himself beyond the usual confines of time, space, and mortality into the reader's "now," an absolutely necessary prelude for the more sexual erotics which then follow.

The stanzas of *Leaves of Grass* that follow the overtly sexualized passage just quoted testify that Whitman fosters this (sexual) communion between speaker and reader not only to proselytize his belief in the need for free expression of sexuality, but also to assert something about the nature of death and the perpetuity of individual identity. The above section is frequently excerpted as if it stood alone. In fact, it is followed by a remarkable meditation on death and immortality that culminates, as do so many of his early poems and as Gould's poem does, in successive assertions (if not active imaginings) of both speaker's and reader's immortality. Thus Whitman's speaker claims that this "communing" not only climaxes in a sense of "peace and joy" but it also gives him "knowledge that pass[es] all the art and argument of the earth." This "knowledge" is expressed as an emergent awareness of the immortality and the oneness of all living things. "[T]he spirit of God," Whitman now realizes, "is the eldest brother of my own," an immortal kinship that extends to "all the men ever born [who] are also my brothers . . . and the women my sisters and lovers." Even the "limitless . . . leaves stiff or drooping in the fields, / And brown ants in the little wells beneath them, / And mossy scabs of the wormfence, and heaped stones, and elder and mullen and pokeweed" are included (Whitman 1996, 31).

In this way, Whitman parlays the intimate sexual communion between speaker and reader that establishes a sense of individual identity and "presence" into a discourse on the immortality of all living things. Although overtly sexual, Whitman's textual erotics function as much to bring a reader to see immortality everywhere—in himself, in all men, even in the "limitless" leaves, ants, moss, bushes and plants—as they do to titillate. And this same realization of the immortality of all things carries over into the next meditation as well, one of the most famous passages in *Leaves of Grass*—that in which the speaker examines a handful of grass and finds death nowhere. In grass, he says, are "hints about dead young men and women, / And hints about old men and mothers, and offspring taken too soon out of their laps," hints that "show there really is no death" and that these "men and women . . . mothers, and offspring . . . are alive and well somewhere" (1996, 32).

Fundamentally, the communion that Whitman seeks to foster in even his most erotic textual moments parallels the communion that marks the sentimental poetry of mourning and memorializing. Indeed, both Gould's address to her son and Whitman's erotic address to his reader "create a thread in the 'woof of time,'" as Kete has described it, that fosters a sense of "presence" and of "communion" regardless of material (in)existence (2000, 249). This presence and communion is sought out over and over again in Whitman's 1855 work, always through his reliance upon apostrophic direct address. Frequently, it is a communion and sense of presence that Whitman overtly parlays into a meditation on the nature of death and the eternality of the individual, as most notably he does at the end of "Song of Myself." Here the speaker invites the reader to converse and commune with him, calling out: "Listener up there! Here you . . . what have you to confide to me?" "I bequeath myself to the dirt to grow from the grass I love, / If you want me again look for me under your bootsoles / [. . .] Failing to fetch me at first, keep encouraged / Missing me one place search another, / I stop somewhere waiting for you" (1996, 88). But whether or not Whitman's moments of direct address actually end in overt meditations on the nature of death, every moment in which he directs his address to his reader is a moment in which he reinscribes himself as an active, vital, reachable presence, capable of being communed with despite his material absence. And he pushed this idea not only throughout 1855, but in successive versions of *Leaves of Grass* as published in 1856, 1860, 1867, and beyond.

To a greater or lesser extent, then, Whitman relied on, troped upon, and borrowed from stylistic conventions central to sentimental literature's culture of mourning and memorializing to make himself a "presence forever accessible to readers of the future . . . able still to confront him, interact with him, even though death and time and space separated them" (Folsom 2006, 282). He could do so because his original readers were preconditioned to respond to such "presence" as powerfully as they did since they were exposed to literature in which apostrophe regularly performed the work of (re)limning important connections. What I now want to suggest is that Whitman was not only aware of the degree to which he was drawing on sentimental literature and literary practices, but he also willingly paid homage to their centrality in his otherwise radical 1855 volume in the latter's design, a design which, in form, size, and color, bears a remarkable resemblance to the period's popular mourning and memorial volumes.

That the 1855 edition of *Leaves of Grass* is a curious physical object has long been observed, and critics have regularly drawn comparisons between its appearance and the physical design of one of the most popular sentimental books of the period, namely *Fern Leaves from Fanny's Portfolio* by Sara Willis Parton ("Fanny Fern").[5] What has been less often noted is that the parlor-table size and floriated covers of Parton's and Whitman's books both approximate the size and design style for nineteenth-century keepsake albums generally (see figures 8.1 and 8.2).

Indeed, in the words of one critic of cultural ephemera, the physical construction of *Leaves of Grass* with its "fancy cloth covers in green, [and] decorated with natural patterns in an oversized format, make this edition difficult to distinguish from a lady's album" (Gernes 1992, 105). Like Harriet Gould's book, such ladies' albums were generally kept as "emblem[s] of life . . . faithful mirror[s] of the minds of the compiler's community." And, as discussed, they were intended to preserve the identity of those who wrote or were written about in them.[6]

When Whitman chose this oversized cover and floriated design, he suggestively imported the material trappings of sentimentality's culture of mourning and memorializing onto his book. As a result, readers familiar with sentimental literary practices would arguably have found the volume to be a curious one only in that moment when they opened it up and found within it not blank white pages waiting to be filled, but lines and lines of verse already printed. What this suggests is that Whitman chose this design because he wished his readers to open the volume prepared to engage in the same spirit of communion or "celebration" of one's loved ones and oneself that they would have brought to the reading or production of any memorial keepsake album, an expectation that his opening lines of poetry reinforce. In this context, Whitman's initial proclamation in *Leaves of Grass*, "I celebrate myself, / And what I assume you shall assume," resonates with the fundamental idea behind the period's mourning and memorial verses (Whitman

Figure 8.1. *Album of Friendship.* Published by John C. Riker. New York, 1850. Used by permission of the University of Missouri-Kansas City Libraries, Dr. Kenneth J. LaBudde Department of Special Collections

1996, 27). When Whitman "celebrates" himself and "assumes" the reader will do so as well, he is essentially inviting that reader to collaborate with him, much as Gould did when she circulated her album among friends. Both sought to generate an object through which a "celebrate[d]" self (or selves) could be made vital and available forever.

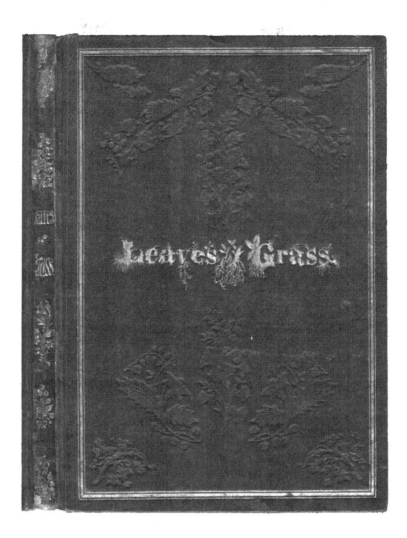

Figure 8.2.   *Leaves of Grass* (1855 edition). Cover of the 1855 edition of Leaves of Grass from Special Collections, University of Iowa Libraries; used with permission of the Walt Whitman Archive (www.whitmanarchive.org).

The cover was not the only element of the text's material design that encouraged readers to see it as a vehicle through which a sense of "presence" and of intimate interpersonal communion could be achieved. Whitman also tipped into the front of his book a photograph of himself (a mass-reproduced engraving of a daguerreotype, to be exact), reinforcing the sense of "presence" that he used apostrophic address to invoke throughout the text. Images of writers appearing as frontispieces were not a remarkable literary practice at this time. The sixteenth edition of Rufus W. Griswold's highly popular

The Poets and Poetry of America (1856) featured a frontispiece depicting the period's most distinguished writers, including William Cullen Bryant and Henry Wadsworth Longfellow. Unlike the images in Griswold's volume, however, Whitman's image was not intended to convey stately literary respectability. Rather, it depicts him in his own everyday idiosyncrasy, arms "akimbo," head and hat cocked to one side, hand in his pocket. Combined with the rest of the book's material design as well as its apostrophic styles of address, this image works to encourage readers to see Whitman's book as something like an archive of the self. As a literary and material synecdoche both representing and "re-presenting" the whole from whom it was drawn, Whitman's folio-sized and finely decorated volume would have nestled rather nicely on parlor shelves next to other sentimental albums whose work and look were in many ways similar to Whitman's own.

CONCLUSION

Like many of the contemporary mourning and memorial volumes that it resembled in its material design and in the way in which it addressed its readers, Whitman's 1855 *Leaves of Grass* sought to create what was, in essence, a death-defying cryptext. It sought to serve as a talisman, medium, and repository not only to house a literary corpus but to "enliven" that corpus in the reader's "presence," ensuring a perpetual connection and communication between them. It was a text that itself formed the foundation for the remarkable poetry that would follow, including Whitman's most critically acclaimed achievement in "re-presenting" himself in a reader's temporal "now," his 1856 "Sun-Down Poem," better known by its 1860 title "Crossing Brooklyn Ferry." Using apostrophic styles of address similar to those in the 1855 edition of *Leaves of Grass* and in the long foreground to that volume, Whitman reaches out from the deck of the Brooklyn ferry to "you that . . . cross shore to shore years hence," "you that . . . are more to me, and more in my meditations than you might suppose" (1856, 211). To this "you," Whitman speaks most intimately in this poem, transcending his own temporality, his own mortality even, while claiming that "It avails not, neither time nor place–distance avails not, / I am with you," "I project myself, also I return—I am with you, and know how it is" (212–13). Such provocative moments of direct address, repeatedly layered amidst seemingly "shared" observations of "river," "crowd," "ships," "seagulls," and "summer-sky," allow Whitman to draw "[c]loser yet" until "you," in perhaps startled agreement, sense the rightness of Whitman's claim that "I am as good as looking at you now, for all you cannot see me" (213, 218). As Whitman describes it, such a sense of shared space, of atemporal communion, "fuses me into you now, and pours my meaning into you," so much so that "you" and "I" are made into a united "we"—in an intimate communion such as lay at the heart of the antebellum literature of mourning and memorializing (218).

At this moment of communion when "you" and "I" seemingly inhabit the same temporal space, "we" come to "feel" our shared immortality, to sense the ongoing vitality and connectedness of our soul(s). "We understand, then, do we not? / What I promised without mentioning it, have you not accepted? / What the study could not teach—what the preaching could not accomplish is accomplished, is it not?" (1856, 219). Such questions, spoken directly to "you," allow "us"—Whitman and reader—to "accomplish," in a sense, what the period's sentimental memorial literature and objects worked to effect for the bereaved, namely, the "communion," even the "(re)union," of the dead with the living. As such, this moment and the many moments of communion similar to it scattered throughout Whitman's poetry grant him a kind of perpetual afterlife in which he remains an available presence for his beloved readers so long as they can read his book. But at the same time, these moments themselves represent a curious literary afterlife of their own. They are the transcendent progeny of a species of sentimental mourning and memorial poetry that Whitman had long been engaged in producing.

NOTES

1. Other scholars have investigated Whitman's relationship to the period's mourning culture, but do so almost exclusively in relation to his Civil War writings. Desiree Henderson's monograph *Grief and Genre in American Literature* (2011) explores Whitman's relationship to mourning culture, arguing that this relationship is writ large in his Civil War book *Drum-Taps*, whose interrupted printings, hasty insertions, and circulation history all give evidence of his attempt to respond in poetically and culturally appropriate ways to the death of a figure like Lincoln. Additionally, Dana Luciano's notable *Arranging Grief: Sacred Time and the Body in Nineteenth-Century America* (2007) investigates Whitman's post-war writing about Lincoln in the context of a larger social and cultural attempt to use grief as a means of reconstructing both a sense of national identity and a sense of historical progression.

2. Direct address and apostrophe are closely allied rhetorical devices, which is why I have chosen to refer to them collectively as "apostrophic styles of address." Direct address targets an absent (but presumed to be at some point available or "listening") reader, and apostrophe targets an absent (but presumed to be reachable or "listening") entity of virtually any kind (prayer is essentially an apostrophic address to God, for instance). In both cases, "communion" is achieved by establishing a sense of the co-presence (in the reader's temporal "now") of both speaker and addressee; that is, such address creates a kind of imagined space of communion and communication—a "psychotextual" space–that seeks to bridge materially enforced distances or dislocations.

3. See Whitman (1963) for similar examples of Whitman using apostrophic styles of address (in "We All Shall Rest At Last," "Each Has His Grief," "Tomb Blossoms," "The End of All," "The Love that Is Hereafter," "The Mississippi at Midnight," "The Play-Ground," "A Sketch," and "The Winding Up").

4. As perhaps the most compelling account to date of where Whitman may have gleaned his mode of address, Ezra Greenspan, in *Walt Whitman and the American Reader*, has shown how in Whitman's 1840s journalism he used direct address in several notable editorials. While Whitman did unquestionably use the device in his journalism to great effect, the fact that his earliest extant poetry and tales, produced before many of the editorials Greenspan brings

forward, relied as' heavily as they did upon such modes of address indicates the need to recognize the centrality of Whitman's involvement in producing mourning and memorial poetry to his later poetic practice.

5. While Fern's work is undoubtedly sentimental, it is important to recognize that as a prodigious and talented writer, she wrote in a wide variety of different styles and genres. Indeed, although arguably half of the selections in the first edition of *Fern Leaves from Fanny's Portfolio* are easily recognizable as sentimental stories or poems that frequently deal with death and mourning, there are nevertheless several selections that are humorous and some that are pointedly satirical. For a more complete treatment of the variety of writing that Fern produced and the significance of this, see Laffrado 2009, Tonkovich 1997, and Samuels 1992.

6. There is a certain slippage between "keepsake" or "memorial" albums and "mourning" albums, and what begins overtly as one might easily end up as the other. A "keepsake" or "memorial" album was generally an album circulated through one's family and friends in which poems, locks of hair, daguerreotypes, flowers, and other objects were collected, generally to mark a bond between individuals. However, such albums always also held the potential to *become* mourning albums when, to echo Lois Gould, "distance or death" hid the "form or face" of those represented in the keepsake album (as quoted in Kete 2000, 287).

Chapter Nine

"Such Verses for My Body Let Us Write"

Civil War Song, Sentimentalism, and Whitman's Drum-Taps

Robert Arbour

On December 30, 1862, the night before the Battle of Murfreesboro, a Union band decided to regale troops with some of their favorite songs, "Yankee Doodle" and "Hail Columbia." Camped nearby were the Confederates. Not to be outdone, the Rebel band launched into its tried-and-true anthems, "Dixie" and "The Bonnie Blue Flag," striking up an impromptu competition. Fueled by patriotic zeal, the contest threatened to go on indefinitely, until the sleepy soldiers agreed on a way to finish it: both bands joined together in a performance of one of the most popular pieces during the Civil War, the parlor song "Home! Sweet Home!" (1823), written by John Howard Payne and composed by Henry Bishop. [1]

Evoking the home on the brink of a battle in the Civil War, which saw more casualties than all earlier American wars combined, the soldiers engaged in more than simple nostalgia. Drew Gilpin Faust has argued that the threat of death became "the most widely shared of the war's experiences" (2008, xiii). Suddenly, the great fear for all Americans, civilians as well as soldiers, was dying away from home, without a "Good Death," one that, following the rituals of the *ars moriendi* tradition, assured mourners they could take comfort in knowing the spiritual state of their dying kin before they passed away (9–10). At home, dying bodies could be interpreted within a coherent narrative; but photographers laid bare the bodies shattered and strewn across the battlefields of the Civil War, giving death a new visibility and a new epistemological significance for Americans. As the soldiers camped in Murfreesboro articulated their longing for home in a sentimental ballad, they turned to a key sentimental symbol associated with an ideal of coherency: their hope for their own bodies as well as for the national bodies they sought to create, their personal aims reflecting their patriotic ones.

Christoph Irmscher has described literary sentimentalism as a "'lingua franca' in the United States," a public "forum for *everyone's* private feelings" (2009, 5). Predicated on the presumption that American readers and writers possessed both shared experiences and a certain emotional transparency, sentimentalism in its heyday in the mid-nineteenth century made possible visions of a national consensus and a unified body politic. Sentimental literary works weren't about tears *per se*, Mary Louise Kete suggests; rather, those tears formed part of a sentimental coding system focused on the domestic and the quotidian, a collaborative literary mode that invited authors and readers to share "in a common cultural or intellectual project" expressed in a language of identifiable feelings and recognizable conventions. At the heart of sentimental discourse, Kete argues, is "a culture invested in imagining itself as a cohesive, integral whole" (2000, xiv, 3). Scholars have uncovered several different sentimental strategies in antebellum America for constructing this emotionally binding sense of cohesion that enabled readers to envision themselves as members of an intimate, if exclusionary, national family.[2] In practice, this meant, as Glenn Hendler has observed, that authors and readers engaged in a fantasy of putting their private feelings on public display and of identifying sympathetically with one another on the basis of the emotional responses they imagined everyone in the nation shared (2001, 9). By its very nature, Joanne Dobson notes, sentimentalism is a "literary idiom" that is understated, conversational, and accessible in order to further its primary aim of creating a sense of "human connection" (1997, 268).

Yet antebellum sentimentalism also offered a mechanism for coping with death or loss. Indeed, as Dobson argues, the loss of a loved one is a theme fundamental to many sentimental texts precisely because loss becomes an occasion for communal bonding and consolation. It is when the loss results in the permanent separation from others that the "sentimental crisis of consciousness" sets in (1997, 267). Consider, for example, a template for the sentimental elegy, Lydia Sigourney's famous "Death of an Infant" (1827). The poem catalogs the parts of the child's body that Death attacks: the "cherub brow," the "cheek and lip," the "veins," the "blue eyes," and finally the voice (1850, 30). But no crisis arises here; instead, the poem closes with a focus on the child's smile, which remains

> So fix'd and holy from that marble brow,—
> Death gazed and left it there;—he dared not steal
> The signet-ring of heaven.
> (1850, 31)

This antebellum vision of death ensures that the child (whose gender is unspecified to make the poem universally applicable) awaits the mother in heaven, and the prospects of the celestial reunion and the restoration of human connection offer readers consolation. The child's body, the subject of the poem, is intact, coherent, and easily interpretable within the domestic space. Paradoxically, while the elegy is generic, it allows readers to focus on the particular (one child in one home) and thus to experience what Max Cavitch has called a "rehearsal of compensatory mourning," which extends to readers the opportunity to reconstruct the semblance of their social ties and social identities (2007, 111). But as the Civil War presented Americans with images of shattered bodies, I will argue, and as the collective losses of Americans accumulated on a new scale and away from home, the war exposed gaps that exist in the model of consolation described here. Consolation for a particular loss became harder to imagine as the dislocations of death alienated readers from the domestic space and from one another, rendering ineffective the trope of the sentimental family as a nationalizing mode.

Especially apparent in conventional poetry, the model of consolation that I have discussed is characteristic of what I will term fireside sentimentalism, the sentimentalism typical of the easily accessible antebellum poetry written to be read by the fireside, with regular rhythms, rhymes, and tropes.[3] No less than poetry, song asked readers to internalize the ideals of fireside sentimentalism and thus to *perform* national belonging. Just as in the antebellum schoolroom and by the fireside, children were made to memorize and recite sentimental poems, so in the parlor, middle-class American families sang the sentimentalized ballads of Stephen Foster. In singing together, antebellum Americans gave their individual voices to a communal set of lyrics, working collaboratively to embody and to share collectively the sentimental values put forth in the songs. Beyond simply recalling the lyrics, Americans were singing themselves into their local communities, constructing a sentimental and nostalgic sense of home that resonated, so the fantasy went, throughout the nation. Indeed, Nicholas Tawa asserts that, to a greater extent even than poetry, Americans consumed popular song and committed it to memory (1984, 7); by the 1850s it became known as a democratic "music for the millions" (vii).[4]

While parlor songs continued to enjoy enormous popularity well into the Civil War, the tensions of the war soon tore apart families and individual (white) bodies, thrusting Americans into an ideological crisis that raised questions about the songs' representation of the nation. As early as 1861, new Civil War songs expressed melancholic concern for broken families, fragmented bodies, and soldiers dying alone. With the national body fractured, national coherence and consensus seemed impossible. Perhaps no one in America understood this shift better than the poet Walt Whitman, whose highly musical volume of Civil War poetry, *Drum-Taps* (1865), moves from poems enthusiastically welcoming the war to pieces that morbidly catalogue and lament the decaying corpses the war piled up. By looking closely at the connections between Civil War songs and *Drum-Taps*, this essay will seek to understand *Drum-Taps* as a response to popular American concerns about the security of the Union and the legitimacy of sentimental consensus during the Civil War. Drawing directly on the conventions of sentimental song, Whitman weaves the broken bodies of soldiers into a musical tapestry, enfolding them into the corpus of a book in which the national family is displaced by the figure of the all-embracing poet.

Before the Civil War, Americans had immersed themselves in music, singing hymns in church and camp meetings, attending operas and minstrel shows, and listening to concerts by solo performers and singing groups. In less formal settings, too, they performed music enthusiastically, with members of the middle class playing "ballads," a loose term for a variety of simple songs (Tawa, 1975, 69), on their parlor pianos. In ways very different from our view of "intellectual property" today, nineteenth-century Americans in fact understood songs as shared property: communal and customizable. Music was printed and sold in stores, to be sure, but many Americans also copied sheet music by hand and memorized it. At home, they could use tunes or lyrics different from the published versions. Nor did composers and lyricists stand in the way of such improvisation and inventiveness. The title pages of parlor-song sheet music often explicitly permitted changes to the scores (Tawa, 1975, 74–75).

Precisely because Americans viewed antebellum parlor music as communal property, when a number of parlor songs made their way into the Civil War songsters that soldiers on both sides carried in their pockets, vocal music transcended the boundaries between North and South. While the North had all of the major music publishing houses like Root and Cady (Chicago) and Oliver Ditson (Boston), Northerners and Southerners of all races heard and sang most of the same songs. Practically the entire country had, as Caroline Moseley puts it, "a common musical experience" (1984, 6), one that appeared to provide democratic access to all, civilians and soldiers alike. In the tradition of parlor music, Northerners and Southerners shared even the new partisan songs of the war, with some variations. It was not uncommon for a patriotic Northern song such as "The Battle Cry of Freedom" (1862), written and composed by George F. Root, to be reworked into many equally fervid anthems for the South, or vice versa.[5] In the absence of international copyright law, moreover, the Confederacy's secession enabled Southerners to publish Northern songs freely without penalty.

If antebellum popular song did not erase regional or class divisions in the mid-nineteenth century, it did make those divisions appear less important or less noticeable to American listeners, even during the war, supplying them with shareable, collective property and a common reservoir of readily identifiable sounds, images, tropes, and phrases that were easy to remember and to internalize. Before the war, the less distinctive the divisions between Americans became, the easier it was to maintain the illusion of homogeneity and consensus.[6] It comes as little surprise, then, that what united the Union and Confederate soldiers at Murfreesboro was a nostalgic and sentimental song about home. One imagines the soldiers in each camp, their faces partially illuminated by the fire, as they cast their voices into the darkness, harmonizing with invisible counterparts from the opposing camp, to deliver with a tinge of irony the second verse of "Home! Sweet Home!": "An Exile from Home splendor dazzles in vain, / Oh! give me my lowly thatch'd Cottage again!" (Bishop and Payne, [1823] 1852, 3). The soldiers draw on antebellum sentimental discourse to find common ground in the home, a conventional site of national consensus.

In the decades just before and during the war, the home played a key role in both literary sentimentalism and sentimental parlor music, serving as a symbol of the consensus and unity of the fireside family, a microcosmic model of the American national family. The scene of the soldiers singing by firelight evokes an image the great sentimentalist Henry Wadsworth Longfellow conjured up in "The Fire of Drift-Wood: Devereux Farm, near Marblehead." In this poem, friends build a fire in an old and drafty farmhouse at sunset, the dying light slowly leaving the companions in darkness as they tell one another stories of the past: "Our faces faded from the sight, / Our voices only broke the gloom." Soon, the flames appear to merge with those of a driftwood fire outside of the farmhouse, and the poem closes:

> O flames that glowed! O hearts that yearned!
> They were indeed too much akin,
> The drift-wood fire without that burned,
> The thoughts that burned and glowed within.
> (1901, 185)

In Longfellow's representation of the work of fireside sentimentality, the common stories and voices dissolve all the individual bodies and identities into one collective space made coherent by sentimental rhetoric. The oral performance of the stories, resembling communal song or the recitation of poetry, brings the companions together into one (national) body, which encompasses everything outside of them as well. The flames and hearts were "too much akin," the speaker tells us, a reminder that, through the sentimental mode, the friends are part of one (national) family, which is unified by a consensus of feelings The home becomes here, as in sentimental song, a socially normative and secure space that fosters national consensus, an ideal emblematized by the emotionally transparent family and the united communal body. Everyone in this family of ideal sentimental readers responds to the stories and the environment in the same way. Thus, as the soldiers at Murfreesboro sang together in the darkness, they put into practice the ideals of antebellum sentimentalism, escaping momentarily from the war that was tearing those ideals apart, and participating in a discourse shared by both sides that capitalized on sentimental tropes, bonding the two sides in their shared longing for home.

Unsurprisingly, sentimental images of the home, the national family, and the unitary national body predominated in Civil War propaganda, which cast the national division in terms of fractures within a single family, pitting "brother against brother." A Civil War envelope (see figure 9.1), for example, shows two young brothers dueling with wooden swords and military hats fashioned from newspapers. One holds a Union flag, the other a Confederate banner, and the caption reads "As It Is—." Underneath this image, in the corner of the envelope, is a picture of "As It Will Be." Here, the brothers fall asleep together in one bed, covered in a blanket of the Union flag, and guarded by a maternal angel who assures readers, "God Watches Over Them."

This envelope suggests the pressures the Civil War put on sentimental ideals. The conflict must be temporary and child's play, the second image suggests, because the Union depends on emotional universality. After the battle, the brothers' intact bodies seem fused together, as the envelope draws directly on two common conventions in sentimental parlor music: nostalgia and the glorification of the mother. Although it reverses the typical juxtaposition of an "idealized past and an alien present" that we see so frequently in the songs composed by Foster, according to Susan Key (1995, 146), implied is the recovery of an idealized common past with the reunification of the national family. The angel watching over the boys evokes the veritable cult of motherhood in music especially popular during the middle of the Civil War. In 1863 alone songs with the titles "Who Will Care for Mother Now?," "Keep Me Awake, Mother," "Dear Mother I've Come Home to Die," and "The Dying Mother's Advice to Her Volunteer Son" were produced.

But even as sentimental verse and song idealized the fireside family and Unionist propaganda promoted an emotionally transparent national family, these ideals of sentimentalism began to erode during the war. There was no more concrete example of the sentimental national family circulating around the United States than the Hutchinson Family Singers, a wildly popular singing group aligned with the temperance movement, abolitionism, and other reform causes.[7] A family from New Hampshire, the Hutchinsons gave concerts throughout the country in the mid-nineteenth century and performed frequently for the Union troops during the Civil War. Singing to civilians and soldiers, the Hutchinsons served as a strong link between the home front and the battlefield and reinforced the image of the sentimental national family in harmony, an image Union soldiers had pledged to safeguard. With the

Figure 9.1. "Angel watching the Union and Confederate 'brothers' envelope." Envelope. Berlin & Jones. 1861–1865. The Library Company of Philadelphia, Civil War Envelope Collection.

Hutchinsons' sheet music in hand, families all across the Union could sing their songs in parlors, performing the very national and sentimental bonds the songs portrayed. By 1864, however, the sentimental coherence that the Hutchinsons offered to families in their songs had been crippled by the war. Their song "Tenting on the Old Camp Ground," written and composed by Walter Kittredge, begins with typical sentimental nostalgia and the soldiers' request for a cheerful song. But in the last two verses, it takes a dark and pacifistic tone:

> We are tired of war on the old Camp ground,
> Many are dead and gone,
> Of the brave and true who've left their homes.
> Others been wounded long,
> We've been fighting today on the old Camp ground,
> Many are lying near;
> Some are dead, and some are dying,
> Many are in tears.
> (Kittredge, 1864, 4)

After the final verse, the refrain shifts from "Tenting on the old Camp ground" to "Dying on the old Camp ground," this last line marked "(ppp)" (5) on the sheet music to indicate it should be played extremely softly, like a dying gasp, as the mass of corpses the song suddenly builds up completely smothers, and kills, the music. [8] By bifurcating the national family, removing soldiers from the safety of the home, and flooding both civilians and soldiers with images of fragmented bodies, the Civil War ripped at the very foundations of sentimentalism. And it did not take long for songs about the war to reflect the citizens' misgivings about the sentimental paradigm for imagining the nation. As the war wore on and emotional universality seemed increasingly unlikely, sentimentalism appeared to fail as a representational strategy for the Union, forcing poets and composers alike to search for different modes of representation.

As we have seen, antebellum sentimental song and verse envisioned the Union as an emotionally transparent national family comprising citizens whose universal feelings allowed them to merge indistinguishably into one coherent national body. Galvanized by Unionist propaganda, this model for the nation would survive during the Civil War, but only in a fragmented and nearly vestigial state, as sentimental ideals quickly broke down. I will now consider some songs from the first few years of the war, when those ideals came under immediate pressure from a sudden national preoccupation with broken bodies and scenes of mass death, challenging the representation of the Union as a coherent national family situated safely in the home. As the war threatened the conventions of sentimental song, it seemed also to undermine the representability of the Union.

Even the war's earliest songs, those most optimistic about a quick and restorative conflict, abound with references to decaying bodies and the threat of dying. One of the best known songs of the war, "John Brown's Body" (1861), transforms the controversial abolitionist—a politically polarizing figure—into a national martyr by concentrating on his rotting corpse. Singers repeat three times, "John Brown's body lies a mould'ring in the grave," before asserting confidently that "His soul is marching on!" (1861, 3) and moving into the hymn-like chorus of "Glory! Glory Hallelujah!" (4). The verses that follow picture Brown's incarnated soul marching to heaven with a knapsack. The penultimate verse breaks from the narrative to proclaim "They will hang Jeff Davis to a tree" before the final verse returns the focus to the Union and the living: "Let's give three good rousing cheers for the union, / As we're marching on" (4, 5). In the name of universality, Brown is here sanitized, made appealing to and representative of all of the singers in the Union. Moldering along with his body is his history of violent abolitionism. Purified of his partisan sins, Brown becomes a model Union soldier, and this image of Brown as patriot allows Unionist singers to envision for him the heavenly consolation typical of sentimental song and verse. Franny Nudelman notes that because the song pivots on the contrast between Brown's corpse and his soul, it has the effect of "reminding soldiers that they died on behalf of a greater cause," but at the same time, "it did not allow them to ignore the difficult reality of violent death" (2004, 15). The song, in short, made his death representative.

So representative is Brown in these lyrics that the sheet music Oliver Ditson published for this song (innocuously titled "Glory! Glory! Hallelujah!") in 1861, prints not only Brown's name in the lyrics but, above it, the name "Ellsworth" (see figure 9.2). The reference is to Elmer Ellsworth, reportedly the first Union casualty of the Civil War, who died on May 24,1861, and was immediately made into a martyr for the United States. Privileging the less provocative Ellsworth over Brown, the sheet music thus encourages readers to think according to the logic of substitution, mobilizing sentimental universality in order to celebrate the idea that anyone might die in service of the Union, even as Ellsworth's and Brown's names stack up on the score like so many corpses on a battlefield or so many names in the death lists that newspapers printed daily. [9] As it appears in the Ditson version, the song makes an ironic comment on sentimental music as a shared experience. Everyone in the Union might share in the death the war brought, as well as in the flattening of reputation, in order to force-fit a sentimental paradigm of universality or sameness onto the nation. The song would, after all, form the basis of Julia Ward Howe's "Battle Hymn of the Republic" (1862), further collapsing the image of the republic and the image of the corpse. As she adds an evangelical purpose, Howe quickens the rhythm of the lyrics, replacing "John Brown's body" with "Mine eyes have seen the glory" (1862, 3). Envisioning a millennial resolution to the war, the speaker of Howe's song, a representative citizen, tacitly appropriates Brown's corpse, the speaker's eyes standing in for Brown's body. The corpse becomes the speaker's poetic and prophetic inspiration, the foundation of a new, divinely purified Union.

In its veneration of dead bodies, "John Brown's Body" characterizes patriotism in terms of the expectation that one will die for one's country, even when this results in the dissolution of the sentimental family. While "John Brown's Body" and, later, the "Battle Hymn of the Republic" maintain at least the emotional universality of sentimentalism, other early war songs, such as Gustav Gumpert's "The Dying Volunteer" (1861), begin to question whether the representative citizens of traditional sentimental calls to battle exist at all. A memorial to a soldier who was killed in the Baltimore Riot of 1861, "The Dying Volunteer" opens with a soldier who bids his wife and child farewell at the doorstep: "The bugle sound I hear; / It calls me to the bloody strife, / It calls the volunteer" (1861, 2). Twice, the "volunteer" is the object of the sentence, and the rhyme with "hear" underscores the idea that his decision to enlist in the army is less than fully voluntary. The music compels the soldier to leave his family. As he ventures from home into the exterior world, he predicts his own death, asking his wife to care for their son "when I die, / Beneath that starry flag" (3). In the second verse, the soldier reveals another reason he chose to fight in the war:

Figure 9.2.   Sheet Music for "Glory! Glory! Hallelujah!" Oliver Ditson & Co. 1861. Courtesy of The Lilly Library, Indiana University, Bloomington, Indiana, Sam De-Vincent Collection.

> My father died on freedom's field,
> I promised on his knee,
> That I would fight and never yield,
> Until our land was free.
> (4)

The combination of the sentimentalized music with universal appeal and the soldier's nearly compulsive focus on his father's corpse forces him off to battle, suicidal though his act may be. In the context of the Civil War, sentimentalism looks suddenly like coercion, particularly when, after the soldier does die in combat, the narrator of the song meditates on his "grave" and resolves: "The Union still we'll save. / All hail to the Stars and Stripes!" (3). Gumpert here dramatizes the creation of a structure of feeling designed to march men off to war, and this feeling involves simultaneously a fear of death and a craving for it. One implication, of course, is that the son, too, will try to save the Union just as his dead father did, perpetuating the pattern. A concern with death and patriotism drives the song. No longer reflective of emotional universality, sentimental verse is reduced here to a prod, reminding the soldier of his obligation to his ancestors and destroying, in fact, the coherent sentimental family. "As he died to make men holy, let us die to make men free" (5), Howe would write one year later in the "Battle Hymn of the Republic" in a paradoxical sentimental vow to sacrifice members of the national family, as Christ was sacrificed, for the sake of the Union.

George F. Root's "The Vacant Chair" (1861), written for Thanksgiving Day, presents the aftermath of scenes like the one Gumpert gives us. When their son Willie, a flag bearer, dies in battle, his family mourns for him. Although they try to take comfort in the conventional expectation of heavenly consolation, assuring one another in the beginning of the song that "We shall meet, but we shall miss him" (1861, 3), for the rest of the song they remain fixated on the past and their loss. At the center of the song (in the second of three verses) is a fireside scene. But as they stare at the vacant chair by the hearth, the only story they can tell there is the one they've been told of Willie's bravery on the battlefield, which fails to satisfy them. "Our hopes in ruin lie," they say at the end of the first verse, and the final verse dwells darkly on the juxtaposition of the weeping family inside the home and Willie's "green and narrow bed" outside (4). A sense of vacancy pervades the entire song. Deprived of their son and unable to find consolation in sentimental conventions, the family has been emptied of all emotions except for utter despair in what amounts to a gloomy Thanksgiving carol. "There will be one vacant chair" (5), the chorus reminds us, with the loss of Willie disrupting the coherence of the sentimental family and resonating out to describe a fractured body politic. Like the national body and the bodies of many soldiers, the family has suffered an amputation, a wound that has challenged the coherence they know and that causes sentimentalism to fail. It is, moreover, a wound that sentimentalism cannot heal.

From the beginning of the war, the fractured body appeared frequently in Civil War music, with isolated soldiers voicing fears about death and wounds, and reflecting on a new scale a national anxiety about death and a divided body politic. Ethelinda Beers's poem "The Picket Guard" (1861), set to music in both the North and South, follows a drowsy sentry keeping watch along the Potomac River. When the sentry begins thinking of his wife and children at home, he becomes distracted and, failing to spot the rifleman who kills him, cries: "'Ha! Mary, good-by!' / And the life-blood is ebbing and plashing." As quiet returns to the Potomac, the narrator comments cruelly in the song's final line: "The picket's off duty forever!" (2005, 66). The sentry's indulgence in sentimentalism brings about his death, shattering his body, as Beers calls attention to the incompatibility of the sentimental mode and a war that makes emotional universality impossible. "Mother dear, your boy is wounded" goes the chorus of George F. Root's "Just After the Battle" (1863), a song narrated by a soldier who lies on the battlefield, "Strewn with dying and with dead" (5, 4), after he's been struck by a Minié ball. He hopes to survive until morning and thinks of mother and home. It's likely, however, that he will not make it back. While in parlor songs the nostalgic longing for home and mother is safe daydreaming, most Civil War lyricists writing about wounded soldiers do not allow the soldiers to return home, suggesting that something fundamental has changed about their bodies, preventing their reintegration into a sentimental community. By challenging the sentimental tenets of emotional universality, the transparent national family, and the coherent national body, popular song during the Civil War points to significant anxieties over the representation of a nation that has been fragmented by citizens who no longer subscribe to sentimental ideals.

It was this same sense of large-scale fragmentation that preoccupied Walt Whitman as he wrote about the war. On December 22, 1862, after he had rushed to Virginia to check on his brother, George, who had been wounded in the Battle of Fredericksburg, Whitman recorded in his notebook a sight that frightened him in the camp of the Army of the Potomac: "at the foot of tree, immediately in front, a heap of feet, legs, arms, and human fragments, cut, bloody, black and blue, swelled and sickening" (1984, 504). At the end of his life, as he reflected on the war in *Specimen Days*, images of the war's dead stayed with him: "the dead, the dead, the dead— *our* dead—or South or North, ours all, (all, all, all, finally dear to me)" (1963, 114). Both from visiting George, whose wound, it turned out, was not serious, and from tending to injured and dying soldiers in the many military hospitals of Washington, DC, Whitman had seen firsthand how the war was damaging individual bodies and threatening the national body. As a poet, he had long been concerned with celebrating the Union and containing American multitudes in his project, *Leaves of Grass*, the first edition published in 1855. But it was the war Whitman chose to take up in a new book of poetry he called *Drum-Taps*. He published *Drum-Taps* in 1865 and then appended a revised version of it to the fourth edition of *Leaves of Grass* in 1867. As the title suggests, Whitman's war poetry reflects his interest in music. [10] "Taps," Justin Kaplan notes, was a term that signified at the beginning of the Civil War "a reveille tattoo," but changed by the end of the war to mean "lights out, last post, a farewell to earth, sounded on the bugle." This shift, according to Kaplan, parallels a shift in attitude visible in Whitman's war poetry. While Whitman's early poems express an unbridled celebration of a war that he, like many Americans, thought would be short and purgative, his later poems are subdued and mournful dirges for soldiers (1986, 299).

It seems appropriate that Whitman chose a musical title for his volume. Though he had no formal training in music, he took every chance he got to listen to it. Despite his initial skepticism, he fell in love with Italian opera when the *Brooklyn Daily Eagle* sent him to review a performance in 1847, an experience, John Dizikes argues, that "gave him the structure and form of his verse" (1993, 187). He cackled along with the rest of the audience at minstrel shows, and he admired the parlor songs of Stephen Foster, the best music in America, he thought (Reynolds, 1995, 183). He was also a devotee of the Hutchinson Family Singers, a group he revered for their stripped-down simplicity, their choral performance, and their distinctively American focus on the common experiences of ordinary citizens (Reynolds, 1995, 181). Given his delight in popular American music and his interest in shared experience, it seems strange that in literary studies Whitman is so often placed in opposition to sentimentalism. He probably had much to do with that legacy. Ever since he published the sappy temperance novel *Franklin Evans* (1842) in *The New World*, Whitman worked to distance himself from every vestige of sentimentalism. That novel was "damned rot—rot of the worst sort," he told his disciple Horace Traubel in 1888 (1906, 93); it was a source of embarrassment for him throughout his career. And so in *Drum-Taps* he declares that he is no "pale poetling" and that he will offer his readers "No dainty rhymes or sentimental love verses" (2002a, 237, 236). But, as we have seen, nineteenth-century sentimentalism was not marked simply by the emotional excess Whitman describes here. Rather, I argue, his use of music in *Drum-Taps* shows just how consistent his poetic project is with sentimental song, as he responds to the concerns about broken bodies and the broken body politic in Civil War song, searching for a way to recover both the Union and the virtues of sentimentalism.

From the start of *Drum-Taps*, Whitman emphasizes the work's musicality with three distinct calls to battle. In the 1881 arrangement of *Drum-Taps*, Whitman would underscore that these poems are military summonses by moving them all to the beginning of the volume, within the first five poems.[11] The opening poem, "First O Songs for a Prelude" (known until 1881 as "Drum-Taps"), is addressed to "Mannahatta," Whitman's feminized personification of his home, Manhattan.[12] "First O Songs" imitates conventional calls to battle like William Cullen Bryant's "Our Country's Call" (1861), which transposes lumberjacks and farmers from the forests and fields to the battleground and thereby naturalizes the work of war. All the men in Manhattan from the "mechanics" to the "salesman" leave their places of occupation, "by common consent," and find a place in Whitman's army. But these men have not consented to enlist without any persuasion. Calling to his muse, Mannahatta, Whitman asks her to tell "How your soft opera-music changed, and the drum and fife were heard in their stead, / How you led to the war, (that shall serve for our prelude, songs of soldiers,) / How Manhattan drum-taps led." Just as the men are to turn in their trades for roles in the military, Mannahatta exchanges "soft opera-music" for "the drum and fife," which then "prompt" the civilians of Manhattan to march to battle (2002a, 235). Shifting, like Whitman himself, from opera music to drum-taps, the music of Manhattan woos the civilians to battle. Everyone remains silent and entranced; even the parting scene Whitman envisions between mother and son happens wordlessly: "Loth is the mother to part, yet not a word does she speak to detain him." The cannons and guns that appear in the field are also silent, but this will soon change, the narrator assures us, when they "begin the red business." This celebratory poem, which closes by asking Mannahatta to "smile with joy" (236), prepares civilian readers, too, for the noises of war, as the poet almost blithely approximates the home front and the battlefield, capitalizing on sentimental universality.

Whitman's sentimental optimism doesn't last long, however. While the first call to battle plays on the motif of music as a shared experience, a music for the millions that evokes a common response, with the drum-taps equivalent to the aria, the poem that would become the second call, "Beat! Beat! Drums!," reveals a more cynical perspective closer in tone to the understated irony in Gumpert's "Dying Volunteer." Here, just two poems later, Whitman rehearses and revises the call to battle in "First O Songs." The speaker begins each of the three seven-line stanzas with the forceful command: "Beat! beat! drums!—blow! bugles! blow!" Again, the music visits all of the civilians in Manhattan, but this time their participation is far from voluntary. "Like a ruthless force," the music must burst into the church and "scatter the congregation," and do the same to the "peaceful farmer" (2002a, 237). The drums and bugle no longer resemble the aria. They now grow discordant and shrill to annoy and attack those who are resistant to enlisting in the army. While, before, the lawyer left his office without a second thought, now the drums must "rattle quicker, heavier" to drive him out of the courtroom. And while in "First O Songs" the music encouraged the people to act in pantomime, moving to the battlefield without any words, here the drums and bugle must compete with and drown out voices: "Let not the child's voice be heard, nor the mother's entreaties" (2002a, 238). Not only does the martial music take away the democratic voices of the people in this call to battle, but it distorts their voices, forcefully making them over into the "common consent" that "First O Songs" celebrates, in a process not unlike the martyrdom in "John

Brown's Body" that rids Brown of any political peculiarities. This shift from "First O Songs" to "Beat! Beat! Drums!" thus throws into relief the contrast between sentimentalism as a nationalizing paradigm and sentimentalism as a coercive tool of the state, with even Whitman's own bugling free verse, emblematic of his poetic voice, in "First O Songs" reined in by regular, militaristic stanzas in "Beat! Beat! Drums!"

The third call to battle in *Drum-Taps* is the most unconventional and introduces a new strategy for unifying the nation, when sentimental universality fails. Michael Moon notes that "Song of the Banner at Daybreak" is both polyvocal and musical, as Whitman experiments with "the effects of opera and related dramatic forms of vocal music" (1991, 178). Here, the dramatis personae are a poet, a pennant, a banner, a child, and his father. Inspired by the banner flapping in the wind, the poet wants to create "a new song, a free song," a song that is part of the "open air" and that will transcend mere "book-words" (2002a, 239). The poet comes to see the banner, the symbol of the nation, and the pennant, the symbol of war, as vehicles for his message, vessels into which he can pour his feelings to speak to his audience. When he sings of the "banner broad and blue" and the "starry banner" (241), the poet evokes nationalistic Civil War anthems like the Confederate "Bonnie Blue Flag" (1861), with the chorus "Hurrah! for the Bonnie Blue Flag that bears a Single Star!" (1861, 4). But unlike typical anthems, the poet's message here is not a universal one. He designs the flag and pennant to appeal specifically to the child, even as the child's father aims to discourage him from fighting, trying to redirect his attention instead to material possessions.

In using a banner to entice a child to enlist, the poem draws on common tropes in Civil War songs. Willie, the son killed in battle in "The Vacant Chair," was a flag bearer in the army. Another popular song called "The Drummer Boy of Shiloh" (1862), written and composed by Will S. Hays, memorializes a child drummer who dies a model death on the battlefield, praying to God and sending a message to his mother before he perishes. Children led off to battle in war songs, then, typically do not return home and, instead, inadvertently tear apart their families. In Whitman's "Song of the Banner at Daybreak," however, rather than leave the boy's fate up to this version of the sentimental fireside family, the poet intervenes by targeting the child directly. Searching for a new song and a new mode, that is, the poet chooses to reconfigure the fireside family in order to absorb the nation's losses himself. Like the others, this call to battle contains a catalogue of prospective soldiers on the home front, but this catalogue is mediated through the poet's perspective: "I see numberless farms, I see the farmers working in their fields or barns, / I see mechanics working" (2002a, 241). Rather than try to create a consensus, the poet considers the people subjectively and approaches them individually, making use of interpersonal contact to convince them to go to war.

Even as the poem illustrates the decline of the coherent national family, Whitman, whose own family was in shambles during the war,[13] provides a solution to this challenge to sentimental ideals. As the poet endows the banner with meaning and the child decides to turn away from his father in favor of the banner and the pennant, the poet exclaims, "My limbs, my veins dilate, my theme is clear at last" (2002a, 243). Just as his message absorbs the child, the poet's body absorbs him, too, swelling as the child joins his cause. Indeed, in his search for a song and a theme, and in his growth when he gains a subject for singing, the poet becomes a figure for Whitman's volume of poetry itself, evocative of *Leaves of Grass*, a volume that, since its first printing, bore a picture of Whitman as its frontispiece. Whitman described himself in 1855 as a "rough," a probable pun on the rough quality of *Leaves of Grass*, a book that would expand and change with him throughout his life. In 1876, he would add to the title page of *Leaves of Grass* a short poem that begins "Come, said my Soul, / Such verses for my Body let us write." The poem closes with "Signing for Soul and Body, set to them my name," and underneath, Whitman included his signature (2002b, 2). Increasingly, I suggest, Whitman came to see the material books he produced as surrogate bodies, corpuses capable of restoring coherency to fragmented verses, fractured families, and damaged bodies. As a volunteer at Washington hospitals, Whitman often wrote letters for soldiers and stood in for their family members at their bedsides. Through *Drum-Taps* and *Leaves of Grass*, he could create a repository for a suffering nation and a proxy for his own body, which began to ache after his exhausting hospital work came to a close in 1864.

Significantly, the textual body the poet constructs in "Song of the Banner at Daybreak" is not like the body Whitman builds in the poem "1861." There, the speaker figures the year "as a strong man erect, clothed in blue clothes, advancing, carrying a rifle on your shoulder." The year's "masculine voice" begins its call to battle in Manhattan but soon broadens its scope to include other states: Illinois, Indiana, Pennsylvania, Ohio, and Tennessee. After hearing its voice, the speaker declares: "I repeat you, hurrying, crashing, sad, distracted year" (2002a, 237). Full of Whitman's early optimism, this poem builds up the national body and makes the poet's role simply to repeat and reflect the consensus he observes, a sentimental move despite the poem's explicit rejection of "sentimental love verses" (236). As Whitman witnessed more and more destruction in the war, however, he saw his hopes for a unitary national body dashed. In "Song of the Banner at Daybreak," he at once disintegrates the national family and dissolves the idea of any national body based on consensus. Instead, he hopes to create individual sympathetic connections with subjects and readers, preserving their differences as he binds them together in the form of his book.

Whitman informs *Drum-Taps* with recognizable tropes from sentimental war songs. "Come Up from the Fields Father," for instance, portrays a mother surrounded by her daughters as she reads a letter that reports her son has been injured in combat: "Sentences broken, *gunshot wound in the breast, cavalry skirmish, taken to hospital, / At present low, but will soon be better.*" The broken sentences here convey the son's broken body; the narrator of the poem explains that the son "is dead already," and the mother wants only to "withdraw, / To follow, to seek, to be with her dear dead son" (254). Evoking songs like "The Vacant Chair" and "Just After the Battle," this poem is also reminiscent of the song "Dear Mother, I've Come Home to Die" (1863) in which a dying soldier calls to his bedside his mother, brother, and sister. Whitman's "The Artilleryman's Vision," which appears to describe posttraumatic stress disorder, gives us another kind of fractured family as a former soldier suffers from nightmares while trying to sleep next to his wife in bed. As she slumbers quietly, he hears "the sounds of the different missiles, the short *t-h-t! / t-h-t!* of the rifle balls," "the great shells shrieking as they pass," "the cry of a regiment charging" (266), "the chaos louder than ever," "the sound of the cannon far or near," and "bombs bursting in air" (267). For this soldier, the noises of war pervert the music of sentimentalism, making communion with his wife impossible. In "Dirge for Two Veterans," the "great drums" pound and the "small drums" whir (264), as the speaker watches a double funeral procession for a father and a son, concluding: "O my soldiers, my veterans, / My heart gives you love" (265).

And this cacophony, ultimately, is what Whitman's poet offers readers of his work. The music of war clashes unevenly with sentimental music in *Drum-Taps*, with some personae finding consolation and resolution, while others, like the mother in "Come Up from the Fields Father," remain withdrawn in despair. But, as "Dirge for Two Veterans" implies, Whitman in the role of minstrel positions himself in the volume both as singer and as drummer. He plays one sort of taps to celebrate the soldiers who march to war and another sort to lay them to rest as they die. It is perhaps significant that bandsmen in the Civil War didn't simply entertain the troops with songs and play in funeral processions. When a battle began, if they were lucky enough not to be sent to the front lines with rifles in hand, their help would probably be enlisted in constructing field hospitals, digging trenches for the dead, running the wounded on stretchers from the battle lines to the hospitals, nursing the dying and wounded in camp, and, when they had a spare moment, lightening the mood in the hospitals by playing a few ditties.[14] As Whitman doubtless knew, the persona of war nurse that he cultivated in Washington, D.C., overlapped nicely with the persona of bard that he had been cultivating since the first edition of *Leaves of Grass*.

In his poems about the hospital like "The Wound-Dresser," which Whitman would move to the center of the volume in 1881, we see his attempts to recuperate the scenes of mass death, fragmentation, and division that were so threatening to mid-nineteenth-century readers and listeners. Figuring the speaker as an "old man bending" over "new faces," Whitman reminds us that his service in war hospitals took a toll on his body and aged him. In this poem, the "young men and maidens" approach the speaker and ask him for his stories about the war (2002a, 259). The speaker then describes his hospital work, omitting any and all names: "To the long rows of cots up and down each side I return, / To each and all one after another I draw near, not one do I miss." He sees a boy and exclaims: "poor boy! I never knew you, / Yet I think I could not refuse this moment to die for you, if that would save you" (260). For Whitman, the anonymity in this scene functions as a *tabula rasa*; his speaker concentrates on the wounded bodies, which he catalogues in the fourth, and last, section of the poem, and the kisses and embraces he receives in particular moments of individual contact. Whitman's persona thus provides coherence through a particularized version of sympathy. Capable of absorbing everyone, his poet prizes contact over universalism, and as with "Song of the Banner at Daybreak," he encourages readers to respond sympathetically and to coalesce through the medium of the poet. Enfolding the dead and wounded in his book, as he does in this poem with his embraces, Whitman resists seeking consensus and instead treats each soldier as an improvisational song collected in a song book; rather than flatten them all into a stereotype or two for easy identification, he uses his poetic inspiration to weave them together and create a sympathetic bond for each of them individually.

In individualizing and particularizing his sympathy, Whitman acknowledges a rupture in sentimental universality and experiments with form and genre to arrive at a reconfigured version of sentimentalism that can engender sympathy even when no consensus exists. He thus looks through the representation of music in *Drum-Taps* to rescue and recuperate the sense of shared experience and common emotional response so vital to mid-nineteenth-century song and so critical to a sense of union in America. After the war's challenges to the national family, corporeal coherence, and emotional transparency shook the sentimental paradigm for the nation to pieces, Whitman collects those pieces through the conventions of sentimental song and links them together by constructing a new surrogate national body in the form of the book that allows for difference and extends sympathy to the individual. He revisits sentimentalism, but he also revises it, creating a version of sympathy that is much more subjective than anything mid-nineteenth-century readers and listeners knew. Perhaps this is why scholars tend to be so adamant about making Whitman into a proto-modernist, the experimentalist who challenges everything that comes before him and inaugurates the age of subjective poetics in postbellum America.

Whitman and the Civil War changed American poetry, to be sure. But to view Whitman in this way is to commit the very mistakes he wanted to avoid in *Drum-Taps*, smoothing over his rough edges to place him neatly into convenient categories for easy identification. Despite our preferences for a more sophisticated poetic genius, we must remember that Whitman is the author of *Franklin Evans* as well as *Leaves of Grass* and that just as much as he enjoyed the opera, he delighted in the sentimental music of Stephen Foster. To do otherwise would be to read ourselves back on to Whitman, to overlook the continuum between sentimentalism and modernism in American literary history, and to ignore the crucial role the Civil War played in sparking the search for new and exciting poetic modes descriptive of a nation that was fast changing even as it was coming back together—as well as it could with the illusion of consensus evaporating, that is.

NOTES

1. For versions of this story, see Manjerovic and Budds (2002, 125). See also Charles Hamm (1979, 231).

2. For some scholars, like Jane Tompkins, these strategies are gendered, as female writers design sentimental novels "to reorganize culture from the woman's point of view" (1985, 124). Others see in sentimentalism more inclusive efforts to unite American readers in spite of their differences. Kete, for instance, examines the strategies of Henry Wadsworth Longfellow and Lydia Sigourney to encourage readers to envision "multiple, various Americas," each of which reflects the poet's "own personal situations and political agendas" (2000, 117). Peter Coviello argues that antebellum writers employed whiteness as a language to construct national "dreams of affiliation" that served to unite far-flung and anonymous American readers (2005, 4). See also Glenn Hendler's suggestion that sympathy, as it is represented in antebellum sentimental texts, is "a paradigmatically public sentiment," a structure of feeling that engenders the fantasy of "an unmediated interpersonal communication of affect" (2001, 12).

3. For studies of fireside sentimentalism, see Haralson (1996), Gruesz (1999), Sorby (2005), and Irmscher (2009).

4. According to Tawa, in antebellum America "only a fraction of the populace read American literature." Rather, "ordinary men and women" preferred "a commonplace symbolism that wandered from favorite song to favorite song" (1984, 7).

5. Among the many lyrical adaptations of "The Battle Cry of Freedom" was a Confederate version by William H. Barnes and Herman Schreiner (published by J. C. Schreiner & Son) that was sung to the same tune and took the same title. See Cornelius (2004, 50).

6. This illusion of consensus, however, had no place for blacks in America. Moseley (1984) argues that while blacks may have sung some of the same popular songs as whites, those songs were all written by and for whites. With few exceptions, the lyrics represent blacks according to buffoonish stereotypes and express yearning for the days of antebellum slavery (2–3). By remaking the songs of white America and creating their own songs, blacks instead displayed a creative resistance to the consensus of sentimentalism, carving out an identity in opposition to the sentimental universality that ignored blackness.

7. For the definitive study of the Hutchinson Family Singers, see Gac (2007).

8. Crawford (2005, 271) remarks that "Tenting on the Old Camp Ground" "explored the gap between the heroic and the sentimental, pondered what war could lead decent men to do, and thus reached a level of understanding that neither standard approach could manage."

9. Further contributing to this logic of substitution was a likely spurious origin story for the song. George Kimball claims that the song was the invention of soldiers in the Second Massachusetts Battalion of Infantry to ridicule a fellow soldier, named John Brown. "This can't be John Brown—why John Brown is dead," the camp wits would quip, inspiring the composition of "the most nonsensical, doggerel rhymes" (1889, 372). While the identity of the lyricist for "John Brown's Body" remains uncertain, the song's tune is commonly attributed to the South Carolina composer William Steffe.

10. For studies of the relationship between music and *Drum-Taps*, see in particular Picker (2000) and Davis (1992). For studies of the influence of music on Whitman, see Reynolds (1995, 154–93) and Dizikes (1993, 184–88).

11. My discussion of these poems follows the arrangement of *Drum-Taps* in the 1881 edition of *Leaves of Grass*. See Genoways (2006) for a persuasive argument that the arrangement of the 1865 edition was motivated by financial decisions rather than artistic ones. Whitman would experiment with the arrangement in the 1871–1872 edition of *Leaves of Grass*, grouping the poems into three clusters distributed throughout the volume. The 1881 edition consequently represents the most concentrated and reflective sequencing of the poems.

12. Picker notes insightfully that in converting the name "Manhattan" to "Mannahatta," Whitman effects "the transformation of the name of his home into percussive taps," as military music begins to change Whitman's own poetic rhetoric (2000, 4).

13. On Whitman's troubled family, see Hutchinson (2003, 137–138). See also Roper (2008).

14. See Manjerovic and Budds (2002, 124–125). Picker makes a similar connection between Whitman and the hospital activities of Civil War bandsmen, arguing that Whitman positions himself first and foremost as an instrumental bandsman in *Drum-Taps* (2000, 6–7).

Chapter Ten

Psychological Sentimentalism

Consciousness, Affect, and the Sentimental Henry James

George Gordon-Smith

The great feminine novelist of a feminine age of letters. —F. W. Dupee on Henry James

Despite diverse scholarly attempts to challenge the gendering of sentiment as uniformly feminine, critical discussions of Henry James as a sentimental writer are sparse. Devoting an entire chapter to James, Kristin Boudreau's *Sympathy in American Literature* explores the dangers of sympathy and its "unpleasant, unexamined side effects," but focuses more on James's distaste for the sentimental politics of suffrage and women's rights than on his use of sentimental tropes themselves (2002, xii). Amanda Claybaugh's *The Novel of Purpose*: *Literature and Social Reform in the Anglo-American World* highlights James's transatlantic role in creating character types important to realist reform literature, but gives most of its attention to George Eliot's role in actually evoking sympathy through characterization (2007, 31–51). Cindy Weinstein's otherwise convincing attempt to expand the sentimental canon looks at Melville and Twain but only mentions James briefly (2004, 10). Such important texts on American sentimentalism and realism as Caleb Crain's *American Sympathy* (2001) and Margaret Cohen's *The Sentimental Education of the Novel* (1999) fail to reference James at all.

Glenn Hendler was the first scholar to take seriously the proposition that James's texts drew on sentimental conventions and culture. Taking *The Structural Transformation of the Public Sphere* by Jürgen Habermas as his starting point, Hendler explores what he calls the "politics of affect" in nineteenth-century American texts. Contra those who view sympathy as "a primarily privatizing emotional exchange," Hendler argues that not only was it "a paradigmatically public sentiment" in nineteenth-century culture (2001, 12), but it was transformative as well, reshaping the lives of individuals and institutions, arts and politics, through the role it played in the public sphere. Like Boudreau, Hendler takes as given James's unease with the political and affective power of sympathy, especially in the hands of women's rights advocates. However, the fact that nineteenth-century culture publicized interiority through various forms of "affective exchanges" including not just letters and biography but fiction also is, Hendler argues, central to James's writing. Hendler's argument is useful because it helps shed light on James as a male author participating in the same type of affective exchange that Adam Smith first suggested promotes sympathy—this despite the fact that he distanced himself as much as possible from sympathy politics itself. As we shall see, Hendler's argument is also useful in its emphasis on the public performance of interiority in a period, which, Hendler contends, turned personality into theatre. If, as Ann Douglas opines, "sentimentalism cannot exist without an audience" (1988, 254), James's characters, even at their most intimately domestic (as when experiencing love or the death of a loved one) can be seen from this perspective as performing what they "feel" (2001, 147–83).

Despite the persuasiveness of Hendler's work, critical resistance to a sentimental James continues. This could be because we are still reluctant to deconstruct the archaic gender roles that align men with reason and the marketplace, not with emotion, or it could be because earlier misreadings of the "sentiment" in sentimental fiction as solely an emotional device lacking any cognitive forethought persist. Readers will find that this chapter addresses both alternatives: it challenges the nineteenth century's unilateral assignment of men to rationality and the marketplace, and it rethinks conventional notions of what "sentiment" entails in nineteenth-century fiction. More specifically, it undertakes to reevaluate Henry James's inscription as an unsentimental writer and confronts the archaic segregation of the sentimental as a solely feminine trope. Instead, it contends that sentiment is as much a rational process as it is an emotional one and that this is how James depicts it.

In calling James a rational sentimentalist, or, preferably, a male author practicing what I call psychological sentimentalism, I recognize that I am associating him rather more closely than many will find comfortable with a group of fiction writers whom he scorned. Nevertheless, in this essay I will demonstrate the following points: first, James's reputation as an anti-sentimentalist notwithstanding, he uses typically sentimentalized characters in his texts, (e.g., orphans, widows, betrayed wives, and secret lovers). Second, these sentimental characters validate sympathetic exchanges with each other through what Hendler identifies as performative or theatrical representations. Third, through kinesics, or the active interpretation of body language (facial expressions, gestures, and so on), these nonverbal performances of feeling make sympathetic exchanges possible. The study of this latter element in

James's writing uncovers a cognitive and psychological component to sentimental and emotive expression in his fiction.

IMAGINATION VERSUS EMOTION:
THE FEMINIZATION OF SENTIMENT

To explain Henry James's role within what Shirley Samuels calls "the culture of sentiment" (1992, 6) requires a theoretical and historical revision of the traditional association of sentimentality with femininity and emotion. At its eighteenth-century inception, primarily male writers, not female, represented what was then called sensibility and the broader culture of sentiment. Laurence Sterne, Samuel Richardson, Henry Mackenzie, and Johan Wolfgang von Goethe all promoted what Hendler terms "sympathetic identification," the process by which people are asked to feel both like and with another person (2001, 5). The most prominent theorist of sympathetic identification was Adam Smith, who described the cognitive and affective dynamic underpinning the politics of sympathy in *The Theory of Moral Sentiments*.

Contrary to what one might expect, Smith speaks very little about emotion per se in his explanation of how sympathy is created, describing it rather in terms of how the mind works: "It is," he writes, "*by the imagination only* that we can form *any conception* of what are [the] sensations [of our brother on the rack] . . . by the imagination we place ourselves in his situation, we conceive ourselves enduring all the same torments" (Italics mine. Smith [1759] 1976, 9). It is Smith's emphasis on the actual mental processes involved in the generation of sympathy that is important. Both imagination and conception are aspects of cognition, which was identified as a masculine function not only by Smith and his audience but also by realist authors such as James a century later. Where James diverged from his fellow realists (and from Smith) was that for them sentiment and sympathy were cognitive processes directed toward evoking emotive responses in the interest of eliciting remedial action on behalf of social reform. For James, sympathy was still rooted in the mind, but its *apolitical* role in emotive exchanges between private individuals was of paramount interest to him.

By the middle of the nineteenth century, sentiment and sympathy, together with sentimentality—the term especially favored by those who used it derisively to discredit social reform movements such as abolition and women's rights—were largely relegated to female authors and to the domestic sphere. Mary Chapman and Glenn Hendler argue that this development was exacerbated by and a symptom of a binary which split nineteenth-century culture between male-dominated public and female-driven private spheres (1999, 3). Different ideologies developed around the home and marketplace

demanding distinct literary representations of social experience with the result that, as Jane Tompkins has argued, sentiment, sympathy, sensibility, and
sentimentality all became thoroughly feminized. Emotion became the domain of women, and by the time Henry James began writing fiction in 1871,
the "man of feeling" had been replaced by the crying mother and "the story
of salvation through motherly love" (Tompkins 1985, 125). The 1852 publication of Harriet Beecher Stowe's *Uncle Tom's Cabin* sounded the death
knell of masculine sensibility in fiction.[1] Sympathy, sentiment's most highly
valorized emotional form and the emotion critical to most nineteenth-century
reform platforms, had cemented itself in readers' minds as a feminine (sentimental) trope.

Yet as Cathy Davidson and Jessamyn Hatcher point out, the unilateral
ascription of sentiment and sentimentality to women in the first half of the
nineteenth century was not so complete as this picture suggests nor as rigid
as the doctrine of separate spheres would seem to make it (2002 10–12).
Originally published in 1977, Ann Douglas's *The Feminization of American
Culture* was the first major scholarly re-evaluation of the feminization of
sentiment in the United States. Although Douglas consistently aligns sentimentality, whose "dishonesty" (1988, 12) she deplores, with the "feminization" of American culture, she also draws attention to a disestablishment
clergy, who replaced Calvinism's harsh Old Testament deity with the softer
image of Christ, and to long ignored male authors of sentimental fiction,
whose writing she found no less "rancid" than that of their female peers
(254). Outraged by the blatantly antifeminist component in Douglas's polemic, feminist scholars took on the "project . . . of rehabilitating the sentimental," launching challenge after challenge to the apoliticism of the binary the
separate-spheres doctrine represented (Sedgwick 2008 154). Jane Tompkins's *Sensational Designs* (1985), Philip Fisher's *Hard Facts* (1985), and,
more recently, Amanda Claybaugh's *The Novel of Purpose* (2007) all stress
the cultural "power" that accrued to women when they used sentimentality to
enact progressive reform agendas. Scholars such as Julia A. Stern and Hendler, meanwhile, explored the roles of male writers in sentimental culture,
also contending that sympathetic identification is not strictly a feminizing
and private emotion. Stern does this by arguing that sentiment and mourning
are interrelated because they draw the individual away from the domestic
sphere into culturally accepted methods of public emotive expression (1997,
68). Hendler does so by describing what he calls "the logic of sympathy," his
language pointing to the cognitive nature of sentiment (2001, 5). As Hendler's work, and indeed two essays in this volume, testify, one result of all
this scholarship is that long-established canonical male authors such as Whitman and James are now being re-evaluated for their "sentimental" component.

THE UNSENTIMENTAL SYMPATHIZER

For an author labeled by his critics past and present as decidedly unsentimental, Henry James develops a surprising number of characters and situations that would be conventionally deemed sentimental. The population of his fiction by ostracized women, orphans, dead lovers, infants, and widow(er)s would seem to indicate that James's fiction is full of pathos. Yet his earliest critics dismissed him as devoid of "elemental passions" (Edel 1977, 39). One commentator suggested that his "genuine scientific interest" made the reader aware of "all that was distressing," arguing that James failed to rise "above the painfulness of [scientific scrutiny] by any passion of sympathy." James's "exceeding cleverness is of too unemotional a character to be employed on pain," this critic went on to say (Review, 1876, 425). Another reviewer remarked that James's work lacks the "profound and universal human sympathy which is needed to temper the severity of his scientific apprehension" (in Hayes, [1877], 1996, 6). For these critics, James was, it seems, too rational, his objectivity and proclivity to dissect character disabling his ability to express such "universals" as sympathy and passion. But an alternative inference can be drawn from James's refusal to display "elemental passions"— namely, that as one averse to public displays of what was finally private experience, James, in writing as he did, sought to advance a modality of affectivity that could be appropriately expressed in public. In this sense he wanted, that is, to keep the private private even while making a public performance of it.

In a review of *The Princess Casamassima* (1886), one of James's most consciously sympathetic novels, William Dean Howells came closest to the mark. Disagreeing with most of James's critics, he insisted that "there is a sympathy for the suffering . . . in the book which should be apparent even to the critical groundlings." James's work, he maintained, does indeed evoke sympathy, but "forbears, as ever, to pat his people on the back, to weep upon their necks, or caress them with endearing and compassionate epithets and pet names" (1887, 829). Howells—a good friend of James and a theorist who helped shape his aesthetic—clearly saw sentimental tropes in James's fiction despite the lack of many of the conventional cues such as tears and "endearing and compassionate epithets." And James's review of Charles Dickens's *Our Mutual Friend* supports Howells's claims: "A story based upon those elemental passions in which we seek the true and final manifestations of character must be told in a spirit of intellectual superiority to those passions" ([1865] 1957, 75–79). "Elemental passions" were James's subject, but the method in which he treated them did not itself partake of these passions. Because his work seemed to lack "sensuous imagery" and "human feeling," his critics viewed him as "unsympathetic," when in fact he expressed his sympathy in a very different way, a way not legible to them (Review 1876, 425).

While James's early reviewers praised his precision and the psychological subtlety with which he paints his characters, his suppression of emotion in favor of intellectuality confused them. For James, sentiment—and more specifically the moral passion, sympathy—were more a matter of cognition than of emotion, and it needed to be approached dispassionately, through the critical intellect, not the heart. A particular character's "passion of intelligence," he tells us in the preface to *The Princess Casamassima*, "is . . . his highest value for our curiosity and our sympathy" (69). Thus he maintains that the writer of a tale must employ the *mind* to express fully the *passions* of characters, writing "in a spirit of intellectual superiority to those passions" he depicts, and thereby maintaining his distance from them ([1865] 1957, 75–79). The goal was to master these passions and hold them up to scrutiny, yet have them still shape his characters' actions. Put another way, James favored a psychological expression of sympathy in his novels. While critics have been correct in arguing that his fiction lacks deeply emotional interaction between characters, to claim that James's work lacks human feeling is to grossly misunderstand his aesthetic goals. James was more interested in promoting mindful sentiment in his fiction, that is, private emotive sympathy that could be conveyed publicly, than he was in his characters' making a public exhibition of emotion.

James's claim to "intellectual superiority" plays itself out in texts that require the reader to assess the deeply psychological motivations behind characters' actions together with their emotional consequences. James's attention to body language, his emphasis on psychological subtlety, and his intellectualism all evince his preference for conscious development over the use of more physical signs of sentimentality, for example, tears—which he conspicuously omits in many of his stories even though, thematically speaking, they seem called for, as, for example, in stories of love betrayed. For James, as for Adam Smith, perceiving sentiment is first a cognitive response. This is to say, James's work internalizes sentiment by intellectualizing emotions. Despite Oscar Wilde's allegation in his review of *The Turn of the Screw* (1898) that James never "arrive[s] at a passion" (Sicker 1980, 9) and Rebecca West's chastisement of Isabel Archer of *The Portrait of a Lady* for marrying without the "consciousness of passion" (1916, 70), James does introduce sentiment into his works—only, in a way unlike that of any other author of his time, he treats it as primarily a mental, rather than an embodied, process.

Jane Thrailkill's rebuttal in *Affecting Fictions* (2007) of W. K. Wimsatt's arguments for "the Affective Fallacy," a term he coined in 1954 (see "Affective Fallacy," Wimsatt 1954, 21) can help clarify what I mean by this last remark. A major figure in the New Critical movement of the 1930s and

1940s, Wimsatt maintained that texts should not be valued for their emotional impact—which, he said, could only lead to impressionism and relativism—but for their intrinsic worth as works of art, which was subject to rational analysis. In *The Verbal Icon: Studies in the Meaning of Poetry*, Wimsatt states, "Emotion . . . has a well known capacity to fortify opinion, to inflame cognition, and to grow upon itself in surprising proportions to grains of reason" (1954, 26). Drawing on twenty-first-century neuroscience and cognitive psychology, Thrailkill reverses this formula. In her reading of *The Wings of the Dove*, she observes that James links words and violence in gestures that point to the presence of thoughts in emotions (2007, 211). Emotions, she states, are "[n]ot isolated to the interiors of individual bodies," but rather "involve events that enter language and are negotiated in the social world of relations" (213). For Thrailkill emotions are expressed through the cognitive function of language before they can enter the social world. Of course, James eschews articulated sentimental words, but he does offer us glimpses of his characters' emotive minds and suffering consciousnesses. James moves beyond language and places the cognitive function of nonverbal communication in the conscious emotions expressed in his characters' minds. In *Wings*, Merton Densher's perceptions of his role in Milly Theale's pain. for example, occur within his own mind as he observes her decaying body: "The facts of physical suffering, of incurable pain, . . . had been made at a stroke, intense, and this was to be the way he was now to feel them" (*Wings* 347). Rather than verbally express his emotions and fear and pain at Milly's deathbed, Densher thinks them for us. Densher feels the *facts* of Milly's suffering. As Thrailkill suggests, the cognizance of Milly's pain is not isolated to the interior. Rather, it enters language in order to negotiate the social world of relations. But if, as I have suggested, James's characters think their emotions, how are these emotions expressed if not through language? How do James's characters express sympathy for each other if not through words?

James's characters negotiate the social world of relations through thinking and observing, rather than feeling and doing. In fact, a quick look at his short stories suggests that a cognitive awareness of suffering through observation is the impetus for sentiment in his fiction. Taking up the sentimental theme of the death of a lover, "Longstaff's Marriage" illustrates James's ability to put cognition before emotion in what otherwise might seem a very bizarre relationship indeed. In this story, which contains not one but two deathbed scenes, Reginald Longstaff proposes to Diana Belford while on his deathbed, only to be refused, which incites him to recover in order to win her. When Diana later becomes sick herself and, dying, proposes to Longstaff, he, unlike her, accepts. But the result is ambiguously ironic. Diana, far from getting better, lets herself die, convinced that it is only through her death that she can show her love for him. As Longstaff becomes a spectator to Diana's dying, we become aware that James is removing the physicality inherent in marriage and allowing Diana to die before she and Reginald can consummate their love. Reginald can only immortalize her and forever remember a virginal and unattainable image, recollecting not the physical expression of their love but the intellectual assessment of what that love now means for him.

"The Altar of the Dead," in which George Stransom "needed no priest and no altar to make him forever widowed" after his fiancée dies (1996, 452), and "Maud-Evelyn," in which a young man believes he is the widower of a woman who died years before he was born, are additional examples of James's short stories that prioritize the human imagination of suffering over sentimental turmoil and overt physical expressions of feelings. This lack of emotional fulfillment frustrated contemporary critics and readers of James not only because had they been accustomed to expect overt expressions of sentiment in their literature, but also because like Wimsatt's naïve readers, they relished being moved. Modern critics, on the other hand, praise James for this very lack of emotion, celebrating what we now call his psychological realism but failing to note that "emotion," albeit cognitively rendered, is still at the heart of James's art. At the same time, however, one of the undesirable side effects of James's eliding of physicality in favor of imagination is that his main characters often linger on the sidelines, watching, making them seem emotionally bloodless even when they are not. In this sense, nineteenth-century reviewers had something on their side when they said James's characters lacked passion.

WATCHING THE PAST: HENRY JAMES AND
MORAL PHILOSOPHY

As I suggested earlier, to understand how James works sympathy into his fiction, one must first understand Adam Smith's description of sympathetic identification. An ideal example is found in *The Theory of Moral Sentiments* when Smith explains how a mother comes to *feel* pain after *witnessing* the suffering of her child:

> What are the pangs of a mother, when she hears the moanings of her infant, that, during the agony of disease cannot express what it feels? In her idea of what it suffers, she joins, to its real helplessness, her own consciousness of that helplessness, and her own terrors for the unknown consequences of its disorder; and out of all these, forms, for her own sorrow, the most complete image of misery and distress. (Smith [1759] 1976, 8)

How little Smith actually describes emotional behavior in this passage is, I think, important. Although he refers to the mother's "pangs," "terrors," and "sorrow," he indicates that he focuses on the "idea of what [the baby] suffers" and a "consciousness of that helplessness." Ironically, while the mother's emotions are there, the production of sympathy itself is presented as the result of cognition. Only after the mother reaches "consciousness" of the suffering of her child and her own "helplessness" are her "terrors of the unknown consequences" emotionally realized in all their fullness (1976, 8).

The image of a mother witnessing a sick child unable to help itself is likely to stir emotion in even the most hard-hearted of observers, but in Smith's description, the emotive response of tears, pleading, and melancholia so beloved of mid-nineteenth-century American sentimentalists takes abstract form at best in references to "pangs," "terrors," and "sorrow." Smith's attention is not on the grieving of this mother but on her intellectual response. In bypassing cognitive processes, nineteenth-century sentimentalists, on the other hand, were, like Wimsatt's implied author, guilty of the "Affective Fallacy." That is, albeit in a "good" cause, they wanted "to fortify opinion" and "inflame cognition," using words and images that could guarantee the stirring up of emotions without the need for thought. While many realists out of concern for their political agendas also sought to appeal to their readers' emotions—most notably Eliot and Howells—this puts James's own psychological realism in clear opposition to sentimentalism and helps explain why the sentimental component in his writing has not been recognized. For him, more than any other nineteenth-century fiction writer, consciousness not only preceded emotion but contained it, rendering it open to rational exploration.

It is unsurprising, therefore, that so many critics have labeled James's fiction not just unsentimental but "scientific." Intellectual developments of the late nineteenth century—including the emergence of evolutionary biology, physiological psychology, neurology, and pragmatist philosophy—were crucial to the burgeoning exploration of the interconnectedness of human thoughts and emotions. Aware of these scientific developments, realist writers increasingly became attentive to the corporeal components of human perception that mediate our sympathies with the physical world. Henry's brother William James, too, sought to develop a language animated by a predominance of the "*in-between* words and phrases where the *fact of feelings* are contained"; that is, he theorized a discourse in which subjective experiences such as sympathy and passion could be viewed as epistemologically sound (Richardson 2007, 115).

It was Henry, however, who actually sought to create this kind of language in his writing, "deploying lexical and syntactic adaptations to stretch into new psychological territory" (Richardson 2007, 115). Indeed, while both brothers in some way lived their father's aphorism—"the 'feeling' mind is measured . . . by the verbal style that it invents for itself" (W. James [1885] 1993, xxix)—it was left to James's fiction to evolve a scientifically oriented, formal language with which to describe both sentiment and knowledge. Admittedly, James's fiction is not particularly laden with "feeling," yet it *is* with "consciousness," which Smith has taught us is a prerequisite to sympathetic identification. While his contemporaries enlisted the sentimental to activate mimesis and promote sympathy for the oppressed, James conceptualized the structure of mindful affect. Purging emotion from the body, he placed it in the mind instead, making consciousness a "feeling circuit of reception" indispensable for the acquisition of pragmatic knowledge about how human beings both think and feel (Richardson 2007, 115).

In *Thinking in Henry James*, Sharon Cameron takes a similar approach when she explores the relationship between thinking and feeling in James's fiction. Taking his interest in nonverbal communication to the outer extreme, she argues that his "characters suppose they have access to each others' minds without reference to their speech" and calls this type of communication "the ventriloquism of thinking" (1989, 85). If, as I argue, emotion is rooted in the brain for James, her argument suggests a fascinating connection between sentiment and cognition in James's work, in which characters identify sympathetically with other characters merely by thinking about them. However, this sympathetic thinking must express itself in some way in order for it to be a sympathetic exchange. And indeed, it is through body language and kinesics that James's characters seem to have access to each others' minds at moments when words are inadequate to express their inner feelings. As an example of James's interest in this kind of wordless "communication" between characters, I look to Maggie and Amerigo in *The Golden Bowl*. Amerigo is having an affair with Maggie's friend, Charlotte. Maggie and Charlotte were childhood friends; Charlotte married Maggie's father, changing their relationship to one of stepmother and daughter. Maggie suspects infidelity between Charlotte and Amerigo and wants to convey her love for her husband upon his return from a trip to Cloucester with Charlotte. The first quotation below represents what she imagines saying to him. Note the tremendous understanding that Maggie, without words, conveys for her husband and then note how Amerigo is able to interpret what she is communicating through his mind's eye:

> You've seemed these last days—I don't know what: more absent than ever before, too absent for us merely to go on so. It's all very well, and I perfectly see how beautiful it is, all around; but there comes a day when something snaps, when the full cup, filled to the very brim, begins to flow over. That's what has happened to my need of you—the cup, all day, has been too full to carry. So here I am with it, spilling it over you—and just for the reason that's the reason of my life. . . . I'm as much in love with you now as the first hour; except that there are some hours—which I know when they come, because they almost frighten me—that show me I'm even more so. They come of themselves—and ah they've been coming! After all, after all—! (2004, 2.323)

Although Maggie is demanding from her husband sympathy in the form of affection, James notes that "[s]ome such words as those were what didn't ring out"; that is, Maggie never actually says what she's thinking to Amerigo, at least not verbally. James then portrays Amerigo's response:

> yet it was as if even the unuttered sound had been quenched here in its own quaver. It was where utterance would have broken down by its very weight if he had let it go so far. Without that extremity, at the end of a moment, *he had taken in what he needed to take*—that his wife was testifying, that she adored and missed and desired him. (2004, 2.323–24)

Amerigo does not need to hear what Maggie is thinking, because with his mind he can understand what she wants him to know, (i.e., "[*take*] *in what he needed to take*"). Such use of the mind to interpret emotion is well documented in nineteenth-century psychological discourse when, as Thrailkill points out, emotion was not limited to its corporeal components. For "writers, readers, and theorists of the late nineteenth century," she writes, "affective experience was conceptualized as both rooted in the body and as mindful" and not as an entity separate from either (2007, 4). Henry James's work seems to advance a similar theory insofar as he treats cognition as systemic to the emotions of his characters and, like emotions, accessible to others without words. Maggie's words to the husband she is losing "didn't ring out" because verbalizing her love would have "broken down" her utterance "by its very weight," and when Amerigo looks at her this is what he "sees."

Similar to Smith's example of a mother sympathizing with a sick child—sympathetic identification occurring after the observer becomes conscious of suffering—Amerigo becomes aware of Maggie's love for him before he feels her love. There are no words that can accurately express Maggie's feelings, nor is there for James an appropriate public forum to express such powerful private emotions. In this sense, scholars such as Wendy Graham and Philip Sicker are right: James does not express heights of emotion as do his contemporaries. But James does state that the sentiments Maggie needs to verbalize are too heavy for words, so she finds another way to express them. Indeed, we know she expresses them somehow because despite her aphonic speech, Amerigo "take[s] in what he needed to take" and understands what Maggie is trying to say to him: that she is aware he is slipping away. Both are thinking about their feelings for the other and somehow convey the latter without actually speaking. Although Cameron suggests that James's characters may "have access to" each others' minds, something more seems to be taking place during these moments of extreme emotion. Before Maggie even begins to think about her love for her husband, she and Amerigo exchange a "silent look" that causes her to think rather than to speak her mind. And after each understands the other, as the passage suggests, Maggie later remembers that "something . . . had passed between them" (2004 2.323). In fact, "how he had looked," she adds, when "something had happened, rapidly with the beautiful sight of him," is what causes them to understand and express their love for each other.

Like Cameron and Thrailkill, Hendler believes that the characters who populate nineteenth-century novels often communicate "fellow feeling" without actually speaking. In his reading of Walt Whitman's *Franklin Evans* it is the "unnatural redness" of Evans's face and the "pale" and "color-less[ness]" of his daughter's that express feelings before words can (quoted in Hendler, 2001, 39). Likewise Hendler's reading of Nathaniel Parker Willis's *Paul Fane* finds that the "inner and more true character" of Winifred is "embodied in the expression," an expression, Willis adds, of which the "lineaments," or the features and details of the face and body, "were to be the presence and language" (quoted in Hendler, 2001, 164). It is uncommon to read sentimental literature in this way, focusing on the body as a material expression of sentiment, but Hendler appears to appreciate the performative *and* silent expression of emotion in the nineteenth century. As Hendler rightly points out, however, few were more skeptical of the public expression of sentiment than Henry James. In his fiction it is Miss Birdseye of *The Bostonians* who represents the unseemly results of mixing sympathy with publicity. The most interesting aspect of Miss Birdseye's public displays of sympathy is its effect on her physical form. Described as an "essentially formless old woman," with "no more outline than a bundle of hay," associating with other people in a "vagueness of boundary," Miss Birdseye loses both her physical and personal identity because of her boundless public expression of sympathy (James [1886], 2009, 27). For James, Miss Birdseye's public sympathies threatened the distinction between the feminine domestic and masculine spheres. It would appear that in addition to sympathy, excess public emotion also threatened both physical and personal identity for James. In fact, it is only within this modality of aphonic performative sympathy that characters can communicate their private sentiments openly without risking their identities. James takes what Hendler calls "distressingly public sentiments" such as those expressed by Miss Birdseye and internalizes them in a manner that allows James to be sympathetic without engaging in overt public sentimentality (Hendler, 2001, 147). Conventional sentimentalism clearly makes distressing emotions too public for James. Yet, as we have seen with Maggie and Amerigo, these emotions must somehow be expressed.

The Golden Bowl illustrates James's ideal of internalized, privatized, yet appropriately public sentiment. In one of the most poignant and conversationally sparse dialogues in James's fiction, one can see the "performance" of sentiment threatening but never actually spilling over into inappropriately public behavior: the confrontation between Maggie and Charlotte on the balcony at Fawns, well in view of Maggie's husband, Amerigo, and Mr. Verver, her father and Charlotte's husband:

> Charlotte was still and grave—she had even uttered her remark about the temperature with an expressive weight that verged upon solemnity; so that Maggie, reduced to looking vaguely at the sky, could only feel her not fail of her purpose. "The air's heavy as if with thunder—I think there'll be a storm." She made the suggestion to carry off an awkwardness—which was a part her companion's gain; but the awkwardness didn't diminish in the silence that followed. Charlotte had said nothing in reply; her brow was dark as with a fixed expression, and her high elegance, her handsome head and long straight neck testified through the dusk to their inveterate completeness and noble erectness. It was as if what she had come out to do had already begun, and when, as a consequence, Maggie had said helplessly "Don't you want something? Won't you have my shawl?" everything might have crumbled away in the comparative poverty of the tribute. [Charlotte's] rejection of it had the brevity of a sign that they hadn't closed in for idle words, just as her dim serious face, uninterruptedly presented until they moved again, might have figured the success with which she watched all her messages penetrate. (2004, 2.489–90)

This scene draws its importance less from what Charlotte and Maggie actually say to each other than from the way in which they engage both through speech and silence and through body language. For example, Maggie's manner (she glances "vaguely" upward, speaks "helplessly") reveals that she believes Charlotte will win this conversational duel before it even begins, and Charlotte's responding silence confirms this belief. Correspondingly, Charlotte's adamant silence and aristocratic presence and demeanor make clear that she assumes she will win. Charlotte overpowers Maggie and Maggie fumbles about in awareness of Charlotte's stronger presence, offering her former friend a shawl, which Charlotte without a word refuses. Both know that the real struggle is over possession of Amerigo, but Amerigo himself is left to watch, as is Mr. Verver. Maggie does not know whether her father is aware of their spouses' affairs.

In this all but silent battle, affect translates into skeletal muscle responses even more than into words but, of course, Maggie has become cognizant of Charlotte's affair well before this confrontation. Charlotte had, in fact, "done nothing but meet her eyes"; yet these "demonstrations," as Maggie puts it, reveal "the secret behind every face . . . as [Charlotte] tried to look at her *through* it and in denial of it" (2004, 483). It is precisely these "demonstrations," hidden revelations of her infidelity, that leave Charlotte with "the strangest of impressions . . . deeper than any negation," which "seemed to speak on the part of each" (483). Although Maggie is nervous when Charlotte asks if she has done anything to offend her, Maggie is determined to exhibit a body posture of aggression. She "summon[s] all her powers" against Charlotte in order to hide her apprehension and manages to "avoid at least the disgrace of looking away" (493). At this point Maggie "performs" for Charlotte what she knows and wants in an effort to make Charlotte know that Maggie is cognizant of the affair without actually making a scene. "[E]verything in [Maggie], from head to foot crowded it upon Charlotte that she knew," that she is aware of the infidelity and wants Charlotte to know that she is conscious of it (492). All of Maggie's body except her own voice wants Charlotte to feel the weight of her cognizance of the affair. Yet Maggie cannot publicly perform her emotions—she cannot cry and scream—because to do so would expose Charlotte as an adulteress to her father, Mr. Verver.

Save stating that Maggie does not answer Charlotte's questions, James does not elaborate on what she does to convey to Charlotte that she is conscious of the affair. But of course Maggie cannot risk making a public scene that would ruin Mr. Verver's happiness. All we know of Charlotte is that she responds in like fashion—each must show appropriate modes of feminine reticence while simultaneously addressing the issue of infidelity as their husbands witness this exchange. Neither Maggie nor Charlotte can descend into public verbal accusations and weeping. By privatizing their emotions and conveying them through their bodies and through broken and sometimes irrelevant conversation rather than through explicit words, Maggie and Charlotte publicly express their private emotions in a manner that does not draw attention to themselves. In the end, neither can declare victory because neither can verbalize the truth. Ironically, as James has noted earlier, Maggie's feelings are too heavy to be articulated in words so she performs them. Charlotte and Maggie lie to each other in the sense that they *say* all is well between them even as their body language reveals a deeper alienation than they could ever admit through speech—Maggie "saw it in Charlotte's face and felt it make between them, in the air, a chill that completed the coldness of their conscious perjury" (2004, 2.495). Both know the truth (that Charlotte wants Amerigo for herself); they have felt it, but will not verbalize it to each other. J. Hillis Miller aptly describes this conscious perjury as a performative utterance that serves as a speech act, meaning that although Maggie's and Charlotte's true sentiments are never actually articulated—they lie to each other—each is cognizant of how the other feels because they have expressed their emotions kinesically (2005, 231).

SENTIMENTAL JAMES

James would appear to argue that witnessing and imagining mental suffering, or the consciousness of suffering, stirs within readers an emotional response equal to our sympathy with the misery of an immigrant, prostitute, or factory worker. But he would add that rich American expatriates, though not impoverished, abused by employers, or unable to speak English, experience an exquisite anguish that also demands our sympathies. Suffering indeed demands sympathy. This formula is foundational to sentimental writing, and James's characters suffer. The themes of widowhood, death, and failed love dominate sentimental novels and James's fiction, but these tropes of affective loss have been ignored in his fiction because they manifest themselves through internal psychological turmoil. We learn of his characters' suffering through their inner dialogue, not tears, through authorial portrayal of their mental anguish, not wailing, through body language, not sobbing.

James's work is "scientific" and "unemotional," as most of his critics conclude. He does avoid physical passion and omit emotive signs and responses typically important to sentimental fiction. Yet James's fiction is deeply sentimental. He leads us to uncover the acute suffering of his characters as happiness eludes them and death closes in on them while they cope with the psychological trauma of their experiences. The fact that his characters shed no tears in public and appear emotionally indifferent to their suffering breaks with typically sentimental writing, but it also forces readers to explore the mental suffering the characters' behavior denotes. James wants us to be absorbed into his mind, to focus on the affect of things exterior to ourselves such as witnessed suffering so that we assimilate it into our own psychological architecture. Ultimately, James encourages us to imagine his characters' suffering through spectatorship, and, as Smith explains the process, to recognize it cognitively before letting our emotions interfere. In sum, he puts forth a new ontology of sentiment, one that requires a close examination of the role of the mind in sentimental discourse. The only way to touch and express those hidden "elemental passions" (Edel 1977, 39), which for him were, as he stated, "the true sentiment and. . . manifestations of character" ("*Our Mutual Friend*" [1865] 1957, 75–79), while also keeping them beneath the surface, is to hide them verbally, yet express them through the body. As an artist, he took it as his goal to reveal this private sentiment of the brain and show us how to witness and express emotion and learn from it without resorting to overt sentimental gestures.

NOTE

1. Chapter IX of *Uncle Tom's Cabin*, "In Which it Appears that a Senator is but a Man," has been read both as an example of the influence of the feminine sensibility in the home and as an example of masculine sensibility. But the Senator's claims that "we mustn't suffer our feelings to run away with our judgment" and that the issue is "not a matter of private feeling" also indicate the disparity and threat of a man's separation of private and public sentiments, a separation illustrated by the Senator's public support of the 1850 Fugitive Slave Law despite his private feelings about it (2001, 114).

Afterword

Mary Louise Kete

Fifty years ago Thomas Kuhn in his *Structure of Scientific Revolutions* somewhat wistfully tried to restrict the use of his term "paradigm shift" to the hard sciences. Nonetheless, the essays in *Sentimentalism in Nineteenth-Century America: Literary and Cultural Practices* illustrate the degree to which something very like a Kuhnian paradigm shift has occurred in the field of nineteenth-century American studies. Certainly, these essays demonstrate the ongoing currency of debates about how to define sentimentality and how to account for the various kinds of work it performed for nineteenth-century Americans; and such questions are typical of the period following a paradigm shift, during which the new parameters of the field are explored, tested, and expanded.[1] But in revisiting sentimentalism, these essays also do something that is less typical. In resisting the tendency of new paradigms to erase the traces of their own history, they remind us of how central the study of sentimentality has become to what need no longer be called the "new Americanism."[2]

Such a history would go something like this: by the beginning of the twenty-first century, the concept of sentimentalism became indispensable to answering the new kinds of questions that were being asked by those trying to recover the cultures that had been pushed to, or even off, the margins of American literary, cultural, and intellectual histories. Mary De Jong reminds us in her introduction to this collection that this occurred neither instantaneously nor as the result of a coherent project. Rather, scholars working from various critical positions and on a variety of problems in American literary history found themselves challenged by the inadequacy of critical theorizations of sentimentalism. Because so much about sentimentality in all its forms had escaped New Critical approaches on the one hand and, for very different reasons, escaped conventional historical approaches on the other hand, sentimentalism lay outside—beneath or beyond—what Hans Robert Jauss described as the horizon of expectations against which mid-twentieth century scholars responded to literature.[3] That these scholars should fail is not surprising for many reasons, but most importantly because sentimentality troubles the analytical opposition between text and context in ways most other modes of representation do not or do in lesser degrees. Scholars needed a new kind of poetics—a poetics of culture—whether literary sentimentality was the central topic of concern or whether the subject under discussion was, say, the discourse of marriage law, the genre of the American slave narrative, or the role of nostalgia in popular music. Quite simply, in the study of sentimental praxis, text and context could not be divided from each other.

In teasing out these matters, literary scholars became what Claude Levi-Strauss would have described as *bricoleurs*—appropriating and redeploying to their own purposes insights and methodologies from various academic disciplines, especially those from the social sciences and from philosophy.[4] Today one would be hard put to find courses in nineteenth-century American culture or literature, no matter what the topic, that do not link the conventionally aesthetic questions of "what" and "how" with more conventionally rhetorical or historical questions such as "by whom," "for whom," "to what effects," and "under what material contingencies." In the process, what had once been rather easily dismissed under an unexamined and derogatory label—sentimentalism—has become visible as a complicated and compelling constellation of literary, rhetorical, and material gestures. Once confined to special interest graduate courses, works such as Harriet Beecher Stowe's *Uncle Tom's Cabin*, Frederick Douglass's *Narrative*, and Harriet Jacobs's *Incidents in the Life of a Slave Girl* now figure prominently in general courses on nineteenth-century literature, their sentimental aspects no longer at odds with their status as "literature." Indeed, insofar as graduate and undergraduate seminars devoted to the question of American or British sentimentality now share space quite regularly with courses on the narrative and lyric, it might not be inaccurate to suggest, as De Jong has done, that something like sentimentality studies has emerged over the past ten years.

All this is to say that what in the 1980s and 1990s had posed a clear "problem" for nineteenth-century literary and cultural history—sentimentality—now seems to offer answers to some of the most pressing questions in the field. One of the biggest stresses on the previous paradigm governing the field of American literature and cultural studies was the recovery of texts by women and other non-elites, especially those by African Americans. Long ignored because of their putatively sentimental character, which marked them as presumably "sub-literary," these texts became rallying points for new generations of literary scholars concerned with the cultural work such literature did. The question of the canon—what should be studied and why—remains contentious in and out of the academy even today, but it has also been instantiated as one of the characteristic critical questions of the new discipline. The "canon wars" of the 1990s made much-needed space for the work of authors of color, women, and other non-elites that troubled a triumphalist history of American exceptionalism, while the inclusion of such writers also brought with it a new understanding of the contingency of literary value itself.

But if "lost" authors such as Stowe, Jacobs, and Douglas now receive their full measure of appreciation, we have also, as several essays in this collection make clear, come to appreciate something harder to see: those authors who despite their vociferous claims to being unsentimental were also deeply indebted to what Shirley Samuels has called "The Culture of Sentiment." [5] It might seem as if George Gordon-Smith's essay, "Psychological Sentimentalism: Consciousness, Affect, and the Sentimental Henry James," revisits sentimentalism only in order to recuperate some of the reputation James has recently lost in the reshuffling of the canon by arguing that his "fiction is deeply sentimental." Gordon-Smith's argument, however, goes well beyond proving that the male author James is not immune to the culture of sentimentality. Indeed, most nineteenth-century scholars now freely admit that male authors participated as fully in this culture as did their female peers. Rather, Gordon-Smith turns to models of sentimentalism that emphasize how and to what degree sentimentality shapes subjectivity to intervene in stalled arguments about James's explorations of the growth and operation of consciousness. James may have despised sentimentalists, but the characters that populate his fiction—orphans, widows, betrayed wives, and unfaithful lovers—are straight from the sentimental playbook, and his examinations of their consciousness is dependent on his reworking of the sentimental tropes they represent.

Like Gordon-Smith's, Adam Bradford's essay takes on an author, in this case, Walt Whitman, who made protestations of unsentimentality part of his masculine persona. Bradford elucidates the way Whitman's celebration of himself uses the functional poetics of sentimentality to enlist his readers in a collaborative act of resistance to the radically alienating experience of death. Far from standing for individualism, the self that Whitman celebrates in *Leaves of Grass* invites the reader to join in a shared effort of anticipatory mourning with the promise that such an effort will facilitate the ongoing "'communion,' even the '(re)union,' of the dead with the living." Whitman demonstrates a practiced and innovative deployment of sentimental poetics to resist the disruptions of distance, death, and time by inviting collaboration in the creation of an imagined self (Whitman's) who can stand in not only for those who are mourned but, also, for those who are mourning. Reorienting the study of James and Whitman in relation to sentimental models expands our understanding of sentimentality in ways that are otherwise impossible, and, therefore—at least implicitly—revise and reassert the claims made for these authors for inclusion in the new canon.

Robert Arbour, too, raises the specter of a sentimental Whitman. Like several others in this collection, however, his essay depends upon insights drawn from work on another kind of problem of recent concern among scholars, namely the intersection between the experience of culture that is affected by what used to be called "the text itself" and material circumstances—that is, changes in the literary marketplace and changes in the technologies of printing and reading. As a discourse that, by most definitions, violates established boundaries in order to renegotiate them, sentimentality has been at the heart of such inquiries since Cathy Davidson's pathbreaking work on Susanna Rowson's *Charlotte Temple*. In her study, "The Life and Times of *Charlotte Temple*: The Biography of a Book," sentimentality is the nexus through which the history of the book, the study of gender performance, and the study of narrative theory meet. For Arbour, models of sentimentality help him to unpack the relationship between popular music of the Civil War and Whitman's compelling but critically elusive *Drum-Taps*. In Arbour's account, Whitman is not just alluding to the content of sentimental popular music but also attempting to co-opt the collaborative force of the shared experience of group singing to "engender sympathy even when no consensus exists."

Susan Toth Lord's chapter, "Lydia Maria Child's Use of Sentimentalism in *Letters from New-York*," examines not only how Child uses sentimental representations in her letters but also how the *Letters* themselves are sentimental gestures meant to constitute a "public sentiment" that could meliorate the cultural differences that were increasingly defining the experience of American class identity. Similarly, by studying the way in which Sarah Josepha Hale enlisted the "various features of *Godey's Lady's Book*—editorials, essays, illustrations, fashion plates, the Health Department"—in her project of fashioning maternal authority, Kara Clevinger demonstrates that Hale was fashioning the authority of her magazine as well. Neither problem—how to understand the nature of Hale's argument over maternal authority, nor how to understand the history of magazine publishing itself, in which Hale played such a prominent role—can be treated without reference to sentimentality's ability to work in, through, and across media.

For the most part, the essays in this collection explore the implications that sentimentality studies have for the present field of nineteenth-century studies. But they also show how the effort to understand the poetics of sentimentality is part of a broader, increasingly important argument about the nature and history of American subjectivity under the conditions of liberalism and neoliberalism, an argument now at the center of disciplinary concern. One reason for this is that the question of gender remains a defining aspect of American subjectivity even as it continues to be the topic of intense political debate on the public stage and in popular media. The question of feminine subjectivity in nineteenth-century America led to some of the earliest attention to sentiment as a rhetorical mode, and while this topic has not been exhausted, sentimentality has increasingly been seen to hold the key to how gender conventions were constituted, performed, and negotiated. Kristen Proehl revisits one of the touchstone texts for sentimentality studies, Louisa May Alcott's *Little Women*, reevaluating the techne of sentimentality in order to demonstrate how attention to gender opens up consideration of other ways through which subjectivity is expressed or determined. While Proehl's main concern is with the relationship between literary sentimentalism and the emergence of the tomboy character—a staple figure in posbellum American fiction—her argument points readers to how sentimentalism facilitates the entanglement of key political dimensions of American subjectivity (gender, class, and race) in the Civil War's immediate aftermath. For Proehl, "femininity and sympathy are intertwined" in Alcott's novel since both these ways of experiencing and performing in the world are structured by sentimentalism.

Among the most important reasons why sentimentality studies is central to current arguments about American subjectivity, however, is that scholars of liberalism have been paying attention to the relevance of sympathy and empathy to the theory and experience of liberal subjectivity. Since sympathy is the definitive affect of sentiment, political philosophers such as Simon Critchely and Slavoj Zizek have had to wrestle with the limits and possibilities of "feeling with" another. [6] As Maglina Lubovich, Ken Parille, Elizabeth Petrino, and D. Zachary Finch show, in this respect there is much to learn from the way that nineteenth-century authors themselves recognized, struggled with, and exploited the problem of the relationship between sympathy and the liberal self. Lubovich, for example, focuses on the place of sympathy in the battle to define American identity and the efficacy of sentimentality as a vehicle to claim or enforce this ideal. According to Lubovich, this is the problem that Donald Grant Mitchell addresses in his *Reveries of a Bachelor* of 1850. The material facts of the protagonist's whiteness, maleness, and wealth, all of which should legally guarantee his liberal status, are, Lubovich argues, nevertheless insufficient within a society constructed along sentimental lines. In such a society, where "right citizenship" also demands participation in the affective bonds of marriage and family, Mitchell's bachelor protagonist uses his reveries to ensure belonging. Sharing the imaginative experience of loss of a wife and child that he never actually had, Mitchell's speaker (re)creates himself as the kind of object of sympathy capable of integration into the sentimental union of notional citizenship.

As Lubovich and Finch both point out, however, nineteenth-century writers did not treat the ethics of the sentimental model of the American subject uncritically. Finch focuses on the work of postbellum author Sarah Piatt, whose poetry, much of it devoted to the mother-child relationship, expresses nostalgia for antebellum sentimentalism but also a deep suspicion of its utopian promises. For Finch, Piatt's writing exemplifies what he calls an "Ethics of Postbellum Melancholy," an ethics both produced by and dependent upon the sentimental ethics it replaced. The ethics of melancholy, as expressed by Piatt, allow her to perpetuate the ideal of the sympathetic subject even while it marks the dangers of such idealism to the self and to her offspring, whom the mother risks infecting with her own nostalgia for a time more imagined than real. In neither the antebellum nor the postbellum examples these two scholars treat are the authors free to imagine without anxiety a liberal subject who is not also sympathetic. On the contrary, in these authors, the sentimentalization of sympathy is itself put into question.

No less attentive to the complex role sympathy played in adult-child relationships, Ken Parille and Elizabeth Petrino also explore the limits of sentimentality as it serves the sympathetic subject. Each does this by focusing on antebellum arguments about pedagogy, articulating both voiced and unvoiced assumptions about the nature of individual subjectivity. Parille discusses a range of child-rearing authorities from Horace Mann and Catharine Beecher to the anonymous authors of domestic advice who populated magazines. Within an explicitly American and liberal political context, these authorities grappled with sympathy's limitations as a pedagogical tool. Without sympathy, one remains an animal—a nonself; without sympathy, there are no grounds for a union. But as Parille points out, "boy-nature" was itself viewed as inherently unsympathetic, making the rearing of boys a more critical problem than the rearing of girls. Not only are boys figured as without sympathy for others but also as peculiarly unsympathetic (in the sense of attracting sympathy) to their mothers. While some authorities nonetheless clung to sentimentalism as a means to "civilize" boys, others worried that too much sympathy allowed them to follow their "animal" nature. These authorities encouraged a "pragmatic approach" to the rearing of boys in which discipline played a key role.

As Petrino suggests, the critical study of pedagogic sympathy offers unique and sometimes troubled insights into the question of how the self knows and communicates with others. In a period when the deaf and the blind were segregated and feared minorities within the greater society, Sigourney was concerned with the practical problem of their education. Her association with them both as teacher and patron led her to rethink Romantic theories of language and the self. Among the questions Sigourney pondered was whether and how one could communicate with the physically challenged and what the experience of those without access to symbolic language was and how it could be molded. Tracing the trajectory of Sigourney's argument for the existence of supra-lingual, nonmediated forms of communication, Petrino shows how Sigourney invented a method that made it possible for her disabled students to express themselves and for others to understand them: the "unspoken language" of sympathy. But Sigourney's great faith in this language faltered when she encountered Julia Brace, a blind and deaf student. As Petrino puts it, "deaf and blind children raise[d] the specter of incommunicability" and challenged Sigourney to interrogate "the limits of human understanding and the very definition of personhood" as she understood it. Sigourney thus took a stand within the broader Romantic argument about the nature of subjectivity, making one's personhood dependent upon the ability to recognize and be recognized by others, even while in her treatment of Brace she admitted the possibility that, for all our sympathy, we may never know fully how others feel.

Petrino's essay points to the fourth concern that distinguishes the current field of American literary and cultural studies from its predecessors, namely its willingness to explore the ways that nineteenth-century America contributed to intellectual, social, and economic movements that transcended national boundaries. Although the particular focus of the volume is on North America, essays like Petrino's contribute to our re-evaluation of Romanticism, and essays like Gordon-Smith's and Finch's contribute to our re-evaluation of a nascent Modernism. But if, as I'm suggesting, some knowledge or theory of sentimentalism has become fundamental to answering the questions that are now privileged in the field of American literary and cultural studies, collections such as this also underscore how much still remains for scholars to do.

NOTES

1. First published in 1962, Kuhn's *Structure of Scientific Revolutions* introduced the now ubiquitous terms "paradigm" and "paradigm shift" in his effort to understand the history of science. By paradigm, he meant the explanatory model governing the pursuit of "normal science"—the fundamental assumptions about how the world works, the kind of questions that are explored, and the approved methods for answering those questions. The history of science, Kuhn argued, has been marked by a few revolutions during which normal science is interrupted because the governing paradigm is unable to account for an increasing number of anomalies. After a period during which it seems as if there is no dominant paradigm, an implicit contest between competing models results in the accepted dominance of a new paradigm; "normal science" resumes but under a new set of assumptions. One marker that such a "revolution" has occurred is that the assumptions and values of the old paradigm are so incommensurate with those of the new that they can hardly be recognized as valid.

2. Donald Pease and Robyn Weigman are most associated with the term the "New Americanists," which became the name of a pathbreaking book series from Duke University Press and the focus for a now long-standing summer seminar on the future of American Studies that has done much to articulate what is at stake in the replacement of one set of assumptions and associated concerns and methodologies by another. But the term derived from a 1988 review essay by Frederick Crews, where he identified a significant challenge being posed to the theory and practice—the science or knowing—of American literature and culture being posed by a varied set of critics including Sacvan Bercovitch, Russell Reising, Myra Jehlen, Jane Tompkins, and Philip Fisher, who had all recently published important revisionist studies of the American Renaissance.

3. Along with Kuhn, Hans Robert Jauss (1982) offered a theory to account for the history of fields of study. In *Toward an Aesthetic of Reception* he laid out an argument for theorizing the role that the reader plays in the production of meaning by texts. He also theorizes the role the reader plays in the changes that can be seen, over time, in what is and is not recognized as having enduring cultural value. He offered a powerful metaphor drawn from the natural world—the horizon—to explain the interactive and mutually dependent relationship of the text and the reader. The horizon changes dependent upon the nature of the expectations of the reader. These are relative, in the case of literature, not to altitude or air quality but to social contingencies that might include education, politics, gender, race, and even, the particular circumstances in which one is reading (the classroom, for example, versus the beach). Other theorists from a variety of disciplines, including Hayden White and Pierre Bourdieu, contributed a set of competing and complementary challenges to our theorizing of disciplines and disciplinary change.

4. Although *bricoleur* was picked up as a useful critical term by later literary and cultural theorists such as Jacques Derrida, the anthropologist Claude Levi-Strauss introduced this term in his pathbreaking 1962 study *The Savage Mind* (Paris: Librairie Plon). It connotes the kind of seat-of-the-pants work done by quilters, tinkerers, or home cooks who transform heterogeneous or otherwise found elements to solve an immediate need and in that process often create works of new and unexpected beauty.

5. Samuels's 1992 edited collection *The Culture of Sentiment* did much to lay out the full set of stakes involved in rethinking critical commonplaces concerning sentimentalism. Though elaborated by numerous later critics, Samuels is the first to draw on Pierre Bourdieu's work to argue that sentimentalism was one of the structuring structures—the invisible tenets—of the habitus or set of unexamined, habitual dispositions of nineteenth-century American culture. Playing on the slippage between Bourdieu's French term "habitus" and the English "home," she suggests that the nineteenth-century American "home" depends upon sentimentality.

6. Among Americanists, Lauren Berlant has given this perhaps the most extensive treatment and opened up an important line of inquiry. Recent debates between Simon Critchley and Slavoj Zizek over the nature of the political subject and of political association have had to contend with the concept of sympathy as theorized by eighteenth-century philosophers, especially those of liberalism. Critchley and Zizek have returned to the project of imagining the grounds for association that are not mandated by external authority and produced by some kind of force and, thus, to the related questions of the subject and sympathy that nineteenth-century Americans were exploring within their everyday praxis. See Critchley's 2012 *Faith of the Faithless: Experiments in Political Theology* and Zizek and Glyn Daly's 2004 *Conversations with Zizek*.

References

Abate, Michele Ann. 2006. "Topsy and Topsy-Turvy Jo: Harriet Beecher Stowe's *Uncle Tom's Cabin* and/in Louisa May Alcott's *Little Women.*" *Children's Literature* 34: 59–82.
———. 2008. *Tomboys: A Literary and Cultural History* . Philadelphia: Temple University Press.
Abbott, Jacob. 1837. *Rollo at Work.* Boston: T. H. Webb.
———. 1839. "Advantages of Discerning Peculiarities of Character in Pupils, and of Adapting Oneself to Them." *American Annals of Education and Instruction* 9: 23–32.
———. 1841a. *Lucy at Play.* Boston: T. H. Webb.
———. 1841b. *Rollo at Play.* Boston: T. H. Webb.
Adams, Rachel and David Savran, eds. 2002. *The Masculinity Studies Reader.* Malden: Black-well.
Adorno, Theodor W. 1998. *Critical Models: Interventions and Catchwords.* Translated by Henry W. Pickford. New York: Columbia University Press.
Alcott, Louisa. 1890. *Louisa May Alcott: Her Life, Letters and Journals.* Edited by Ednah D. Cheney. Boston: Roberts Brothers.
———. 1995. *The Selected Letters of Louisa May Alcott.* Edited by Joel Myerson, Daniel Shealy, and Madeleine B. Stern. Athens: University of Georgia Press.
———. 1997. *The Journals of Louisa May Alcott.* Edited by Joel Myerson, Madeleine Stern, and Daniel Shealy. Athens: University of Georgia Press.
———. [1868] 2004a. *Little Women: Or, Meg, Jo, Beth and Amy.* Edited by Anne K. Phillips and Gregory Eiselein. New York: W. W. Norton.
———. [1888] 2004b. "Recollections of My Childhood." In Alcott (2004a): 428–33. "A Mother's Love." 1845. *The Mother's Magazine* 13: 115–16
Ariès, Philippe. 1962. *Centuries of Childhood: A Social History of Family Life*, translated by Robert Baldick. New York: Vintage.
Arthur, T. S. 1845. *Married and Single; or, Marriage and Celibacy Contrasted, in a Series of Domestic Pictures.* Philadelphia: Henry F. Anners.
Barnes, Elizabeth. 1996. "Affecting Relations: Pedagogy, Patriarchy, and the Politics of Sympathy." *American Literary History* 8: 597–614.
———. 1997. *States of Sympathy: Seduction and Democracy in the American Novel.* New York: Columbia University Press.
Baym, Nina. 1998. "Women's Novels and Women's Minds: An Unsentimental View of Nineteenth-Century American Women's Fiction," *Novel* 31 (3): 335–50.
Beecher, Catharine. 1842. *A Treatise on Domestic Economy.* Boston.
B[eers], E[thelinda]. 1861. "The Picket-Guard." *Harper's Weekly* 5 (257): 766.
Bell, Michael. 2000. *Sentimentalism, Ethics, and the Culture of Feeling.* New York: Palgrave.

Bennett, Paula. 1995. "'The Descent of the Angel': Interrogating Domestic Ideology in American Women's Poetry, 1858–1890." *American Literary History* 7: 591–610.

———. 2003. *Poets in the Public Sphere: The Emancipatory Project of American Women's Poetry, 1800-1900.* Princeton: Princeton University Press.

Bennett, Paula Bernat, Karen L. Kilcup, and Philipp Schweighauser, eds. 2007. *Teaching Nineteenth-Century American Poetry.* New York: Modern Language Association.

Bergman, Jill, and Debra Bernardi, eds. 2005. *Our Sisters' Keepers: Nineteenth-Century Benevolence Literature by American Women.* Tuscaloosa: University of Alabama Press.

Berlant, Lauren. 2001. "The Subject of True Feeling: Pain, Privacy and Politics." In *Feminist Consequences: Theory for the New Century*, edited by Elizabeth Bronfen and Misha Kavka, 126–60. New York: Columbia University Press.

Bertolini, Vincent J. 1999. "Fireside Chastity: The Erotics of Sentimental Bachelorhood in the 1850s." In Chapman and Hendler 19–42.

———. 2002. "'Hinting' and 'Reminding': The Rhetoric of Performative Embodiment in *Leaves of Grass*." *ELH* 69 (4): 1047–82.

Bishop, H. R., and John Howard Payne [1823] 1852. "Home Sweet Home." In *Harmonized Songs: Three or Four Voices.* Arranged by James G. Maeder, 3–5. New York: William Hall & Son.

Blight, David. 2001. *Race and Reunion: The Civil War in American Memory.* Cambridge: Harvard University Press.

Bosco, Ronald A., and Joel Myerson. 2003. *Emerson in His Own Time.* Iowa City: University of Iowa Press.

Boudreau, Kristen. 2002. *Sympathy in American Literature: American Sentimentalism from Jefferson to the Jameses.* Gainesville: University Press of Florida.

"Boyhood and Barbarism." 1851. *The American Whig Review* 7: 278–83.

Boym, Svetlana. 2001. *The Future of Nostalgia.* New York: Basic Books.

Brasher, Thomas. 1963. Introduction to *Early Poems and Fiction.* Vol. 9. *Collected Writings of Walt Whitman*, ii–xxii. New York: New York University Press.

Brodhead, Richard. 1993. *Cultures of Letters: Scenes of Reading and Writing in Nineteenth-Century America.* Chicago: University of Chicago Press.

Brown, Gillian. 2001. *The Consent of the Governed: The Lockean Legacy in Early American Culture.* Cambridge, MA: Harvard University Press.

———. 2003. "Child's Play." In Levander and Singley (2003): 13–39.

Brown, Herbert Ross. 1959. *The Sentimental Novel in America 1789–1860.* New York: Pageant Books.

Buell, Lawrence. 2003. *Emerson.* Cambridge: The Belknap Press of Harvard University Press.

Burrows, Edwin G., and Mike Wallace. 1999. *Gotham: A History of New York to 1898.* New York: Oxford University Press.

Burton, Robert. [1621] 1927. *The Anatomy of Melancholy.* New York: Tudor Publishing Company.

Butler, Judith. 1997. *The Psychic Life of Power: Theories in Subjection.* Palo Alto, CA: Stanford University Press.

Cameron, Sharon. 1989. *Thinking in Henry James.* Chicago: University of Chicago Press.

Carpenter, Cari M. 2008. *Seeing Red: Anger, Sentimentality, and American Indians.* Columbus: Ohio State University Press.

Cavitch, Max. 2007. *American Elegy: The Poetry of Mourning from the Puritans to Whitman.* Minneapolis: University of Minnesota Press.

Chandler, Elizabeth Margaret. 1836. *Essays, Philanthropic and Moral, by Elizabeth Margaret Chandler. Principally Relating to the Abolition of Slavery in America.* Philadelphia: Lemuel Howell.

Chapman, Mary, and Glenn Hendler, eds. 1999. *Sentimental Men: Masculinity and the Politics of Affect in American Culture.* Berkeley: University of California Press.

———. 1999. Introduction to *Sentimental Men: Masculinity and Politics of Affect in American Culture*, 1–16. Berkeley: University of California Press.

Cheng, Anne Anlin. 2001. *The Melancholy of Race: Psychoanalysis, Assimilation, and Hidden Grief.* New York: Oxford University Press.

Cherniavsky, Eva. 1995. *That Pale Mother Rising: Sentimental Discourse and the Imitation of Motherhood in 19th-Century America.* Bloomington: Indiana University Press.

Child, Lydia Maria. 1882. *Letters of Lydia Maria Child.* Boston: Houghton Mifflin.

———. [1828] 1989. *The American Frugal Housewife.* Bedford, MA: Applewood Books.

———. [1833] 1996. *An Appeal in Favor of That Class of Americans Called Africans.* Edited by Carolyn L. Karcher. Amherst: University of Massachusetts Press.

———. [1843–1845] 1998. *Letters from New-York.* Edited by Bruce Mills. Athens: University of Georgia Press.

Chudacoff, Howard P. 1999. *The Age of the Bachelor: Creating an American Subculture.* Princeton: Princeton University Press.

Clark, Beverly Lyon. 2004a. Introduction to *Louisa May Alcott: The Contemporary Reviews,* xi–xvii. New York: Cambridge University Press.

———, ed. 2004b. *Louisa May Alcott: The Contemporary Reviews.* New York: Cambridge University Press.

Clark, Elizabeth B. 1995. "'The Sacred Rights of the Weak': Pain, Sympathy, and the Culture of Individual Rights in Antebellum America." *Journal of American History* 62: 463–93.

Claybaugh, Amanda. 2007. *The Novel of Purpose: Literature and Social Reform in the Anglo-American World.* Ithaca, NY: Cornell University Press.

Cleghorn, Cassandra. 1999. "Chivalric Sentimentalism: The Case of Dr. Howe and Laura Bridgman." In Chapman and Hendler 163–80.

Cobb, Lyman. 1847. *The Evil Tendencies of Corporal Punishment.* New York: Mark H. Newman.

Cohen, Margaret. 1999. *The Sentimental Education of the Novel.* Princeton: Princeton University Press.

Cornelius, Steven H. 2004. *Music of the Civil War Era.* American History Through Music Series. Series Ed. David J. Brinkman. Westport, CT: Greenwood Press.

Coviello, Peter. 2005. *Intimacy in America: Dreams of Affiliation in Antebellum Literature.* Minneapolis: University of Minnesota Press.

Crain, Caleb. 2001. *American Sympathy: Men, Friendship, and Literature in the New Nation.* New Haven: Yale University Press.

Crawford, Richard. 2005. *America's Musical Life: A History.* New York: W. W. Norton.

Crews, Frederick. 1988. "Whose American Renaissance?" *New York Review of Books.* 27 October. 68–81.

Critchley, Simon. 2012. *The Faith of the Faithless: Experiments in Political Theology.* New York: Verso.

Culler, Jonathan. 1981. *The Pursuit of Signs: Semiotics, Literature, Deconstruction.* Ithaca, NY: Cornell University Press.

"Danger of Mental Excitement." 1833. *Mechanics' Magazine, and Journal of the Mechanics' Institute* 2: 132 . Accessed July 6, 2011. American Periodicals Series Online, ProQuest (454600102).

Davidson, Cathy N. 1989. "The Life and Times of *Charlotte Temple:* The Biography of a Book." In *Reading in America: Literature and Social History,* edited by Cathy N. Davidson. 157–79. Baltimore: Johns Hopkins University Press.

Davidson, Cathy N., and Jessamyn Hatcher, eds. 2002. Introduction to *No More Separate Spheres! A Next Wave American Studies Reader.* 7–26. Durham: Duke University Press.

Davis, Robert Leigh. 1992. "Whitman's Tympanum: A Reading of *Drum-Taps.*" *American Transcendental Quarterly* 6 (3): 163–75.

Dawson, Melanie. 2003. "The Miniaturizing of Girlhood: Nineteenth-Century Playtime and Gendered Theories of Development." In Levander and Singley 63–84.

De Jong, Mary. [2000] 2011. "Davidson, Lucretia Maria." *American National Biography Online.* Accessed July 6, 2011. http://www.anb.org.libproxy.temple.edu/articles/16/16-00420.html.

Dill, Elizabeth. 2008. "That Damned Mob of Scribbling Siblings: The American Romance as Anti-Novel in *The Power of Sympathy* and, *Pierre.*" *American Literature* 80 (4): 707–37.

Dizikes, John. 1993. *Opera in America: A Cultural History.* New Haven: Yale University Press.

Dobson, Joanne. 1997. "Reclaiming Sentimental Literature." *American Literature* 69: 263–88.

Doriani, Beth Maclay. 1996. *Emily Dickinson: Daughter of Prophecy*. Amherst: University of Massachusetts Press.

Douglas, Ann. 1977a. *The Feminization of American Culture*. New York: Knopf.

———. 1977b. *The Feminization of American Culture*. New York: Noonday Press.

———. [1977] 1988. *The Feminization of American Culture*. New York: Doubleday.

Edel, Leon. 1977. *Henry James: A Life*. New York: Harper & Row.

Elbert, Sarah. 1988. *Hunger for Home: Louisa May Alcott's Place in American Culture*. Newark, NJ: Rutgers University Press.

Elliott, Maud Howe. 1904. *Laura Bridgman: Dr. Howe's Famous Pupil and What He Taught Her*. Boston: Little Brown.

Ellis, Mrs. 1852. "The Mother's Love." *Godey's Lady's Book* 44: 163–64.

Embury, Emma C. 1844. "The Rights of Children." *Godey's Lady's Book* 28: 80–83. Accessed July 6, 2011. American Periodicals Series Online, ProQuest (326957861).

Eng, David L., and David Kazanjian, eds. 2003. *Loss: The Politics of Mourning*. Berkeley: University of California Press.

Farrell, James J. 1980. *Inventing the American Way of Death, 1830–1920*. Philadelphia: Temple University Press.

Faust, Drew Gilpin. 1992. *Southern Stories: Slaveholders in Peace and War*. Columbia: University of Missouri Press.

———. 2008. *This Republic of Suffering: Death and the American Civil War*. New York: Vintage.

Fiedler, Leslie A. [1960] 1966. *Love and Death in the American Novel*. Urbana-Champaign, IL: Dalkey Archive Press.

Finch, Francis Miles. 1867. "The Blue and the Gray." *The Atlantic Monthly* 20:119. September, 1867: 369–70.

Finkelstein, Barbara. 1985. "Casting Networks of Good Influence: The Reconstruction of Childhood in the United States, 1790-1870." In Hawes and Hiner 111–52.

Fisher, Philip. 1985. *Hard Facts: Setting and Form in the American Novel*. New York: Oxford University Press.

Folsom, Ed. 2006. "Nineteenth-Century Visual Culture." In *A Companion to Walt Whitman*, edited by Donald D. Kummings, 272–89. New York: Blackwell.

Foote, Stephanie. 2005. "Resentful Little Women: Gender and Class Feeling in Louisa May Alcott." *College Literature* 32: 63–85.

Ford, Thomas. 1965. "Emily Dickinson and the Civil War." *University Review of Kansas City* 31: 199–203.

Foster, Travis. 2010. "Grotesque Sympathy: Lydia Maria Child, White Reform, and the Embodiment of Urban Space." *ESQ* 56: 1–32.

Foucault, Michel. 1978. *The History of Sexuality*. New York: Pantheon Books.

Freud, Sigmund. 1948. *Collected Papers, Volume 4*. Edited by Ernest Jones. Translated by Joan Riviere. London: Hogarth Press.

———. [1917] 1963. "Mourning and Melancholia." In *General Psychological Theory: Papers on Metapsychology*, Introduction by Philip Rieff. Translated by Joan Riviere, 61–78. New York: Collier Books.

———. 1989. *Civilization and Its Discontents*. New York: Norton.

Gac, Scott. 2007. *Singing for Freedom: The Hutchinson Family Singers and the Nineteenth Century Culture of Reform*. New Haven: Yale University Press.

Gardiner, Judith Kegan. 2002. "Theorizing Age and Gender: Bly's Boys, Feminism and Maturity Masculinity." In *Masculinity Studies & Feminist Theory: New Directions*, edited by Judith Kegan Gardiner, 90–118. New York: Columbia University Press.

Gaul, Theresa Strouth, and Sharon M. Harris. 2009. Introduction to *Letters and Cultural Transformations in the United States, 1760-1860*. 1–14. Burlington, VT: Ashgate.

Genoways, Ted. 2006. "The Disorder of *Drum-Taps*." *Walt Whitman Quarterly Review* 24 (2): 98–117.

Gernes, Todd. 1992. "Recasting the Culture of Ephemera: Young Women's Literary Culture in Nineteenth-Century America." PhD dissertation. Brown University.

Ginzberg, Lori D. 1992. *Women and the Work of Benevolence: Morality, Politics, and Class in the Nineteenth-Century United States.* New Haven, CT: Yale University Press.

Graham, Edward K. 1908. "The Necessary Melancholy of Bachelors." *Putnam's Monthly and the Reader.* Vol. 4: 695–97.

Graham, Wendy. 1999. *Henry James's Thwarted Love.* Palo Alto, CA: Stanford University Press.

Grant, Julia. 1998. *Raising Baby by the Book: The Education of American Mothers.* New Haven, CT: Yale University Press.

Gray, Janet Sinclair. 2004. *Race and Time: American Women's Poetics from Antislavery to Racial Modernity.* Iowa City: University of Iowa Press.

Greyser, Naomi. 2007. "Affective Geographies: Sojourner Truth's *Narrative*, Feminism, and the Ethical Blind of Sentimentalism." *American Literature* 79 (2): 275–305.

Gruesz, Kristen Silva. 1999. "Feeling for the Fireside: Longfellow, Lynch, and the Topography of Poetic Power." In Chapman and Hendler, 43–63.

Gumpert, Gustav. 1861. "The Dying Volunteer of the 6th Massachusetts Regiment." Philadelphia: G. André & Co.

Haight, Gordon S. 1930. *Mrs. Sigourney, the Sweet Singer of Hartford.* New Haven, CT: Yale University Press.

Hale, Sarah J. 1842. "Editors' Table: Conversations at the Editors' Table." *Godey's Lady's Book* 25: 58–59. Accessed July 6, 2011. American Periodicals Series Online, ProQuest (326953271).

———. 1845. "Editors' Table." *Godey's Lady's Book* 31: 44–46. Accessed July 6, 2011. American Periodicals Series Online, ProQuest (326962481).

———. 1845. "The Empire of Woman," *Godey's Lady's Book* 31:12. Accessed July 6, 2011. American Periodicals Series Online, ProQuest (326962341).

———. 1858. "Editors' Table: OUR LITLE CHILDREN, SHALL THEY LIVE?" *Godey's Lady's Book* 57: 81–84. Accessed July 6, 2011. American Periodicals Series Online, ProQuest (336745861).

Halttunen, Karen. 1982. *Confidence Men and Painted Women: A Study of Middle-Class Culture in America, 1830–1870.* New Haven, CT: Yale University Press.

Hamm, Charles. 1979. *Yesterdays: Popular Song in America.* New York: Norton.

Hanawalt, Jean Allen. 1981. "A Biographical and Critical Study of John James and Sarah Morgan (Bryan) Piatt." PhD dissertation, University of Washington.

Haralson, Eric. 1996. "Mars in Petticoats: Longfellow and Sentimental Masculinity." *Nineteenth-Century Literature* 51 (3): 327–55.

Harris, Susan K. 1990. *19th-Century American Women's Novels: Interpretive Strategies.* New York: Cambridge University Press.

Hawes, Joseph, and N. Ray Hiner, eds. 1985. *American Childhood: A Research Guide and Historical Handbook.* Westport, CT: Greenwood Press.

Hayes, Kevin J., ed. 1996. *Henry James: The Contemporary Reviews.* Cambridge: Cambridge University Press.

Hays, Sharon. 1995. *The Cultural Contradictions of Motherhood.* New Haven, CT: Yale University Press.

Henderson, Desiree. 2011. *Grief and Genre in American Literature, 1790-1870.* Burlington, VT: Ashgate.

Hendler, Glenn. 1991. "The Limits of Sympathy: Louisa May Alcott and the Sentimental Novel." *American Literary History* 3: 685–706.

———. 2001. *Public Sentiments: Structures of Feeling in Nineteenth-Century American Literature.* Chapel Hill: University of North Carolina Press.

Hendler, Glenn and Mary Chapman, eds. 1999. *Sentimental Men: Masculinity and the Politics of Affect in American Culture.* Berkeley: University of California Press.

Hewitt, Elizabeth. 2004. *Correspondence and American Literature, 1770–1865.* Cambridge: Cambridge University Press.

Hoeller, Hildegard. 2006. "From Agony to Ecstasy: The New Studies of American Sentimentality." *ESQ* 52.(4): 339–69.

Hollis, C. Carol. 1964. "The 'Mad Poet' McDonald Clarke." In *Essays and Studies in Language and Literature*, 250–67. New York: Duquesne University Press.

Homestead, Melissa J. 2006. Review of *Our Sisters' Keepers: Nineteenth-Century Benevolence Literature by American Women. Journal of the Midwest Modern Language Association* 39 (1): 174–77.

Howard, June. 1999. "What Is Sentimentality." *American Literary History* 11.(1): 63–81.

Howe, Julia Ward. 1862. "Battle Hymn of the Republic." Boston: Oliver Ditson & Co.

Howells, William Dean. 1874. "Recent Literature." *Atlantic Monthly* 34: 201. July 1874: 104–5.

——. 1887. "Editor's Study." *Harper's Monthly* 74: 829.

Hutchinson, George. 2003. "Race and the Family Romance: Whitman's Civil War." *Walt Whitman Quarterly Review* 20 (3): 134–50.

Irmscher, Christoph. 2009. *Public Poet, Private Man: Henry Wadsworth Longfellow at 200*. Amherst: University of Massachusetts Press.

Jackson, Charles O. 1977. *Passing: The Vision of Death in America*. Westport, CT: Greenwood Press.

Jackson, Virginia. 2005. *Dickinson's Misery: A Theory of Lyric Reading*. Princeton, NJ: Princeton University Press.

James, Henry. [1878] 1920. "Longstaff's Marriage." *Master Eustace*. New York: Thomas Seltzer.

——. [1865] 1957. *"Our Mutual Friend." Literary Reviews and Essays by Henry James*. Ed. Albert Mordell James. New York: Twayne.

——. [1895] 1996. "The Altar of the Dead." *Henry James: Complete Stories, 1892-1898*. New York: Library of America.

——. [1899] 1997. "Maud-Evelyn." *Henry James: Complete Stories, 1898-1910*. New York: Library of America.

——. [1902] 1999. *The Wings of the Dove*. New York: Signet Classics.

——. [1904] 2004. *The Golden Bowl*. New Milford, CT: Toby Publishing.

——. [1886] 2009. *The Bostonians*. Oxford: Oxford Classics.

James, William. 1993. *The Correspondence of William James*, Vol. I. *William and Henry, 1861-1884*, edited by Ignas K. Skrupskelis and Elizabeth M. Berkeley. Charlottesville, VA: University Press of Virginia.

Jauss, Hans Robert. 1982. *Toward an Aesthetic of Reception*. Minneapolis: University of Minnesota Press.

["John Brown's Body."] "Glory! Glory! Hallelujah!" 1861. As Sung by the Federal Volunteers Throughout the Union. Boston: Oliver Ditson & Co.

Johnson, Barbara. 1986. "Apostrophe, Animation, and Abortion." *Diacritics* 16 (1): 28–47.

Jones, Gavin. 2003. "Poverty and the Limits of Literary Criticism." *American Literary History*. 5: 765–92.

Kaplan, Amy. 1998. "Manifest Domesticity." *American Literature* 70 (3): 581–606.

Kaplan, Justin. 1986. *Walt Whitman: A Life*. Touchstone Edition. New York: Simon & Schuster.

Karcher, Carolyn L. 1994. *The First Woman in the Republic: A Cultural Biography of Lydia Maria Child*. Durham, NC: Duke University Press.

Kazin, Alfred. 1997. *God and the American Writer*. New York: Knopf.

Kelly, Gary, ed. 2008. *Lydia Sigourney: Selected Poems and Prose*. Buffalo: Broadview Press.

Kent, Katherine. 2003. *Making Girls into Women: American Women's Writing and the Rise of Lesbian Identity*. Durham, NC: Duke University Press.

Kerber, Linda. [1980]1986. *Women of the Republic: Intellect and Ideology in Revolutionary America*. New York: Norton.

Kete, Mary Louise. 2000. *Sentimental Collaborations: Mourning and Middle-Class Identity in Nineteenth-Century America*. Durham, NC: Duke University Press.

Key, Susan. 1995. "Sound and Sentimentality: Nostalgia in the Songs of Stephen Foster." *American Music* 13(2): 145–66.

Kidd, Kenneth. 2004. *Making American Boys: Boyology and the Feral Tale*. Minneapolis: University of Minnesota Press.

Kimball, George. 1889. "Origin of the John Brown Song." *The New England Magazine* 7 (4): 371–77.

Kincheloe, Pamela J. 1997. "Through the Claude Glass: Nineteenth-Century American Writers and Monumental Discourse." PhD dissertation, Southern Illinois University, Carbondale.

———. 1999. "Two Visions of Fairyland: Ireland and the Monumental Discourse of the Nineteenth-Century Tourist." *Irish Studies Review* 7: 41–51.

King, Pendleton. [1884] 2003. "Notes on Conversations with Mr. Emerson." In *Emerson in His Own Time*, edited by Ronald A. Bosco and Joel Myerson, 128–35. Iowa City: Iowa University Press.

Kirk, E. N. 1843. "Useful Monarchs Educated by Mothers." *The Mother's Magazine and Family Library* 11: 167.

Kittredge, Walter. 1864. "Tenting on the Old Camp Ground." Adapted and Sung by the Hutchinson Family: Tribe of Asa. Boston: Oliver Ditson & Co.

Krentz, Christopher. 2007. *Writing Deafness: The Hearing Line in Nineteenth-Century American Literature*. Chapel Hill: University of North Carolina Press.

Kuhn, Thomas. 1962. *Structure of Scientific Revolutions*. Chicago: University of Chicago Press.

Laderman, Gary. 1996. *The Sacred Remains: American Attitudes Toward Death, 1799–1883*. New Haven, CT: Yale University Press.

Laffrado, Laura. 2009. *Uncommon Women: Gender and Representation in Nineteenth-Century U. S. Women's Writing*. Columbus: Ohio State University Press.

"Lament of an Old Bachelor." 1838. *Southern Literary Messenger* 4(8): 523–24.

Lane, Harlan. 1984. *When The Mind Hears: A History of the Deaf.* New York: Random House.

Lane, Harlan, Richard C. Pillard, and Ulf Hedberg, eds. 2010. *The People of the Eye: Deaf Ethnicity and Ancestry*. New York: Oxford University Press.

Leland, Heather Roberts. 2004. "'The Public Heart': Urban Life and the Politics of Sympathy in Lydia Maria Child's *Letters from New York*." *American Literature* 76 (4): 749–75.

Levander, Caroline. 2006. *Cradle of Liberty: Race, Child and National Belonging from Thomas Jefferson to W.E.B. Du Bois*. Durham, NC: Duke University Press.

Levander, Caroline F., and Carol J. Singley, eds. 2003. *The American Child: A Cultural Studies Reader*. New Brunswick, NJ: Rutgers University Press.

Levi-Strauss, Claude. 1962. *The Savage Mind*. Paris: Librairie Plon.

Lewis, Jan. 1997. "Mother's Love: The Construction of an Emotion in Nineteenth-Century America." In *Mothers and Motherhood: Readings in American History,* edited by Rima D. Apple and Janet Golden, 52–71. Columbus: Ohio State University Press.

"Little Hands." 1861. *Godey's Lady's Book* 62: 439. Accessed July 6, 2011. American Periodicals Series Online, ProQuest (337332941).

Locke, John. [1693] 1996. *Some Thoughts Concerning Education and Of the Conduct of the Understanding*. Indianapolis, IN: Hackett.

Longfellow, Henry Wadsworth. 1849. *Kavanagh*. Boston: Ticknor, Reed and Fields.

———. [1849] 1901. *The Seaside and the Fireside*. In *The Poetical Works of Henry Wadsworth Longfellow*, edited by Henry Frowde, 174–93. London: Oxford University Press.

"Look at the Results." 1843. *The Mother's Magazine* 11: 54–59.

Luciano, Dana. 2007. *Arranging Grief: Sacred Time and the Body in Nineteenth-Century America*. New York: New York University Press.

Lyda, Heather. "Textual Editing Project: 'The Deaf, Dumb, and Blind Girl,' by Lydia Howard Sigourney, 1828." 17 November 2006. http://www.westga.edu/~perben/Engl%204125/early_american_fiction_proje.htm.

Macarthy, Harry. 1861. "The Bonnie Blue Flag." New Orleans: A. E. Blackmar & Bro.

Madeley, Edward. 1902. *The Science of Correspondences Elucidated: The Key to the Heavenly and True Meaning of the Sacred Scriptures*. London: James Speirs.

Manjerovic, Maureen, and Michael J. Budds. 2002. "More Than a Drummer Boy's War: A Historical View of Musicians in the American Civil War." *College Music Symposium* 42: 118–30.

Mann, Horace. 1843. *Sixth Annual Report of the Board of Education, Together with the Sixth Annual Report of the Secretary of the Board*. Boston: Dutton and Wentworth.

Marcellin, Leigh-Anne. 2000. "'Singing off the Charnel Steps': Soldiers and Mourners in Emily Dickinson's War Poetry." *The Emily Dickinson Journal* 9 (2): 64–74.

Marshall, David. 1988. *The Surprising Effects of Sympathy: Marivaux, Diderot, Rousseau, and Mary Shelley.* Chicago: University of Chicago Press.

Marvel, Ik [Mitchell, Donald Grant]. 1850. *Reveries of a Bachelor; or, A Book of the Heart.* Philadelphia: David McKay.

———. [1851] 1893. *Dream Life: A Fable of the Seasons.* Philadelphia: Henry Altemus.

"Maternal Influence." 1835. *Godey's Lady Book* 11: 73.

Matteson, John. 2007. *Eden's Outcasts: The Story of Louisa May Alcott and Her Father.* New York: W.W. Norton.

McIntosh, James. 2000. *Nimble Believing: Dickinson and the Unknown.* Ann Arbor: University of Michigan Press.

McMillen, Sally G. 2008. *Seneca Falls and the Origins of the Women's Rights Movement.* Oxford: Oxford University Press.

Miller, J. Hillis. 2005. *Literature as Conduct: Speech Acts in Henry James.* New York: Fordham University Press.

Mills, Bruce. 1998. Introduction to *Letters from New-York* by Lydia Maria Child, ix–xxviii. Athens: University of Georgia Press.

Moody, Joycelyn. 2001. *Sentimental Confessions: Spiritual Narratives of Nineteenth-Century African American Women Authors.* Athens: University of Georgia Press.

Moon, Michael. 1991. *Disseminating Whitman: Revision and Corporeality in* Leaves of Grass. Cambridge, MA: Harvard University Press.

Moseley, Caroline. 1984. "'When Will Dis Cruel War be Ober?': Attitudes Toward Blacks in Popular Song of the Civil War." *American Music* 2 (3): 1–26.

"Mothers, Do You Sympathize with Your Children?" 1856. In *The Mother's Rule; or, The Right Way and the Wrong Way,* edited by T. S. Arthur. Philadelphia: H. C. Peck and Theo. Bliss.

Myerson, Joel, and Daniel Shealy, eds. 1997. *The Journals of Louisa May Alcott.* Athens: University of Georgia Press.

Noble, Marianne. 2000. *The Masochistic Pleasures of Sentimental Literature.* Princeton, NJ: Princeton University Press.

Nudelman, Franny. 2004. *John Brown's Body: Slavery, Violence, & the Culture of War.* Chapel Hill, NC: University of North Carolina Press.

Okker, Patricia. 1995. *Our Sister Editors: Sarah J. Hale and the Tradition of Nineteenth-Century American Women Editors.* Athens, GA: University of Georgia Press.

Otter, Samuel. 1999. *Melville's Anatomies: Bodies, Discourse, and Ideology in Antebellum America.* Berkeley: University of California Press.

Parris, Brandy. 2003. "Difficult Sympathy in the Reconstruction-Era Animal Stories of *Our Young Folks.*" *Children's Literature* 31: 25–49.

Penry, Tara. 1999. "Sentimental and Romantic Masculinities in *Moby-Dick* and *Pierre.*" In Chapman and Hendler 226–43.

———. 2010. "Sentiment and Style." In *A Companion to American Literature and Culture,* ed. Paul Lauter. 221–36. Malden, MA: Wiley Blackwell.

Piatt, Sarah. 1882. *A Book About Baby. And Other Poems in Company with Children.* Boston: D. Lothrop and Company.

———. 2001. *Palace-Burner: The Selected Poetry of Sarah Piatt.* Edited by Paula Bernat Bennett. Urbana, IL: University of Illinois Press.

Picker, John M. 2000. "'Red War Is My Song': Whitman, Higginson, and Civil War Music." In *Walt Whitman and Modern Music: War, Desire, and the Trials of Nationhood,* edited by Lawrence Kramer, 1–25. New York: Garland.

"Precocious Children." 1859. *Godey's Lady's Book* 58: 153–54. Accessed July 6, 2011. American Periodicals Series Online, ProQuest (336749081).

"Precocity." 1820. *Euterpeiad, or Musical Intelligencer, and Ladies Gazette* 1 (30): 119. Accessed July 6, 2011. American Periodicals Series Online, ProQuest (1118654332).

Proehl, Kristen. 2011. "Battling Girlhood: Sympathy, Race, and the Tomboy Narrative in American Literature." PhD Dissertation, The College of William and Mary.

"Recent Poetry by Women." 1880. *Scribner's Monthly* 19 (4):635.

Review of James's *Roderick Hudson.* 1876. *North American Review* 122: 421–25.

Reynolds, David S. 1988. *Beneath the American Renaissance.* New York: Knopf.

———. 1995. *Walt Whitman's America: A Cultural Biography.* New York: Knopf.

Richards, Z. "Discipline—Moral and Mental." 1855. *The American Journal of Education* 1: 107–19.

Richardson, Joan. 2007. *A Natural History of Pragmatism: The Fact of Feeling from Jonathan Edwards to Gertrude Stein.* Cambridge: Cambridge University Press.

Robbins, Sarah. 2004a. *Managing Literacy, Mothering America: Women's Narratives on Reading and Writing in the Nineteenth Century.* Pittsburgh: University of Pittsburgh Press.

———. 2004b. "Periodizing Authorship, Characterizing Genre: Catharine Maria Sedgwick's Benevolent Literacy Narratives." *American Literature* 76 (1): 1–29.

Roberts, Heather. 2004. "'The Public Heart': Urban Life and the Politics of Sympathy in Lydia Maria Child's *Letters from New York*." *American Literature* 76 (4): 749–75.

Roberts, Jessica. 1997. "The American Poetry of Sarah Morgan Bryan Piatt." Honors thesis. Dartmouth College.

Romero, Lora. 1992. "Vanishing Americans: Gender, Empire, and New Historicism." In Samuels 115–27.

———. 1997. *Home Fronts: Domesticity and its Critics in the Antebellum United States.* Durham: Duke University Press.

Root, George F. 1863. "Just After the Battle." Chicago: Root & Cady.

———. 1861. "The Vacant Chair. Or, We Shall Meet, But We Shall Miss Him." Chicago: Root & Cady.

Roper, Robert. 2008. *Now the Drum of War: Walt Whitman and His Brothers in the Civil War.* New York: Walker & Company.

Rotundo, E. Anthony. 1998. "Boy Culture." In *The Children's Culture Reader* edited by Henry Jenkins, 337–62 . New York: New York University Press, 1998.

Rousseau, Jean-Jacques. [1762] 2005. *Emile.* Abridged. Translated by William H. Payne. London: Appleton.

Rust, Richard Dilworth, et al., eds. 1978. *The Complete Works of Washington Irving.* Volume I: 1802–1823. Boston: Twayne Publishers.

Ryan, Mary. 1982. *Empire of the Mother: American Writing about Domesticity, 1830–1860.* New York: Haworth Press.

Ryan, Susan M. 2003. *The Grammar of Good Intentions: Race and the Antebellum Culture of Benevolence.* Ithaca, NY: Cornell University Press.

Samuels, Shirley, ed. 1992. *The Culture of Sentiment: Race, Gender, and Sentimentality in Nineteenth-Century America.* New York: Oxford University Press.

Sánchez-Eppler, Karen. 1992. "Bodily Bonds: The Intersecting Rhetorics of Feminism and Abolition." In Samuels 92–114.

———. 1999. "Then When We Clutch Hardest: On the Death of a Child and the Replication of an Image." In Hendler and Chapman 64–85.

———. 2000. "Playing at Class." *English Literary History.* 67 (3): 819–42.

———. 2005. *Dependent States: The Child's Part in Nineteenth-Century American Culture.* Chicago: University of Chicago Press.

Sawaya, Francesca. 1999. "Sentimental Tentacles: Frank Norris's *The Octopus*." In Hendler and Chapman 259–71.

Saxton, Martha. 1995. *Louisa May Alcott: A Modern Biography.* New York: The Noonday Press.

Sayers, Edna Edith, and Diana Gates. 2008. "Lydia Huntley Sigourney and the Beginnings of Deaf Education in America: It Takes a Village." *Sign Language Studies* 8 (4): 369–411.

Schiesari, Juliana. 1992. *The Gendering of Melancholia: Feminism, Psychoanalysis and the Symbolics of Loss in Renaissance Literature.* Ithaca, NY: Cornell University Press.

Sedgwick, Catharine Maria. 1835. *Home.* Boston: James Munroe.

Sedgwick, Eve Kosofsky. 1990. *Epistemology of the Closet.* Berkeley: University of California Press.

Shakespeare, William. 1942. *The Complete Plays and Poems of William Shakespeare.* Edited by William Allan Neilson and Charles Jarvis Hill. Cambridge, MA: The Riverside Press.

Shamir, Milette, and Jennifer Travis. 2002. *Boys Don't Cry?: Rethinking Narratives of Masculinity and Emotion in the U.S.* New York: Columbia University Press.

Shelton, F.W. 1853. "On Old Bachelors." *The Southern Literary Messenger* 19 (4): 223–28.

Sicker, Philip. 1980. *Love and the Quest for Identity in the Fiction of Henry James.* Princeton, NJ: Princeton University Press.

Sigourney, Lydia. [1827] 1850. "Death of an Infant." In *Select Poems by Mrs. L. H. Sigourney,* 30–31. Philadelphia: A. Hart.

———. 1835. *Tales and Essays for Children.* Hartford: F. J. Huntington.

———. 1837a. "Do Your Duty to Your Brothers and Sisters." *Youth's Magazine* (July 7, 1837): 230–232.

———. 1837b. *Zinzendorf and other Poems.* New York: Leavitt, Lord and Co.

———. 1838a. "Laura Bridgman, The Deaf, Dumb, and Blind Girl of the Boston Institution for the Blind." *The Lady's Book and Magazine* 16 (June 1838): 252.

———. 1838b. *Letters to Mothers.* Hartford: Hudson and Skinner.

———. 1853a. *The Faded Hope.* New York: Robert Carter and Brothers.

———. 1853b. *Letters to My Pupils, With Narrative and Biographical Sketches.* New York: Robert Carter & Brothers.

———. 1854. *The Western Home, and Other Poems.* Philadelphia: Parry and Macmillan.

Silber, Nina. 1993. *The Romance of Reunion: Northerners and the South, 1865–1900.* Chapel Hill: University of North Carolina Press.

Smith, Adam. [1759] 1976. *The Theory of Moral Sentiments.* Indianapolis: Liberty Classics.

Snyder, Katherine V. 1999. *Bachelors, Manhood and the Novel, 1850–1925.* Cambridge: Cambridge University Press.

Solomon, Robert C. 2004. *In Defense of Sentimentality.* New York: Oxford University Press.

Sorby, Angela. 2005. *Schoolroom Poets: Childhood, Performance, and the Place of American Poetry, 1865–1917.* Durham, NH: University of New Hampshire Press.

Sorisio, Carolyn. 2000. "The Spectacle of the Body: Torture in the Antislavery Writing of Lydia Maria Child and Frances E. W. Harper." *Modern Language Studies* 30 (1): 45–66.

"*Southern Review, The*" 5.10. [1869] 2004. In Clark (2004b): 69.

Spargo, R. Clifton. 2004. *The Ethics of Mourning: Grief and Responsibility in Elegiac Literature.* Baltimore, MD: Johns Hopkins University Press.

Spiro, Lisa. 1999. Introduction. "'Smoke, Flame and Ashes.' A 'Reverie' from Ik Marvel's (Donald Grant Mitchell) *Reveries of a Bachelor*. A Critical Edition with Facsimile." Last modified. Nov. 4. 1999. http://etext.lib.virginia.edu/users/spiro/Contents2.html.

———. 2003. "Reading with a Tender Rapture: *Reveries of a Bachelor* and the Rhetoric of Detached Intimacy." *Book History* 6: 57–93.

Steele, Jeffrey A. 2001. "The Limits of Political Sympathy: Emerson, Margaret Fuller, and Woman's Rights." In *The Emerson Dilemma: Essays on Emerson and Social Reform,* edited by T. Gregory Garvey, 115–35. Athens: University of Georgia Press.

Stern, Julia A. 1997. *The Plight of Feeling: Sympathy and Dissent in the Early American Novel.* Chicago: University of Chicago Press.

Sterne, Madeleine B. 1997. Introduction to *The Journals of Louisa May Alcott,* 3–39. In Myerson and Shealy.

Stowe, Harriet Beecher. [1852] 1981. *Uncle Tom's Cabin; or Life Among the Lowly.* New York: Penguin.

———. [1852] 2001. *Uncle Tom's Cabin: or, Life Among the Lowly.* New York: The Modern Library.

———. 2010. *Uncle Tom's Cabin.* Edited by Elizabeth Ammons. 2nd ed. New York: Norton.

Swedenborg, Emanuel. 1913. *The Path of Life.* Compiled, translated, and edited by John Curtis Ager. New York: The New-Church Press.

Tawa, Nicholas. 1975. "The Performance of Parlor Songs in America, 1790–1860." *Annuario Interamericano de Investigación Musical* 11: 69–81.

———. 1984. *A Music for the Millions: Antebellum Democratic Attitudes and the Birth of American Popular Music.* The Sociology of Music. No. 3. New York: Pendragon.

"The Bright Side." 1856. In *The Mother's Rule; or, The Right Way and the Wrong Way.* Edited by T. S. Arthur. Philadelphia: H. C. Peck and Theo. Bliss. 193–98.

"The Comforts of Playing 'Hookie.'" 1856. *The Mother's Magazine for Daughters and Mothers* 25: 91–92.

"The Profession of Schoolmaster." 1858. *North American Review* 86: 40–59.

Thrailkill, Jane. 2007. *Affecting Fictions: Mind, Body, and Emotion in American Realism.* Cambridge, MA: Harvard University Press.

Tompkins, Jane. 1985. *Sensational Designs: The Cultural Work of American Fiction 1790–1860.* New York: Oxford University Press.

Tonkovich, Nicole. 1997. *Domesticity with a Difference: The Nonfiction of Catharine Beecher, Sarah J. Hale, Fanny Fern, and Margaret Fuller.* Jackson: University Press of Mississippi.

"Training of Boys I." 1845a. *The Mother's Journal and Family Visitant* 10: 117–19.

"Training of Boys III." 1845b. *The Mother's Journal and Family Visitant* 10: 147–49.

"Training of Boys IV." 1845c. *The Mother's Journal and Family Visitant* 10: 164–67.

Traubel, Horace. 1906. *With Walt Whitman in Camden.* Boston: Small, Maynard & Company.

Trobridge, George. 1928. *Emanuel Swedenborg: His Life, Teachings, and Influence.* New York: The New-Church Press.

Vendler, Helen. 2005. *Invisible Listeners: Lyric Intimacy in Herbert, Whitman, and Ashbery.* Princeton: Princeton University Press.

Warhol, Robin. 1989. *Gendered Interventions: Narrative Discourse in the Victorian Novel.* New Brunswick, NJ: Rutgers University Press.

Wait, Gary E. 1992. "Julia Brace." *Dartmouth Library College Bulletin.* Internet. http://www.dartmouth.edu/~library/Library_Bulletin/Nov1992/LB-N92-Wait.html.

Wearn, Mary McCartin. 2006. "Subjection and Subversion in Sarah Piatt's Maternal Poetics." *Legacy* 23 (2): 163–77.

———. 2007. *Negotiating Motherhood in Nineteenth-Century American Literature.* New York : Routledge.

Weinstein, Cindy. 2004. *Family, Kinship, and Sympathy in Nineteenth-Century American Literature.* Cambridge: Cambridge University Press.

West, Rebecca. 1916. *Henry James.* New York: H. Holt.

Wexler, Laura. 1992. "Tender Violence: Literary Eavesdropping, Domestic Fiction, and Educational Reform." In Samuels 9–38.

"What is to be done with Charley?" 1860. *The Mother's Magazine and Family Circle* 28: 14–17.

Whitman, Walt. 1842a. [Untitled]. *New York Aurora,* March 8, p. 2.

———. 1842b. "The Death and Burial of MacDonald Clarke." *New York Aurora,* March 18:1.

———. 1855. *Leaves of Grass.* Brooklyn, New York: Published by the Author.

———. 1856. *Leaves of Grass.* Brooklyn, New York: Published by Author.

———. 1963. *Early Poems and Fiction Vol. 9. Collected Writings of Walt Whitman,* edited by Thomas L. Brasher. New York: New York University Press.

———. [1892] 1963. *Specimen Days.* In *Prose Works 1892. Vol. I: Specimen Days,* edited by Floyd Stovall, 1–295. *The Collected Writings of Walt Whitman.* Series Eds. Gay Wilson Allen and Scully Bradley. New York: New York University Press.

———. [1862] 1984. *Washington.* In *Notebooks and Unpublished Prose Manuscripts. Vol. II: Washington,* edited by Edward F. Grier, 477–933. *The Collected Writings of Walt Whitman.* Series Eds. Gay Wilson Allen and Scully Bradley. New York: New York University Press.

———. 1996. *Poetry and Prose.* Edited by Justin Kaplan. New York: Library of America.

———. [1865] 2002a. *Drum-Taps.* In *Leaves of Grass and Other Writings,* edited by Michael Moon, 234–75. New York: W. W. Norton.

———. [1876] 2002b. *Leaves of Grass.* In *Leaves of Grass and Other Writings,* edited by Michael Moon, 2–491. New York: W. W. Norton.

Willis, Nathaniel Parker. 1864. "Beauty After Death." In *The Poems, Sacred, Passionate, and Humorous, of Nathaniel Parker Willis,* 115. New York: Clark and Maynard.

Wilson, Jno. Stainback. 1858. "Health Department: Popular Errors, Etc." *Godey's Lady's Book* 57: 84. Accessed July 6, 2011. American Periodicals Series Online, ProQuest (336745851).

————. 1860. "Health Department." *Godey's Lady's Book* 61: 80–81. Accessed July 6, 2011. American Periodicals Series Online, ProQuest (336753391).

————. 1862. "Health Department: Why Children Die." *Godey's Lady's Book* 65: 402–3. Accessed July 6, 2011. American Periodicals Series Online, ProQuest (337338111).

Wilson, Sarah. 2004. "Melville and the Architecture of Antebellum Masculinity." *American Literature* 76: 59–87.

Wimsatt, William K. 1954. *The Verbal Icon: Studies in the Meaning of Poetry.* Louisville: University Press of Kentucky.

Wimsatt, William K. and Monroe C. Beardsley. 2001. "The Affective Fallacy." *The Norton Anthology of Theory and Criticism.* Ed. Vincent B. Leitch, 1387–1403. New York: W. W. Norton .

Wyman, Morrill. 1867. *Progress in School Discipline: Corporal Punishment in the Public Schools.* Cambridge.

Zizek, Slavoj. 2000. "Melancholy and the Act." *Critical Inquiry* 26: 657–81.

Zizek, Slavoj and Glyn Daly. 2004. *Conversations with Zizek.* Cambridge, UK: Polity.

Index

abolitionists, 5, 168–169

academic and scholarly work: on Alcott, 106, 119n2; bachelor melancholia in, 124–127; *bricoleurs* in, 198, 204n4; James as sentimentalist in, 181, 199; on literary sentimentalism, 5–9, 12, 29, 123, 162, 197–203, 204n3; nineteenth-century childhood and class divisions treatment in, 108; on reader sympathetic identification, 75; Whitman treatment in, 151, 159n4, 199–200; on women and emotion, 29, 44n1, 183–184

Adorno, Theodor, 54, 64

affective: capacity of boys, 30, 33, 34, 35, 38, 39, 40; capacity of girls, 30, 33, 34, 35, 39; communication model, 86; discipline, 31; domestic ideology, 30; exchange, 182, 183, 191; "fallacy", 186, 189; motherhood, 25–26, 29–30; politics, 181. *See also* maternal affective pedagogy

African Americans, 72, 117, 179n6, 198. *See also* slavery

alcoholics and alcoholism, 99

Alcott, Louisa May: academic interest in, 106, 119n2; anti-slavery stance of, 105, 110–111, 115; background and familial history of, 108–110, 114; economic vulnerability for, 17, 108; poverty for, 105, 109, 114–115; sentimental

benevolence of, 3, 10; *See also Little Women*

"Another War" (Piatt), 60–61

antebellum culture. *See* sentimental culture

antebellum sentimentalism: child death and suffering central to, 17; death and loss portrayal in, 19, 162–163; domestic vulnerability in, 17; male/female child distinction in, 30, 32–33, 35, 37; nostalgia for, 53; parlor songs in, 163

anthropomorphic presence: apostrophic direct address to create, 144, 145, 146, 147, 148, 150, 151, 152, 152–153, 154, 157, 158; in *Leaves of Grass*, 152, 152–153, 154, 155–157, 158

apostrophic direct address: anthropomorphic presence created from, 144, 145, 146, 147, 148, 150, 151, 152, 152–153, 154, 157, 158; to dead, 148–151; in mourning and memorializing, 144, 145, 145–147, 148–151, 153, 154, 158, 159n2; to reader, 145, 146, 146–147, 149–150, 151–152, 152–153, 158; sentimental writers and common use of, 148

"Army of Occupation" (Piatt), 49–50, 51, 64

"At the Playhouse" (Piatt), 58, 58

bachelor and bachelor melancholia: in academic scholarship and history,

217

benevolence involving, 105, 117, 118;
Stowe's *Cabin* evincing passive, 3;
sympathetic identification and, 1, 118
reader: academic scholarship concerning
sympathetic identification of, 75;
apostrophic direct address to, 145, 146,
146–147, 149–150, 151–152, 152–153,
158; communion with, 151, 152,
152–153, 154, 155–157, 158–159;
sympathetic identification for, 75, 79,
83, 86, 90, 90, 91–92, 97–98, 99,
100–102, 112, 139n11, 144
reason, 25, 34
"Republican Motherhood", 16, 27n2, 27n3
Reveries of a Bachelor (Mitchell), 11, 127,
138n1; bachelor as idle dreamer in, 126,
127, 129, 129, 130–131, 133–134;
home in, 127; identity through
imagined loss/lack in, 137; marriage
and family considered in, 128–131,
134–135, 137; masculine alternative
form in, 124–125, 137; mourning in,
134, 137; public opinion of, 136;
scholarly view of, 124–127;
spectatorship in, 125, 126; sympathetic
letters considered in, 136
rhetorical mode, 5, 7
rights, children's, 24–26, 28n12
"The Rights of Children" (Embury), 24–25
romance, 3

sacrifice, 112
savagery, 35, 37, 45n8
scholar and scholarship. *See* academic and
scholarly work
self and selfhood, 48, 54, 152–153, 158
sensibility, 2
sentiment: body language for expressing,
190–191, 192–194; culture of, 183,
199, 204n5; public, 90, 92, 181, 192,
193–194, 200; public compared to
private, 192, 193–194
sentimental authors and writers: antislavery stance of, 95, 96, 102, 105, 110,
115; apostrophic direct address
common for, 148; bourgeois
subjectivity introduced by, 4; boys and
sympathy disagreement from, 43;
commonality and diversity among, 2;

deafness subject for, 78–85; male, 183,
184, 199; on maternal sympathy, 31,
32, 44n6; of poetry, 142, 143; on
poverty, 115; pragmatic compared to,
32, 38, 40, 42, 43, 44n5, 44n6;
sentimental benevolence in work of, 3,
10, 77–78, 82; sympathetic
identification and, 10, 42, 47, 72, 90,
90, 91–92, 97–98, 99, 100–102, 144,
184, 190; on sympathetic mother as
fiction, 29, 30; women as, 3–4, 198;
women's education championed by, 4,
9. *See also* Alcott, Louisa May; boys
and boyhood; Child, Lydia M.;
children; communion; Hale, Sarah J.;
James, Henry; Mitchell, Donald Grant;
Piatt, Sarah, poetry of; Sigourney,
Lydia Huntley; Stowe, Harriet Beecher;
Whitman, Walt
sentimental benevolence, 87n5; for deaf-
blind, 83–84; deaf education and,
70–72, 71, 73–74, 77–78, 79, 80, 86,
87n7, 87n10, 88n12, 202; defining, 70,
72; education, 73–74; family bonds
expanded in, 73; morality in teaching,
74; nonverbal communication
engendering, 70, 73, 74, 77, 78, 84–85,
86, 87n3; politics and impact of, 87n6;
sentimental writers' work evincing, 3,
10, 77–78, 82; summary of, 86;
sympathetic identification necessary
for, 72. *See also* social justice and
benevolence
sentimental culture, 139n13, 179n4, 183;
boys' portrayal in, 33; defined, 28n7;
heroic gap with, 179n8; maternal
sympathy and, 32, 184; of mourning
and memorializing, 141, 142, 152, 154,
155, 159n1; music shared in, 164, 178;
public and private spheres of, 183, 184;
tomboy narrative incongruity with, 107,
114
sentimentalism and sentimentality: in
American literary history, 197–198,
203n2; American subjectivity impacted
by, 200–201; bachelor melancholia as
subset of, 8, 11, 123, 124; bachelor
melancholia divergence from, 124, 125,
138n4; Christianity and Christian home

and undermining, 7, 10, 183; sentimentalism on family bonds relation to, 70, 87n4; sentimentality, middle-class women, and, 3–4; in sentimental texts, 3, 10, 96, 97–99; sympathetic identification for, 92. *See also* sentimental benevolence

society. *See* sentimental culture

The Southern Literary Messenger, 126–127, 136, 138n7, 138n8

speaker. *See* apostrophic direct address

spectatorship, 125, 126

spirituality, 92–93

spoken word, 74

Stowe, Harriet Beecher, 3, 107, 199; anti-slavery stance of, 105, 115; boy/girl child-rearing distinction for, 30, 35; passive racism in work of, 3; sentimental benevolence in work of, 77–78; social justice in sentimentalism of, 3; *See also Uncle Tom's Cabin*

subjectivity, American, 200–201, 202

sublime, 78

suffering, human: bachelor melancholia adopting, 133; child, 17, 20; in marriage, 134; sentimentality in response to, 7, 187–188, 188–189, 193, 194–195; sympathetic identification from, 191

Swedenborg, Emmanuel, 93, 95

sympathetic identification: with bachelor, 133, 135; in child-rearing, 38, 42; for class divisions, 106; collaboration in, 89, 92, 94, 97, 102, 139n11; consciousness central to, 189; with deaf-blind, 82, 83, 86; defined, 107, 131, 183; education/social advocacy for disabled promoted through, 10, 72; with immigrants, 100–102; marriage and, 135; middle-class women and racial, 106; with poverty, 100; public morality raised by, 10; racial, 1, 118; reader, 75, 79, 83, 86, 90, 90, 91–92, 97–98, 99, 100–102, 112, 139n11, 144; requirements and limitations of, 72, 108; sentimental benevolence relying on, 72; sentimental writers and, 10, 42, 47, 72, 90, 90, 91–92, 97–98, 99, 100–102, 144, 184, 190; Smith on, 1,

183, 188–189; for social justice and benevolence, 92; from suffering, 191

sympathy, 44n1; bachelor impacted by, 132; collaboration in exchange of, 89, 92, 94, 97, 102; crafted privacy engendering, 90; critics on effectiveness of, 89; disability providing avenue for, 75; family as foundation of, 135; femininity intertwined with, 106, 108, 183–184; gender subversion relationship with, 106, 114; James eschewing politics of, 182, 183; language for expressing, 187, 189; letters of, 136; in Mitchell and Stowe's work, 133, 136; moral and ethical behavior stemming from, 89, 132; motherhood and fiction of, 29, 30; national identity formed from, 89, 132, 201; personal, 7, 92; as political force, 10–11, 184; sentimentality relationship with, 31, 119n1; sentimental writer and reader exchange of, 90, 90; social differences bridged through, 10, 97–98. *See also* maternal sympathy

temperance. *See* alcoholics and alcoholism

theater, 63, 182

The Theory of Moral Sentiments (Smith), 1, 89, 132, 183, 188–189

"There Was a Rose" (Piatt), 61–62

tomboy narrative, 106–107, 112, 113, 117, 119; *See also Little Women*

Tompkins, Jane, 4, 5, 43, 183

tragedy, 56

"Training of Boys", 37, 42

Uncle Tom's Cabin (Stowe), 3, 5, 115, 195n1, 198; boyhood discipline and maternal sympathy in, 40, 42–43; domestic ideology in, 43; *Little Women* protagonist compared to, 107; maternal affective pedagogy failing in, 40–42, 43; maternal sympathy engendered in, 36, 184; motherhood sympathy fiction in, 30; passive racism evinced in, 3; sentimental benevolence in, 77–78; sympathy in, 133; white motherhood valorized and idealized in, 41–42, 43, 45n10

About the Contributors

Robert Arbour is a doctoral candidate at Indiana University. His dissertation, "A Sentimental War: American Poetry and the Civil War," tracks changes in sentimental poetry as a nationalizing mode during and after the Civil War.

Adam Bradford, Florida Atlantic University, is completing a book manuscript entitled "Communities of Death: Walt Whitman, Edgar Allan Poe, and the Nineteenth-Century American Culture of Mourning and Memorializing."

Kara B. Clevinger, Ph.D., English, Temple University, was a fellow at the Center for the Humanities at Temple and the Philadelphia Center for History of Science while completing her dissertation, "A Pure Influence: Domestic Dreams in Antebellum Literature."

Mary Gosselink De Jong, Penn State Altoona, has published many articles on American literature and culture on such topics as Frances Osgood's poetry and nineteenth-century hymnody. She coedited *Popular Nineteenth-Century American Women Writers and the Literary Marketplace.*

D. Zachary Finch is currently a Lecturer at Dartmouth College. His publications include criticism for *Jacket* and *Boston Review* and poetry in *American Letters & Commentary, Poetry, Tin House,* and *Sentence.*

George Gordon-Smith, a Ph.D. candidate at Emory University, studies nineteenth-century American literature with an emphasis on sentiment and disability. His dissertation explores the role of disability in abolitionist literature as a tool for inciting sentimental action against slavery.

Mary Louise Kete, University of Vermont, wrote *Sentimental Collaborations: Mourning and Middle-Class Identity in Nineteenth-Century America.* She has published and lectured widely on American literature and is working on another book, *Slavish Ekphrasis: Representation, Slavery, and the Liberal Self.*

Susan Toth Lord, Kent State University, published "Women's History, Women's Empowerment: Lydia Maria Child's *Ladies Family Library Series*" in *Womanhood in Anglophone Literary Culture: Nineteenth and Twentieth Century Perspectives.*

Maglina Lubovich, Fond du Lac Tribal and Community College, wrote a doctoral dissertation on critiques of marriage by bachelors and spinsters in nineteenth-century American literature. She has published in *Legacy* and coedited a book on male beauty.

Ken Parille, East Carolina University, has published many articles on nineteenth-century American boyhood and education. He is the author of *Boys at Home: Discipline, Masculinity, and "The Boy-Problem" in Nineteenth-Century American Literature* and coeditor of *Daniel Clowes: Conversations.*

Elizabeth Petrino, Fairfield University, is author of *Emily Dickinson and Her Contemporaries: American Women's Verse, 1820-1885* and coeditor of *Jesuit and Feminist Education: Intersections in Teaching & Learning for the Twenty-First Century.* Her articles have appeared in *The Emily Dickinson Journal, ESQ, Tulsa Studies in Women's Literature,* and *Legacy.*

Kristen Proehl, Clemson University, is working on a book project titled *Battling Girlhood: Sympathy, Race, and the Tomboy Narrative in American Literature.* Her article on the cultural memory of the Harpers Ferry raid appears in *The Afterlife of John Brown.*

Made in the USA
Las Vegas, NV
10 January 2022

41018200R00141